DICTIONARY OF FREE-MARKET ECONOMICS

In memory of my parents, Tina and Otto Foldvary, who encouraged and supported my pursuit of meaning and knowledge.

ACKNOWLEDGMENTS

Many thanks to Charles Rowley for his assistance in initiating this project, Bertrand Lemennicier for suggestions of some names of French free-market economists, Aeon Skoble for help with the Ayn Rand concepts, John Cobin on allodialism, members of the libprofs e-mail list for much help, my wife Janet for language insights, and many others who helped me with concepts, resources, definitions, and sources.

ABBREVIATIONS

abbrev.	abbreviation
acc.	accounting
Br.	British
ec.	economics
eth.	ethics
fin.	finance
Fr.	French
Ger.	German
Gk.	Greek
Lat.	Latin
leg.	legal
log.	logic
n.	noun
OED	Oxford English Dictionary
phil.	philosophy
pl.	plural
Russ.	Russian
sci.	science
syn.	synonym

A

a posteriori. *Lat.* Afterwards, or following; known from experience and INDUCTION rather than deductively (DEDUCTION) derived.

a priori. *Lat.* From what goes before: beforehand, or prior to. *A priori* PROPOSITIONS are prior to derivations therefrom. Deductive (DEDUCTION) reasoning is also referred to as *a priori*. The term is also used for propositions that are self-evident or derived deductively, without using experience regarding specific events, though the premises for such reasoning are ultimately based on general EMPIRICAL experience. LUDWIG VON MISES held that an *a priori* is one which cannot be traced to a logically prior cause, and is thus a FOUNDATIONAL premise. See also APRIORISM.

A–D. ADVANCE–DECLINE RATIO.

AAA. **1** The highest credit rating assigned to securities (for example corporate and municipal bonds) by the Standard & Poor and Moody's rating agency; pronounced 'triple A.' Lesser ratings are AA (double A) and A (single A), followed by B ratings, and so on. Such a rating system is also applied by agencies to banks and shares. **2** *Abbrev.* American Automobile Association, Agricultural Adjustment Act, American Accounting Association, American Arbitration Association.

ab invito. *Lat.* Coerced (COERCE), compulsory. For example, a transfer *ab invito*.

ABA. American Bankers Association.

ABA transit number. The number assigned to a US financial institution. It is inscribed on its checks.

abalienate. To transfer title of. *Syn.* alienate (ALIENATION).

abandon. **1** To desert or forsake PROPERTY, giving up CLAIM (2) to it. Abandoned property is that for which an owner (OWNERSHIP) has permanently given up POSSESSION and all RIGHTS. **2** To permanently plug a well.

1

abandonment.   1 *Economic* The act of willingly deserting or relinquishing PROPERTY, unilaterally giving up CLAIM (2) to it. 2 *Ethics* The absence of objective values or meaning of life due to the absence of God, hence human beings need to determine these without divine guidance. Contrast: FORFEITURE.

abandonment cost.   The cost of ABANDONMENT (1). See also SHUT DOWN COSTS. The cost can be SOCIAL as well as PRIVATE.

abate.   1 To reduce or eliminate. 2 To deduct or discount part of a payment. Abatement of TAXES is a reduction after an ASSESSMENT or tax has been levied. 3 *Law* To annul. 4 To calm or quiet.

abduction.   1 *Law* Kidnapping; forcibly and illegally carrying off a person. 2 *Phil.* A type of reasoning (REASON), neither deductive (DEDUCTION) nor inductive (INDUCTION), in which one originates a HYPOTHESIS or a premise based on the creative analysis of facts and prior theory. The term was introduced by Charles Saunders Peirce.

ability.   The POWER to ACT. The socialist (SOCIALISM) slogan, 'From each according to his ability; to each according to his need,' originated with Louis Blanc (1811–82), *Organisation du Travail* (1839). This principle is applicable to family economies. In a free market CATALLAXY or EXTENDED ORDER, rewards are 'to each according to his ability' when applied to production, and needs are met by equal and unhampered access to NATURAL OPPORTUNITIES, along with charity to those with inability.

ability to extract.   See ABILITY TO PAY.

ability to pay.   1 A rationale for TAXATION based on social OBLIGATION and the availability of funds not vital to survival, hence extractable without undue SACRIFICE. The concept also can refer to equal tax payments from those with equal INCOME or WEALTH. The main alternative rationale is the BENEFIT PRINCIPLE of PUBLIC FINANCE. 2 A bond issuer's ABILITY to obtain sufficient revenue to pay the interest and principal of the debt.
    The concept of 'ability to pay' (1) is typically based on the EQUAL SACRIFICE of UTILITY (absolute, proportional, or marginal). Richer payers allegedly lose less utility per dollar of tax than poorer ones, due to DIMINISHING MARGINAL UTILITY. Aside from the issue of INTERPERSONAL comparing of utilities, the rationale may in practice be implemented as the 'ability to extract,' GOVERNMENT taking funds where it can most effectively extract them, just as thieves rob banks because 'that's where the money is.'

Although 'ability to pay' (1) is incorporated in GRADUATED or PROGRESSIVE tax rates, such tax rates may not in practice tap some of the richest incomes, which may be sheltered from taxation, but tax lower income more easily tapped, such as payrolls and sales.

Whether 'ability to pay' (1) is equitable (EQUITY) depends on the ethical (ETHIC) standard used; typically, equal sacrifice is presumed without any explicitly derived ethical standard. Whatever the rationale in equity, the ability to pay principle sacrifices EFFICIENCY, since even the wealthy have less incentive to exert effort and to invest resources as the tax rate increases, reducing expected PROFITS. Higher marginal tax rates also create an incentive for tax AVOIDANCE and EVASION, reducing the gains from higher tax rates.

abject.   Severe; worst; wretched.

abject poverty.   Wretched POVERTY, leaving people suffering from hunger, sickness, and harsh weather. This is normally due to interventionist (INTERVENTION) policies which stifle prosperity, for as Henry George (1883, p. 78) wrote, 'There is in nature no reason for poverty.' See also NATURE.

abjure.   Renounce by oath.

abolish.   Eliminate, destroy, or repeal, as in abolishing slavery (SLAVE) or BARRIERS to trade.

abomination.   Something EVIL and/or repugnant, such as a TAX system that is not only costly to the payers, but has a high social cost (SOCIAL COSTS AND BENEFITS) of compliance and is ARBITRARY and invasive of privacy.

aboriginal.   The first of their kind, such as aboriginal people being the first human beings to settle some TERRITORY.

aboriginal land rights.   The NATURAL RIGHTS of aboriginal people to the land they homesteaded (HOMESTEADING), rights retained after being invaded and losing possession. This is a current issue in Australia, Canada, the USA and other countries.

abortive benefits.   The failure (FAIL) of intended BENEFITS to achieve their purpose. A GOVERNMENT program which imposes greater social costs (SOCIAL COSTS AND BENEFITS) (including the EXCESS BURDEN OF TAXATION) than benefits has abortive benefits, since it decreases net WELL-BEING.

above par.   A share of stock with a market value greater than its par value or face value.

above the line.   1 The INCOME-TAX 'line' is GROSS INCOME; income is listed above the line, deductions BELOW THE LINE. Gross income less deductions is adjusted gross income. 2 Before-tax revenue and expenditure.

absentee landlord.   An owner of REAL ESTATE who does not live on the property and administers it through an AGENT (2).

absenteeism.   The practice of employees taking unauthorized time off work, possibly as an expression of a grievance.

absolute.   Complete, independent, unrestricted, and pure. As in ABSOLUTE ADVANTAGE, absolute authority, absolute governance, absolute truth. Contrasted with relative, comparative, mixed or impure, partial, or restricted. 'The absolute' in philosophy is the totality of what exists. See RELATIVELY ABSOLUTE ABSOLUTES.

absolute advantage.   In the theory of EXCHANGE, including INTERNATIONAL TRADE: the ABILITY to produce an item of a certain quality at a lower average COST, due to greater productivity, than another AGENT (1). Contrast: COMPARATIVE ADVANTAGE.

absolute cost advantage.   The ABILITY of a FIRM to produce at a lower average cost than potential entrants to the INDUSTRY (2), due to resources or technology not available to the others, such as PATENTS and PROPRIETARY knowledge. Contrast: COMPARATIVE ADVANTAGE.

absolute income.   The current INCOME of a household (for example during one year) rather than a lifetime income or PERMANENT INCOME.

absolute income hypothesis.   The Keynesian proposition (KEYNESIAN ECONOMICS) that CONSUMPTION is basically a function of current or ABSOLUTE INCOME, a central element of simple Keynesian MACROECONOMIC *MODELS. The HYPOTHESIS states that the first derivative of the function is positive and less than one, and that the marginal propensity to consume is less than the average propensity to consume. This hypothesis is generally not empirically warranted (WARRANT) for the long run. Even if warranted, the relationship between consumption and income is not necessarily linear. Moreover, even if the linear equation $C = c_0 + By_d$ were warranted, total consumption as a function of total income does not warrant its mathematical manipulation into a determination of national income given c and C if the causation is that consumption is determined by income. See also LIFE-CYCLE HYPOTHESIS OF CONSUMPTION.

absolute monopoly.   An INDUSTRY (2) in which there is only one FIRM, or product for which there is only one provider in its MARKET. (See also ENTRY MONOPOLY.) This can be created by GOVERNMENT, as in the postal monopoly with first-class mail, by the complete ownership of a natural or locational resource, or by the MARKET PROCESS. A firm that has an absolute monopoly can set a higher price than if there is competition, resulting in a loss of social welfare, since the price is higher than the MARGINAL COST of the GOOD, unless the firm can price discriminate (PRICE DISCRIMINATION), that is, sell some of the items at lower prices while keeping the high payers. There may be no real welfare loss, however, if the market is such that other firms would not be profitable, price discrimination is not feasible, or if regulation to set a lower price (for example at marginal cost) has its own failures.

There are many locational monopolies, such as the only dentist in a small town, but their MARKET POWER is limited by social relationships and competition from other nearby market areas. The potential of entry of new firms also limits monopoly power. Large absolute monopolies not due to government protection and barriers are quite rare. If any exist, the MONOPOLY PROFIT, or ECONOMIC PROFIT beyond normal returns, can be taxed (TAX) without any effect on output.

Locational or 'natural' monopolies provide a service or resource, such as water or electricity, to a territorial community, and are typically granted a monopoly by government in exchange for regulation. In some cases, such as a telephone service, it is possible to have competitive service using the same infrastructure. For the infrastructure or for resources such as water, providers (including municipalities and governmental districts) could bid for the franchise. These territorial (TERRITORIAL GOODS) services are also subject to COMPETITION among communities.

absolute poverty.   The condition of families who do not have sufficient INCOME to obtain basic NEEDS such as food, shelter, and basic medicine. An income level at or below SUBSISTENCE.

absolute price.   A PRICE measured in MONEY rather than in other GOODS, thus having a number based on a UNIT OF ACCOUNT rather than being values relative to other goods.

absolute priority rule.   That creditors be satisfied prior to owners (OWNERSHIP) in liquidations.

absolute scarcity.   Scarcity plus fixity (FIXED). The condition of there being SCARCE (1) resources fixed in quantity, although the total amount available may be unknown.

absolute tax incidence.   The INCIDENCE of a TAX relative to there being zero taxation. See INCIDENCE OF TAXATION.

absolutism.   *Phil.* The exercise of ABSOLUTE governance. Absolute government is not limited by any internal laws or organizations. See also its subset, TOTALITARIANISM.

absorb.   1 To cancel out or negate, for example when litigation costs absorb PROFIT, hence reducing the profit that would otherwise have existed. 2 Take in and assimilate, including the acquisition of another enterprise and incorporating it into the acquiring firm. 3 To offset sell with buy orders.

absorption.   1 The use of goods by an ECONOMY (1) (see also ABSORPTIVE CAPACITY). 2 The absorbing (ABSORB (1)) of one firm by another.

absorption approach.   A country's BALANCE OF TRADE expressed by the equation $B = N - X$, B being the balance of trade, N national income, and X domestic consumption and investment. B is thus affected by changes in N and X; whether this is more than a trivial residual is the question.

absorptive capacity.   The ABILITY of an ECONOMY (1) to ABSORB (2) INVESTMENTS (an increase in CAPITAL GOODS or human capital) without decreasing returns. If there is no change in technology, eventually marginal productivity declines as investment increases, reducing returns to investments.

abstinence.   Postponing CONSUMPTION to some future date, using resources instead for loans and INVESTMENT. The term was used by NASSAU SENIOR in his theory of INTEREST, in which interest is a reward for abstinence. JOHN STUART MILL proposed that abstinence is also a reward for not using up financial capital. Abstinence or waiting is related in conception to the concept of TIME PREFERENCE, whereby people prefer to have goods in the present than in the future, but the interest premium is not a return on waiting itself but due to the excess of quantity demanded over quantity supplied for loanable items when the interest rate is zero.

abstract.   1 Apart from any concrete or specific exemplar of the concept under consideration. An abstraction such as a model leaves out minor elements of a system, concentrating on the essential ones. See also PRIMACY OF

THE ABSTRACT. **2** A concise summary of a paper or report, often preceding the main body of an academic paper or article. **3** *Law* To take or remove, an abstraction being an unauthorized and injurious taking.

abstract labor. In MARXIST ECONOMICS, LABOR in the ABSTRACT, which is regarded as creating the MARKET value of products. In FREE-MARKET ECONOMICS, labor consists of concrete individual workers who create a MARGINAL physical and revenue product, LAND and CAPITAL GOODS also contributing to value.

abstraction. The outcome of abstracting (ABSTRACT (1)), whereby the particular becomes generalized, simplified, and more theory-laden. JOHN LOCKE regarded abstractions as standards by which actual items are categorized.

absurd. See *REDUCTIO AD ABSURDUM*.

Abu Said ibn Khaldun. Arab historian, sociologist and economist (1332–1406). Held government positions. President Reagan cited Khaldun as supporting the view that a reduction of TAX rates generates larger tax revenues, that is the LAFFER CURVE. Khaldun proposed that human geography complements historical sociology.

abundance. **1** A condition in which there are sufficient GOODS for the set of persons who want them, for example luxury goods can be in plentiful quantity for those who can pay the price. **2** PROSPERITY for all members of a society, all persons being able to obtain the goods that a typical modern household enjoys.

abuse. Improper use. A harmful departure from reasonable use and treatment. For example, the abuse of RENEWABLE RESOURCES can be considered to consist of their wanton destruction, depriving others of their use, whereas proper use would preserve the resource. The abuse of animals is treatment that causes excessive, avoidable suffering. The abuse of power is its exercise contrary to law.

abusus. *Lat.* Using up; wasting.

academese. Jargon and dialects spoken by those doing ACADEMIC work.

academic. **1** Pertaining to scholarly work, such as that done in a university. **2** Theory or concept with slight practical importance, applicability, or relevance.

academic freedom.   The FREEDOM to teach subjects as the instructor wishes, and to publish, without ARBITRARY governmental, institutional, or doctrinal RESTRICTIONS, or regard for any public benefits, so long as the teachings do not constitute deception.

academic tenure.   A permanent grant of a position in a college or university, normally after an initial duration in which the candidate has satisfied requirements such as prestigious publications and the ABILITY to obtain grant funds. Tenure allegedly protects the ACADEMIC FREEDOM of professors, but under a more market-oriented system, the freedom to teach and publish could be safeguarded as well. The costs of academic tenure include the inability to discharge a no-longer effective scholar and teacher, a reduced ability to decrease the size of a faculty when demand decreases, and the payment of WAGES not warranted by performance. The pressure and requirement of tenure also skew pre-tenured professors to the desires of those with authority to decide on tenure rather than the interests and concerns of the scholar. The tenure process can also favor publication over teaching or even certain types of research. (Such considerations are also discussed in the entry of the same title in Block and Walker, 1989.)

academician.   A scholar or teacher.

accelerate.   **1** To apply some FORCE that increases the velocity of an item (such as a rate of output, payment, or cost) or changes its direction. **2** Hence, to speed up an accounting or payment process, such as DEPRECIATION (1) or a maturity date, from its normal schedule.

accelerated cost recovery system.   In US TAX law (the Economic Recovery Act of 1981, modified by the Tax Reform Act of 1986), a DEPRECIATION (2) period shorter than the actual life of the CAPITAL GOOD. The accelerated depreciation reduces the tax burden and stimulates INVESTMENT, since an earlier reduction of taxes frees funds that can earn returns. However, the tax favoring of CAPITAL GOODS relative to LABOR will skew investment away from HUMAN CAPITAL, resulting in a market DISTORTION.

accelerated depreciation.   A TAX *ACCOUNTING of DEPRECIATION (1) that may exceed the actual depreciation, that is the wear and tear, with large deductions in the first years, although also justified when assets are more productive in their earlier years. Such a depreciation schedule stimulates investment, similar to the ACCELERATED COST RECOVERY SYSTEM.

acceleration premium.   More pay for greater output.

acceleration principle. The concept of an ACCELERATOR linking CONSUMP-TION and INVESTMENT.

accelerator. A proposition that INVESTMENT is a function of the rate of change of output, so that for example as output falls, investment falls. As the accelerator interacts with the MULTIPLIER, an initial decline accelerates into a major decline. The concept plays a role in some hypotheses of TRADE CYCLES. The hypothesis posits that net investment equals some coefficient (the amount of CAPITAL GOODS needed to produce a unit of output) times the change in income. The concept does not take into account the structure (differing ROUNDABOUTNESS) of capital goods and the effects of LAND, although some models have taken into account differing reaction times.

accelerator-multiplier model. A model of growth using the ACCELERATOR and MULTIPLIER.

accept. To receive something willingly.

acceptance. An agreement by the recipient to receive an item. The accept-ance of a bill or offer by the person to whom it is drawn typically though not necessarily consists in signing or using it.

acceptilation. The release of a DEBT by the creditor without receiving pay-ment.

access. The ABILITY to approach persons or obtain resources or public records without ARBITRARY *BARRIERS. In REAL ESTATE, access involves rights to adjoin-ing transportation routes. In computing or data processing, access involves obtaining data. Political access depends on the number of governing agen-cies, the degree to which SPECIAL INTERESTS are able to influence legislation, and the size of the voting pool in a jurisdiction.

access/space trade-off. The trade-off between land area and transportation costs, the choice being more space where land is cheap and transport dear further from the center of COMMERCE, versus less space but cheaper access closer to commerce.

accession rate. The number of newly hired workers per month divided by total EMPLOYMENT. This rate is a leading indicator of the BUSINESS CYCLE.

accessions tax. A TAX on assets transferred without a reciprocal exchange, such as by GIFT or inheritance (INHERITANCE TAX), levied on the recipient. If these assets are considered legitimately owned by the donor, then an accessions tax is an INTERVENTION, that is an ARBITRARY taking and alteration of voluntary BEHAVIOR. A donor tax, such as a gift or inheritance tax, is paid by the donor.

accidentalism.   *Phil.* The theory that while all events may be caused, some cannot be predicted.

accommodate.   1 Help in a complementary (COMPLEMENT) way, as when monetary policy accommodates a DEMAND *SHOCK that raises the DEMAND FOR MONEY by expanding the MONEY SUPPLY. 2 Adopt a practice to avoid conflict, without necessarily adapting to or assimilating it.

accommodative monetary policy.   An increase in the MONEY SUPPLY by the monetary authority to temporarily offset higher INTEREST RATES due to government borrowing, or to ACCOMMODATE (1) a demand shock.

account.   1 A CONTRACT between two parties, one of which owns assets or credit and the other of which holds the assets and maintains records of the amounts, as with a BANK account. 2 A record of TRANSACTIONS and assets.

accounting.   The ACTIVITY and resultant reporting of systematically recording transactions, and the analysis and interpretation of the methods and reports.

accounting costs.   The COSTS of a firm as recorded by an accountant, hence the EXPLICIT costs and not the IMPLICIT *OPPORTUNITY COSTS of the owner's resources and of the firm's FINANCIAL ASSETS.

accounting equation.   The identity 'ASSETS equal LIABILITIES plus net worth'. This is a result of double-entry bookkeeping.

accounting identity.   An equation that balances by definition, such as the ACCOUNTING EQUATION and the MACROECONOMIC formula $Y = C + I + G$ where Y is by definition the sum of the terms of the right side (which assumes that SAVINGS equals INVESTMENT).

accounting profit.   Gross revenues minus EXPLICIT *COSTS, that is the costs of exchanged items that an accountant would record. An accounting profit excludes IMPLICIT costs, that is payments for FACTORS owned by the proprietor (PROPRIETARY), which when subtracted from the accounting profit, constitute the ECONOMIC PROFIT.

accounting rate of return. INCOME during some time interval divided by the average amount of the ASSET.

accounts payable. Funds due to suppliers for items received.

accounts receivable. Funds owed from those who received goods.

accretion. See ACCUMULATION (3).

accrual basis. ACCOUNTING based on INCOME and EXPENSES that ACCRUE, in contrast to a CASH BASIS.

accrue. Accumulate, and recorded as an addition or COST, even if no EXPLICIT *TRANSACTION takes place.

accrued expenses. LIABILITIES recorded as incurred but not yet paid.

accumulation. 1 An increase due to continuous additions. 2 In Marxism (MARXIST ECONOMICS), an increase in CAPITAL GOODS. 3 *Fin.* Adding the income generated by an ASSET to the amount of the asset.

achieving society. Concept and name of book by David McClelland (1976). Entrepreneurial (ENTREPRENEUR) achievement involves new ideas and the desire to succeed, a personality trait.

acid test ratio. The sum of cash, securities, and receivables divided by current liabilities, used in financial analysis to measure a firm's solvency. This is also called a 'quick ratio.' It is normally desirable for the ratio to be at least 1:1.

acquaintance, knowledge by. KNOWLEDGE obtained from observation and experience, in contrast to knowledge by description.

acquisition. The absorbing (ABSORB) of one firm by another, especially by purchasing its common stock.

acquisitive offenses. Theft and other crimes against title and POSSESSION of PROPERTY.

across the board. Applying to all members of a group.

ACRS. ACCELERATED COST RECOVERY SYSTEM.

act. **1** An ACTIVITY (1) or a STATE OF BEING. **2** A demonstration and expression of the actor's will, hence a VOLUNTARY exercise of POWER, a CHOICE among options. **3** Laws, decisions, and commands of a government agency.

According to the sociologist T. Parsons, the act (2) is the basic unit of sociological analysis. In law, CORPORATIONS are legal persons and act as an agency.

act of God. An event not caused by human ACTION and which cannot be prevented. Insurance policies have clauses for such events.

act of state. ACTION by a state GOVERNMENT affecting another state government, rather than action by a state government directly affecting its citizens. Such action is inherent in sovereignty, and outside the jurisdiction of domestic courts. In US and British law, an act of state does not apply to citizens or subjects, hence may not be used to violate or restrict constitutional RIGHTS.

act utilitarianism. An ETHIC by which the MORAL *VALUE of an ACT is the amount of additional HAPPINESS, WELL-BEING or utility (UTILITY, MARGINAL) it induces among some set of PERSONS. An act is thus the basis of moral value. See also UTILITARIANISM for rule-utilitarianism. Problems with act utilitarianism include i) the derivation of the ethic; ii) when an act has differing effects on different persons, why the well-being of some outweighs the suffering of others; iii) how to measure WELL-BEING and compare individual utilities. These problems can be resolved if a UNIVERSAL ETHIC is first derived and then applied to acts, although the prime determinant of moral values would be the rules of the ethic rather than unmeasurable utility.

acting. **1** Performing an ACT (2). **2** Representing or substituting for another.

acting man. A term used by LUDWIG VON MISES in *HUMAN ACTION* (1949, 1966) to emphasize that PERSONS *ACT purposefully (PURPOSEFUL).

actio personalis moritur cum persona. *Lat.* The personal RIGHT to ACTION (4) or PROPERTY expires with the death of the PERSON. One application can be to a PATENT or COPYRIGHT that confers a lifetime right that is not inheritable.

action. **1** The PURPOSEFUL pursuit of ENDS. See also HUMAN ACTION. **2** *Fin.* The performance of a stock or an exchange market. **3** An ACTIVITY (1) that is required. **4** *Leg.* A lawsuit or other legal proceeding.

action lag. A duration of time between the decision to enact POLICY and its actual implementation. See also ADMINISTRATIVE LAG.

action of contract.   *Leg.* ACTION (4) to enforce a CONTRACT.

action research.   EMPIRICAL research in the field, in which the researcher becomes a participant in the group studied and may act also as a consultant to the group.

actionable.   Eligible for ACTION (4), such as damage, misrepresentation, negligence, or nuisance.

active.   **1** Having intense ACTIVITY. **2** Productive of return, yield, or PROFIT.

active balance.   The portion of the MONEY stock which has a high VELOCITY, mainly CURRENCY and CURRENT ACCOUNT deposits. The rest of the money supply consists of idle balances. Changes in velocity normally involve transfers between active and idle balances.

active fiscal policy.   Discretionary fiscal policy (DISCRETIONARY POLICY), attempting to influence economic variables as well as obtain revenues, which can result in volatile (VOLATILITY) policy.

active management.   Seeking above-average PROFIT relative to risk.

activity.   **1** A change of state. Contrast: STATE OF BEING. **2** The intensity of activity (1); that is, how busy some AGENT (1) or organization is. **3** Trading volume.

activity analysis.   The determination, such as with linear programming, of optimal combinations processing using a given amount of inputs, each process being an 'activity'.

activity rate.   In the UK, the LABOR force participation rate, or ratio of workers to the relevant population.

activity ratio.   Any of various measures of the intensity of activity in a firm, such as sales divided by assets, generating CASH FLOW, indicating liquidity or EFFICIENCY.

actor.   A PERSON (or group of persons on behalf of an organization) who ACTS purposefully (PURPOSEFUL). An AGENT (1) can be an actor or a person acted upon.

acts/omissions question.   The ethical question of whether moral EVIL is only committed by the ACTIVITY (1) of an ACTOR, or whether moral evil can also be committed by omission, that is the failure to perform some activity. If the latter is the case, then in a pure market (PURE MARKET ECONOMY), AGENTS (1) have positive moral and legal obligations even in the absence of a CONTRACT.

actual.   Existing empirically (EMPIRICAL) rather than hypothetically or what was planned, potential, contracted for, or expected in the future, hence the true, real, correct, physical, or *EX POST* situation.

actual cash value.   The MARKET PRICE or value of a contract when it is or would be cashed out or redeemed.

actual cost.   The PRICE paid regardless of MARKET PRICE or value.

actual market value.   The PRICE an item fetches in a MARKET.

actually existing socialism.   SOCIALISM as it is and was, rather than as it theoretically should be or was alleged to be by government propaganda. This term was used by dissidents.

actuarial.   Regarding insurable RISKS and the probabilities of incurring them, used in computing payable premiums.

ad hoc.   *Lat.* Concerning a particular case, with no systematic justification or general application. The term can be pejorative if it is used for what is claimed (CLAIM (3)) to be general and justified.

ad hominem.   *Lat.* Argument directed to the person, that is one's opponent or object of criticism, rather than *AD REM*. Scientific dialogue is *ad rem*; a discussion of an economist's life and influences is *ad rem* if that is the subject, and not otherwise. The *ad hominem* fallacy consists of *ad hominem* premises and *ad rem* conclusions.

ad judicium.   *Lat.* Argument based on judgment, so named by JOHN LOCKE, for sound, warranted (WARRANT), *AD REM* arguments, that is those using LOGIC and EVIDENCE.

ad libitum.   *Lat.* However one desires.

ad rem.   *Lat.* Relevant to the thing or topic being discussed, as opposed to *AD HOMINEM*.

ad valorem **tax.**   *Lat.* A TAX on the exchange of assets or on assets, measured by the value of the assets. Examples include sales, value-added, and property taxes. With respect to income taxes, it is a FLAT TAX.

ad voluntatem.   *Lat.* According to one's will.

AD.   AGGREGATE DEMAND.

AD–AS.   A MACROECONOMIC *MODEL and analysis using AGGREGATE DEMAND and AGGREGATE SUPPLY curves. In such models, the intersection of the curves determines the equilibrium national output and the price level, although if the AS curve is vertical, only the price level is determined by this intersection, AS being already determined by the labor market and the AGGREGATE PRODUCTION FUNCTION. Some Austrian school economists (AUSTRIAN ECONOMICS), suspicious of aggregates in general, disdain such models.

Adam Smith Institute.   A FREE-MARKET-oriented organization that does POLICY research in London, UK, founded in 1977. There are also ADAM SMITH institutes in other countries.

Adams, John.   Second president of the USA, he was also a political theorist and revolutionary, arguing that the US colonies were not legally under the jurisdiction of the British parliament.

adaptive expectations.   EXPECTATIONS about the values of future variables based on projections from a weighted average of past values, without taking into account theories or models of policies of ACTORS that can change the projection, hence not taking into account all information, in contrast to RATIONAL EXPECTATIONS. However, if the theory or model is a fog, that is, overwhelmingly uncertain, or forecasting errors were made previously, then rational expectations become adaptive. For example, if nothing is known about how interest rates will move, then the rational expectation of the future interest rate is a projection of the recent movement in the interest rate.

addiction.   A strong continuous desire for some item beyond that needed for health, so that deprivation causes distress. Hence the DEMAND is extremely INELASTIC, and some question whether the preferences of an addict are really VOLUNTARY. The policy in a pure market is to allow an adult addict to exercise his PREFERENCE, since one may also choose to end the addiction and enter into remedial therapy. Those advocating RAMSEY TAXES would place a high tax burden on addicts.

adherent.   A supporter and follower of a school of thought or cause.

adiaphora.   *Gk.* Moral indifference or neutrality. In MARKET ETHICS, morally GOOD and neutral ACTS are within the market, and EVIL acts are outside of and violate the MARKET. Acts which are neither good nor evil are morally neutral.

adjudicate.   To decide a problem in a court of law. It is the ultimate process followed by market AGENTS (1) in settling disputes peacefully by having an AGENT (2) with legal authority to determine a decision. Other dispute-resolution methods are arbitration and mediation.

adjunct.   Added or connected but secondary and subordinate, hence, an instructor who contracts with a college or university to teach courses, typically part time and for much lower wages, since there is no ECONOMIC RENT with such employment.

adjust.   To alter to fit a condition, such as adjusting for a change in the PRICE LEVEL.

adjustment lag.   The duration of time in which a variable adjusts to changes in its determinants.

adjustment process.   The EQUILIBRATION of the MONEY SUPPLIES and foreign exchange in international trade so that IMPORTS and EXPORTS balance. In a GOLD STANDARD, movements of GOLD are equal and opposite to movements of other GOODS, so that a country with a surplus of exported goods imports gold, which increases the money supply, increases prices, thus decreasing exports and increasing imports until the trade balances. With a FLOATING EXCHANGE RATE, some money movements offset goods, but mainly the exchange ratios change to balance the payments.

adjustment speed.   The time it takes for a SURPLUS or SHORTAGE to disappear in the MARKET for a GOOD.

administer.   To manage and control an organization, or to carry out a task.

administered prices.   PRICES set by the GOVERNMENT rather than the MARKET such as with a regulated INDUSTRY (2), or by MONOPOLISTIC or oligopolistic (OLIGOPOLY) FIRMS when the costs of changing prices exceed the short-run losses from deviating a bit from MARKET CLEARING, or unilaterally by the management of one FIRM rather than by negotiation with its partner firms.

administrative cost. **1** The overhead in collecting TAXES. **2** Management COST.

administrative lag. The time between the realization by a MONETARY *AUTHORITY that some ACTION is desirable, and the actual action.

administrative law. The branch of law dealing with governmental administrative agencies. In the USA, the right of due process and judicial review are, by legal principle if not practice, protections against ARBITRARY and harmful acts by administrators.

administrative socialism. CENTRAL PLANNING, control, and ownership of productive assets and processes, rather than the SOCIALISM of anarchist (ANARCHISM) workers' cooperatives.

adolescence. Possibly an outcome of INTERVENTION, it is a period of time between puberty and the age of legal maturity or majority, in which a distinct teenage culture creates faddish demands for music, films, clothes, drugs and other items. Adolescence is not a purely natural stage, but is partly an outcome of mandatory school attendance, lack of apprenticeship programs, restrictions on teenage labor, and laws prohibiting teenagers from marrying and assuming adult responsibility. There is also in modern society an absence of rites of initiation into adulthood. The social problems of adolescence are at least in part outcomes from such policies.

ADR. AMERICAN DEPOSITORY RECEIPT.

adult. A fully grown and physically mature PERSON, having attained the age of majority, that is, legal authority and responsibility over one's own life. Much of MARKET theory implicitly has adults as its domain of ACTORS.

adulteration. Mixing a substance not normally included in a product into the PRODUCT (1), without informing the CONSUMER, hence constituting FRAUD.

advance. **1** A loan against expected earnings, or a payment before the provision of a service. **2** An increase. **3** A closing PRICE higher than in the previous period.

advance–decline line. The number of ADVANCES (3) minus declines.

advance–decline ratio.   The number of stocks which ADVANCE (3), divided by those which decline. This is one signal about the overall direction of an exchange MARKET.

advantage.   *N.*   A favorable or better attribute, ABILITY, or condition. See also ABSOLUTE ADVANTAGE, COMPARATIVE ADVANTAGE.

adverse balance.   A deficit in the BALANCE OF TRADE, considered adverse by some because of the mercantilist (MERCANTILISM) conception that EXPORTS are good and IMPORTS bad.

adverse selection.   The problem that those buying insurance are those most likely to receive payouts. When possible, the remedy is to differentiate the customers and CHARGE (1) those with higher risk higher premiums. There can be legal BARRIERS to this remedy, as well as asymmetric information limiting its scope.

adverse supply shock.   An increase in FACTOR prices, creating a SUPPLY *SHOCK that reduces AGGREGATE SUPPLY.

advertise.   To publicize and promote one's BIDS or offerings and increase GOODWILL in order to increase the demand. Most advertising is by private companies, but GOVERNMENTS also advertise (for example, state lotteries). One element in advertising is information, and another is persuasion to change PREFERENCES. Advertising is criticized as a social WASTE, but aside from the information, advertising provides the variety that some customers like, helps build brand reputation, is a vehicle for competition, and pays for media such as newspapers and television. Advertisements directed to children may be problematic, but those directed to ADULTS do not impinge on CONSUMER SOVEREIGNTY so long as there is no deception. See SYNTHESIZED DEMAND.

advisor.   An organization that contracts with a MUTUAL FUND to provide knowledge and advice on investments and their management.

Aenesidemus of Cnossos.   Skepticism is a basic element of scientific, hence economic, method, and skepticism relies on the tropes posited by Aenesidemus, a defender of Pyrrhonism. Some of the tropes involve SUBJECTIVE VALUES and differing perceptions, hence can contribute to the theory of subjectivity in economics.

aesthetics and economics.   Aesthetics is the study of art and beauty. What is pleasing as perceived by the senses involves LOGIC, psychology (genetically determined responses to color, and so on), culture, and personally SUBJECTIVE tastes. The elements of LOGIC and psychology incur an element of objectivity (OBJECTIVE) to aesthetics, so that for example a 'well-written essay' has both objective and subjective elements. Among the relationships of aesthetics to ECONOMICS are: i) aesthetics as a goal of production (rather than purely instrumental utility); ii) the role of aesthetic values in the formation of theory (see ELEGANT); iii) aesthetic values as a PUBLIC GOOD and their PROVISION by the MARKET PROCESS, that is the question of whether there would be more beauty (for example in civic architecture) in an unhampered market or with interventionist planning; iv) the depiction of economic ideas through art (whether visual, poetic, prose, or musical). A question that can be posed is why there seems to be little poetry devoted to the beauty of free markets.

aetiology. Etiology, the determination and assignment of causes.

affairs. In economics, the totality of one's activities and assets, including one's PROPERTY and BUSINESS (1).

affiliated company. A company that has a substantial proportion of its STOCK (2) owned by another company.

affiliated person. A person who can influence the policy of a CORPORATION; for example directors, high-level executives, and major share owners.

affinity card. A credit card affiliated with a nonprofit organization which receives funds in proportion to the amount spent.

affirm the antecedent. In a statement S: 'if X then Y', X is the ANTECEDENT, and to affirm the antedecent is to validly conclude Y from the premises X. Syn. *modus ponens*.

affirmantis est probare. *Lat.* The burden of proof is on one who affirms.

affirmative action. **1** The POLICY of favoring the members of a particular group (previously disadvantaged) among equally qualified candidates. **2** Reverse discrimination in favor of specified previously disadvantaged groups, so that lesser qualified applicants might be admitted in order to satisfy criteria such as the desire for diversity or longer-term equality.

Neither (1) nor (2) necessarily imply quotas as an outcome, since affirmative action *per se* is a PROCESS. Affirmative action creates more temporary inequality in order to more quickly advance long-term equality, hence aggressively 'affirming' the goal of equal opportunity. Both (1) and (2) can be and in practice are mandated by law in the USA and other countries. In a FREE MARKET, affirmative action would be a voluntary option for PRIVATE ENTERPRISE; GOVERNMENT would not engage in (2) and would engage in (1) only to remedy recent negative arbitrary discrimination. Equal opportunity would provide economic justice without discrimination. One cost of reverse discrimination is to lower the esteem of the positions held by members of the group subject to affirmative action, even when obtained by superior merit.

affluence. Having such a high degree of WEALTH and INCOME that much of one's purchasing consists of discretionary items rather than NEEDS such as food, medicine, and shelter.

affluent society. A country in which a large middle- and upper-class have a great deal of discretionary income and wealth. The term was used by John Kenneth Galbraith (1958), who argued that further output should be shifted to GOVERNMENT-determined CONSUMPTION for social services. In this view, since needs and basic comforts have been provided, further wants are artificially created by advertising (ADVERTISE). Such a view is countered by the subjectivity of values, the proposition that human desires are unlimited, the feasible provision of PUBLIC GOODS by private and voluntary enterprise, the social cost of transfer seeking associated with government expenditure, and the excess burden of TAXATION as it has existed in affluent countries. The poor and lower-income classes might also argue in favor of their having greater private consumption rather than more government spending.

afford. Able to pay for something, or able to obtain something without great SACRIFICE.

after-hours trading. Exchanging shares of stock after the closing for normal trading.

after tax. Net, after having paid TAXES. The real return on an asset is after price INFLATION and after taxes.

AG. *Aktiengesellschaft.* A Swiss or German corporation.

against the box. A SHORT SALE of stocks which the seller owns but rather than delivering them, he borrows them from a broker.

Age of Enlightenment. The era in Europe from about 1650 to 1800, during which there was a great advance in philosophy and science, particularly in the recognition of human EQUALITY, LIBERTY, and NATURAL RIGHTS, with greater tolerance for dissent and minorities.

age of majority.   The age at which a youth legally becomes an ADULT and may contract *sui juris*.

Age of Reason.   Congruent with the AGE OF ENLIGHTENMENT, the age of REASON was characterized by the recognition that TRUTH, including social ETHICS and the proper basis of GOVERNMENT, is discovered using reason, rather than relying merely on tradition, authority, or whim.

agency.   1 An entity that ACTS (1). 2 An organization acting on behalf of customers, subjects, members, or citizens. A governing agency is the organization that conducts GOVERNANCE, whether of a GOVERNMENT or an ASSOCIATION.

agency cost.   The COSTS of having an AGENT (2), including the cost of MORAL HAZARD.

agency problem.   A PRINCIPAL–AGENT problem of CORPORATIONS due to their separation of ownership from control. Managers pursue their own goals, such as maximization of their salaries and options, rather than the best interests of the shareholders. A partial remedy is the common practice of payment in stocks and options, especially for the chief executive officer, but executive pay may become greater than warranted by performance and the competition for managers. Legal reforms making it easier to sue while making the loser of lawsuits pay the legal costs of the winner may help.

agency shop.   A virtual UNION SHOP, prevalent in the GOVERNMENT sector in the USA, where workers pay the equivalent of union dues while the union acts as the bargaining AGENT (2), circumventing right-to-work laws.

agency theory.   The theory concerning the relationship between a principal and an AGENT (2), the latter having an agenda that differs from that of the principal who hires him. The two parties may also have differing perceptions of risk. See AGENCY PROBLEM.

agenda.   A list of things to be done. In politics and PUBLIC CHOICE, the agenda consists of the candidates, topics, and items presented to voters (VOTING) and decision makers. If voters only have the CHOICE among the items in an agenda, the agenda setters have great POWER, since they determine and limit the set of choices. The order in which the agendas or items to be voted on are presented can determine the outcomes.

agent. **1** A person or organization which ACTS and through its ACTIVITY achieves some effect. **2** An agent (1) acting on behalf of another. See PRINCIPAL AND AGENT.

agglomeration. A gathered-together dense mass, such as people in a city or stores in a shopping district. See DISECONOMIES OF AGGLOMERATION, ECONOMIES OF AGGLOMERATION.

aggravation. Harm done by a CRIME or tort beyond the defining elements of the crime or tort.

aggregate corporation. A CORPORATION with more than one shareholder.

aggregate demand. *Abbrev.* AD. The totality of DEMAND or EXPENDITURE for all GOODS in an ECONOMY (1), based on NET DOMESTIC PRODUCT. In AD–AS analysis, it is graphed against the PRICE LEVEL, with a downward-sloping curve, since for a given amount of NOMINAL *INCOME (hence MONEY SUPPLY), a lower price level enables buyers to obtain a greater quantity of goods. This aggregate EQUILIBRIUM demand curve shifts with income, thus DEMAND-SIDE analysis posits that greater spending, for example by GOVERNMENT, shifts the curve outward, to more goods, if the AGGREGATE SUPPLY curve is upward-sloping. But that effect also depends on where the funds come from and the relationship between savings and investment. If all savings are invested, then domestic sources of funding do not shift aggregate demand, although foreign spending can shift the curve. If the aggregate supply curve is vertical, a shift in aggregate demand does not change output but only the price level. Some Austrian school economists (AUSTRIAN ECONOMICS) question the usefulness or meaning of the concept of aggregate demand.

aggregate expenditure. The totality of NOMINAL *EXPENDITURE in an ECONOMY (1) during some time period. The significant expenditure categories are CONSUMER and CAPITAL GOODS, but national accounting and analysis thereof typically have as their categories private CONSUMPTION of domestic goods, private domestic INVESTMENT, net EXPORTS, and GOVERNMENT spending, hence $Y = C + I + G + (X - M)$. Syn. national output. See also NATIONAL INCOME.

aggregate output. **1** NATIONAL INCOME calculated by summing value-added, priced at factor cost. **2** GROSS DOMESTIC PRODUCT.

aggregate production function. AGGREGATE EXPENDITURE or national output as a function of MACROECONOMIC inputs or FACTORS, namely LAND, LABOR, and CAPITAL GOODS. In the short-run function, land and capital goods are held constant, with labor variable. In macroeconomic models, the quantity of labor is set by the labor market, and this is then carried to the aggregate production function to determine national output. Some economists think the concept of an aggregate production function is meaningless. It seems, however, that it is conceptually sound to envision greater output when there are more ECONOMY-wide inputs.

Due to DIMINISHING RETURNS on the fixed factors, the short-run aggregate production function has a positive first and a negative second derivative. More workers increase output, but at a declining rate. Note that this is not a model of the growth of the labor supply over time, but of various amounts of labor at a particular moment in time. Most depictions of the function only use two factors, implicitly weaving land into capital goods, whereas in classical and GEO-ECONOMIC theory, the productivity of land is an important distinction.

aggregate supply.   *Abbrev.* AS. The totality of SUPPLY for all GOODS in an ECONOMY (1) (the NET DOMESTIC PRODUCT). The AGGREGATE PRODUCTION FUNCTION determines the aggregate supply as a function of FACTOR inputs. In AD–AS analysis, AS is graphed against the PRICE LEVEL. In the classical macroeconomic model, the AS curve is vertical, since output is determined in the LABOR market, where WAGES are set at MARKET-CLEARING rates.

In DEMAND-SIDE and KEYNESIAN ECONOMICS, the AS curve can be upward-sloping if there are idle resources stuck above market-clearing rates. For example, if NOMINAL wages are stuck above the market-clearing rate, an increase in the money supply raises the price level, lowering the REAL WAGE, hence increasing the quantity of LABOR demanded, thus raising output. Successive increases in the price level thus are associated with successive increases in output.

A question in such demand-side theory is why the wage level would be above market-clearing in the first place, and why there would be ECONOMY-wide rigidities. The long-term wage contract as a rationale for sticky-wage manipulative monetary policy has been shown by Foldvary and Selgin (1995) to be inconsistent with RATIONAL EXPECTATIONS.

aggregates.   *N.* A set of items gathered into a whole. An example is AGGREGATE EXPENDITURE, which sums the expenditures of many items and categories. Aggregation of diverse items, even when they belong to some common category, can mask the importance of diversity within the category. For example, treating CAPITAL GOODS as an aggregate masks the CAPITAL STRUCTURE (1), with some capital goods being more roundabout than other, lower-order, capital goods. Austrian economists especially are suspicious of the meaningfulness of aggregates, including data.

aggregation problem.   The problem of deriving MACROECONOMIC theory variables, and relationships from the BEHAVIOR and variables of MICROECONOMIC items. An example is a SOCIAL WELFARE FUNCTION.

aggression.   The initiation of an unprovoked attack, forcefully invading (INVASION) the DOMAIN of another, in violation of the RIGHTS of the victim. Aggression violates FREE-MARKET principles.

aggressive.   1 Inclined and tending to commit AGGRESSION. 2 Having initiative, bold, active; willing to take risks for large gains.

aggressive growth fund.   An AGGRESSIVE (2) MUTUAL FUND, taking on a high risk to attain superior appreciation.

aggrieved.   Having suffered a loss, harm, or violation of RIGHTS.

aging.   An increase in the median age of a population. The economic impact is a greater proportion of persons not in the LABOR force, hence when there are pay-as-you-go government welfare programs for the aged funded by PAYROLL TAXES, as is common with SOCIAL SECURITY programs, the burden of dependency on workers and employers increases. In traditional societies, except when food is SCARCE (2), the aged are not a SOCIAL PROBLEM because they live with their offspring in extended families and provide child-care services. Dietary and environmental causes of illness contribute to the medical burden of the aged; these causes are significantly increased by intervention subsidizing (SUBSIDY) unhealthy practices (for example by fraudulently implying a product is healthy) and preventing the provision of innovative remedies for disease.

agio.   1 The difference in value between monetary or INTEREST-RATE variables and values, such as present-day funds versus future funds (the agio for interest and discount rates), or gold versus paper currency. 2 A FEE paid to exchange currencies.

agio theory of interest.   The theory that INTEREST is due to TIME PREFERENCE, with present-day goods being more desirable than future goods, the rate of discount being the NATURAL RATE OF INTEREST. The Austrian theory of interest (AUSTRIAN ECONOMICS) is an AGIO (1) theory.

agnostic.   1 Neither believing nor disbelieving, pending warrants, hence having a skeptical attitude and suspending judgment. 2 The view (coined by T.H. Huxley) that some phenomenon such as God cannot possibly be known, that is, proven or disproved, although an agnostic can also be a theist or atheist by faith. By extension, the agnostic doctrine of knowledge is that nothing can be proven, there is no absolute knowledge, and all beliefs are relative.

agora. *Gk.* **1** In ancient Greece, a place of assembly, particularly MARKET places. **2** An Israeli coin, one-hundredth of a shekel. **3** In modern usage, particularly among FREE-MARKET adherents, the market or the free market, used for poetic effect.

agoric. MARKET-like.

agoric systems. Computer systems in which resources are bought and sold in AUCTION-type MARKETS.

agrarian revolution. A major increase in agricultural output due to the use of better CAPITAL GOODS, including superior seeds. There can be a cost in less variety and vulnerability of large-scale single crops to diseases. *Syn.* agricultural revolution.

agreement. A CONTRACT or VOLUNTARY *ACCEPTANCE of terms among PERSONS. Agreement is the basis of FREE-MARKET organizations and TRANSACTIONS. A blanket agreement covers a wide range of items, not necessarily enumerated. A gentlemen's agreement is a verbal agreement based on trust.

agribusiness. A large COMPANY that produces and distributes agricultural products.

agricultural economics. The ECONOMICS of AGRICULTURE, a major branch of economics, with departments and schools (or faculties, as in Europe) devoted to the field.

agricultural reform. The reform of either techniques or LAND TENURE in AGRICULTURE. See also LAND REFORM. Besides better CAPITAL GOODS and training, organizational reform such as the formation of COOPERATIVES, and financial reform such as ACCESS to CREDIT (1), are elements of creating more productive techniques. The reform of land tenure can lead to greater productivity by shifting sites to more intensive and more efficient use, for example from large estates that underuse land or from inefficient state farms.

agricultural revolution. See AGRARIAN REVOLUTION.

agricultural subsidies. GOVERNMENT *POLICY which transfers income to farm owners, including funds and price supports. CONSUMERS and taxpayers bear much of the burden, while the owners of farmland obtain much of the benefit, since such SUBSIDIES become capitalized in the value (CAPITALIZED VALUE) of farmland. Farming interests have concentrated benefits and their representatives use LOGROLLING to obtain these subsidies.

agricultural system. PHYSIOCRACY, called thus by ADAM SMITH in *The Wealth of Nations* 1776, 1976.

agriculture. The production of plant and animal PRODUCTS (1) for food, fiber, and fuel. Agriculture is classified as a sector of an ECONOMY, the other two typically being manufacturing and SERVICES. DEVELOPMENT normally shrinks employment in the agricultural sector.

ahistorical. Presenting a theory as though it had no history, when it does have historical elements. For example, theory which treats human beings as atomistic (ATOMISM) individuals (other than as a conditional premise) is ahistorical, since human beings have historically lived in organized COMMUNITIES.

aid. A transfer of resources; GOVERNMENT aid forcibly transfers resources from taxpayers to foreign and domestic recipients. Much foreign aid has been wasted or diverted from its intended recipients, and a lack of development due to POLICY *BARRIERS may not be overcome with aid.

air rights. The right to use or benefit from the air space above the surface of land owned (LANDOWNER), or collect damages, for example from noisy airplane flights.

airline deregulation. The removal of price controls and other restrictions on airlines. Previous to regulation, airlines in the USA functioned as a CARTEL.

Alchian, Armen (1914–). Professor emeritus at UCLA and author with W. Allen of FREE-MARKET-oriented textbook *University Economics*. Some of his articles are reprinted in *Economic Forces at Work* (Liberty Press, 1977). His paper 'Uncertainty, Evolution, and Economic Theory' (1950) made the point that the MARKET PROCESS is one of survival of the profitably 'fit' firms which do maximize profits.

aleatory contract. An AGREEMENT whose fulfillment depends on uncertain (UNCERTAINTY), uncontrollable events, beyond the will of the parties.

alien corporation.   A domestic COMPANY incorporated abroad.

alienable.   Capable of being transferred or abandoned (ABANDON).

alienation.   1 A transfer of PROPERTY to another. 2 An early Marxist term and concept (derived from Hegel and Feuerbach) for the feeling of detachment, separation, apathy, estrangement and/or resentment felt by the PROLETARIAT because these workers do not own the CAPITAL GOODS and LAND which they work with, hence they see themselves as mere objects, means to others' ends. Contrary to this view, how workers are treated, how much they are empow-ered and their working conditions, has much to do with their identity and SYMPATHY for the COMPANIES they work for, their PRODUCTS (1), and themselves. 3 Estrangement from GOVERNMENT due to its COERCION and the inability of the victim to change the POLICY or to escape from it. 4 The Freudian concept of a psychological estrangement from natural peaceful human inclinations and instincts because of the constraints of civilization that represses these, so that man becomes a stranger to himself. Evidently these constraints are enforced by the state to prevent nature from re-emerging. The economic impact is the enforced consumption of items that natural man would not prefer.

all faults.   A sale in which faults in the PRODUCT (1) which do not change the identity of the GOODS, and in which there is no FRAUD, are covered, hence not ACTIONABLE. *Syn.* as is.

All Ordinaries Index.   A PRICE INDEX of major stocks on the Australian Stock Exchange.

All-Share Index.   *Financial Times* Actuaries All-Share Index of about 700 companies on the London Stock Exchange.

allocation function.   The provision of GOODS and SERVICES by GOVERNMENT. The other two functions in Richard Musgrave's taxonomy are REDISTRIBUTION and stabilization (STABLE). FREE-MARKET thought has been critical of the latter two functions, while the refutation of MARKET-FAILURE arguments, along with PUBLIC-CHOICE theory, has cast doubt on the proposition that allocation too must be governmental, as a general proposition.

allocative efficiency.   The OPTIMAL set of outputs produced in the most EFFICIENT way with the most efficient combination of inputs.

allodari.   Allodiaries (see ALLODIARY).

allodial.   Concerning LAND *TITLE held without any OBLIGATION to another AGENCY such as a lord, STATE, or other co-owner, hence free of any vassalage, fealty, RENTAL payment or TAX. See also FEUDALISM, GEOISM. In allodial policy, the LAND TENURE consists of many holdings rather than a governmental (GOVERNMENT) ALLODIARY.

allodialism.   The social system, or belief in such, based on ALLODIAL *LAND *OWNERSHIP. One proponent is John Cobin.

allodiary.   A PERSON who has title to LAND under ALLODIAL tenure.

allodification.   Making LAND TENURE *ALLODIAL.

allodium.   Land under ALLODIAL *OWNERSHIP.

allowance.   1 MONEY given or paid for a particular reason, or periodically as a GIFT. 2 A DEDUCTION (1) from taxable INCOME.

alpha.   1 *Fin.*, *Gk.* The RETURN of a MUTUAL FUND relative to a general market portfolio of the same RISK (2). Thus, a positive alpha indicates superior performance. See also BETA. 2 Letter commonly used for the constant in a regression equation in econometrics.

altruism.   The practice and desire of selflessly benefitting (BENEFIT) others rather than one's narrow SELF-INTEREST. SYMPATHY differs from altruism in that with sympathy, one derives utility (UTILITY, MARGINAL) from benefitting others, while with pure altruism, one does it from a sense of DUTY or OBLIGATION, although 'altruism' is also used to refer to acts due to sympathy. Followers of AYN RAND disdain such self-sacrifice. In NATURAL MORAL LAW, benefitting others is morally good (GOOD, MORALLY), but not a moral obligation. With a MARKET consisting of VOLUNTARY *ACTION, benefits to others fall within the DOMAIN of free markets. Contrast: egoism.

amalgamated company.   An amalgamation or combination of FIRMS into effectively one firm, which then has great MARKET POWER. *Syn.* TRUST (2).

ambiguity.   Vague, doubtful, uncertain (UNCERTAINTY), unclear, or multiple meanings. Whether of language in a theoretical PROPOSITION or in a CONTRACT, it is good scientific and legal practice to have clear and distinct meanings for key terms.

ambitus.   *Lat.* Obtaining a GOVERNMENT office through purchase rather than by election or appointment by merit.

ameliorations. Improvements.

amenities. **1** The benefits of the PUBLIC GOODS in a COMMUNITY such as swimming pools, also including the natural conditions (views, air, climate). These typically become capitalized (CAPITALIZATION) in LAND *RENT or PROPERTY *VALUE. **2** A negative easement, hence constraining the RIGHTS of the owner.

American Depository Receipt. A security issued by a domestic BANK, which represents and is backed by the holding of the foreign security by the bank, the ADR receiving the DIVIDEND. These trade on the US and UK stock exchanges. Since ADRs represent foreign stocks, there is a CURRENCY *RISK (1) in addition to the value risk (1).

American Economic Association. The major US professional organization of economists. It holds an annual conference in conjunction with other economic societies. Its *The Journal of Economic Literature* presents a record of published work.

American Enterprise Institute. An organization which conducts research on the impact of policy on enterprise and the ECONOMY.

American Institute for Economic Research. Based in Massachusetts, the AIER focuses its research on the BUSINESS CYCLE, MONETARY economics, and land-value taxation (LAND-VALUE TAX). It sells its publications to the public, including booklets on personal finance. The methodology espoused derives from the work of Dewey and Harwood.

American rule. In law, the practice of making the winner of a lawsuit pay his own attorney fees unless statute law or a CONTRACT specifies awarding such fees. In the English rule, the losing party pays the attorney fees of the winning party. The American rule amounts to a TAX on parties who are sued and win their cases. FREE-MARKET economies encompass the ENGLISH TORT SYSTEM.

AMEX. The American Stock Exchange in New York City.

amittere legem terrae. *Lat.* Not protected by the law of the land. This is one way a free society can deal with criminals, or those who refuse to pay for COMMUNITY services, by literally making them outlaws.

amoral. **1** Without regard to MORALITY. **2** NONMORAL.

amortization. The repayment of principal or DEPRECIATION (1) of CAPITAL GOODS value over the life of the loan or ASSET.

ampliative argument. An argument whose conclusions are derived not just from the explicit premises but also from unstated, implicit premises. Coined by Peirce, this characterizes much reasoning (REASON).

amplitude. The difference between output at the peak and trough of a BUSINESS CYCLE.

amusement tax. A SALES TAX on tickets for amusement parks, sports events, and so on, normally *ad valorem* (AD VALOREM TAX).

analysis. The logical (LOGIC) separation of a CONCEPT into parts so that one may study the structure and then derive an explanation for the PHENOMENON.

analytic. 1 Regarding ANALYSIS. 2 Mathematical, stemming from the view that the only vehicle for THEORY is mathematical MODELS, hence that rigorous analysis is necessarily mathematical, a view emphatically rejected by Austrian (AUSTRIAN ECONOMICS) and geo-economists (GEO-ECONOMICS) (see Boettke, 1996). 3 *Phil.* A property of a PROPOSITION, that it is necessarily true, or even a tautology, since it follows from and is already incorporated in the meaning of the terms and premises.

anarchism. The political philosophy of social harmony without any state or IMPOSED *GOVERNMENT. RULES and COMMUNITY *GOODS are instead provided by VOLUNTARY *ASSOCIATION. Anarchist rules derive from an ETHIC by which RIGHTS are mutually respected in peaceful cooperation. Major anarchists include William Godwin, Max Stirner, Benjamin Tucker, Pierre-Joseph Proudhon, MIKHAIL BAKUNIN, Peter Kropotkin, Leo Tolstoy, and MURRAY ROTHBARD. See also ANARCHY, ARCHISM.
   Tucker and Rothbard were libertarians, and Tolstoy a geo-anarchist, and the rest cooperativists (COOPERATIVE), mutualists, or socialists (SOCIALISM). Anarchism is generally split between collectivists (COLLECTIVISM) who advocate cooperative ENTERPRISE and oppose individual PRIVATE (1) PROPERTY, and individualists (INDIVIDUALISM) or anarcho-capitalists (ANARCHO-CAPITALISM) who advocate individual LIBERTY and regard individual property as proper. A third variant is GEO-ANARCHISM, in which LAND is commonly owned but other property is held individually.
   If there are multilevel networks of associations, up to a continental association of associations, then there is a continuum rather than a sharp line between anarchism and MINARCHISM. If most of society is organized in net-

works of associations, then effectively there is a uniform rule of law even under anarchism.

anarcho-capitalism. Individualist (INDIVIDUALISM) ALLODIAL *ANARCHISM, hence a social system with PRIVATE ENTERPRISE, ALLODIAL *LAND *OWNERSHIP, and no IMPOSED *GOVERNMENT.

anarcho-geoism. *Syn.* of GEO-ANARCHISM.

anarcho-syndicalism. The movement and philosophy of trade union ANARCHISM, in which the MEANS OF PRODUCTION is held by labor UNIONS and worker COOPERATIVES.

anarchy. 1 The practice of ANARCHISM. 2 Social CHAOS or violence, often used pejoratively. The term 'anarchy' is misleadingly used in this sense when there is *anomie* or internal conflict, associating the absence of effective GOVERNANCE with conflict, whereas anarchy (1) is peaceful and orderly (ORDER). This negative meaning was due to self-styled anarchists such as BAKUNIN who advocated violent revolution.

anarchy of production. The MARXIST-ECONOMICS notion that the PURE *MARKET PROCESS is not orderly (ORDER) but chaotic (CHAOS).

Anderson, James (1739–1808). Scottish agricultural economist, he pioneered the concept of DIFFERENTIAL RENT as the price for superior LAND, thus influencing DAVID RICARDO.

angel-of-death provision. TAX *POLICY that exempts unrealized gains from taxation on the death of the owner, when the PROPERTY is valued on a stepped-up basis (STEP UP OF BASIS). The effect is to lock in property that is to be inherited; owners borrow funds rather than sell property and pay a CAPITAL GAINS TAX.

angild. In Saxon law, the value of a PERSON or object, which amounted to the COMPENSATION (1) due the victim of a CRIME.

Angliae jura in omni casu libertatis dant favorem.   *Lat.* English law in all cases should be favorable to liberty.

animal rights. The NATURAL RIGHTS of animals, with the view that while human beings have the right to obtain utility (UTILITY, MARGINAL) from animals, animals have the right not to be unduly harmed, such as suffering beyond what is reasonably needed for material utility (not the utility of sadists who enjoy the suffering). If animal rights are recognized, then the implication for the MARKET PROCESS is that acts which violate the rights of animals are prohibited or fined. Some animal-rights advocates go to unwarranted extremes, placing the rights of nonperson animals equal to those of persons.

animal spirits.   **1** Lively vigor. **2** The antiquated notion that sensation and movement depend on a fluid called 'animal spirits.' **3** The term as appropriated by J.M. KEYNES and then Joan Robinson for investment based on emotional factors, for example pessimism or optimism. Animal spirits as an explanation for major turns in the ECONOMY rather begs the question of the cause of the pessimism or optimism, and why sentiments should change.

annual percentage rate.   The true COST of borrowing for t years, calculated as the annual compounded percentage:

$$APR = 100 \left((1 + \text{total credit payment})/\text{amount of credit}\right)^{1/t}.$$

annual report.   A publication by CORPORATIONS of their finances and operations during their fiscal or calendar year. Investors and lenders use it to evaluate the FIRM.

annuity.   A periodic payment for a fixed number of years or for the life of the annuitant. One annuitizes a lump sum by transforming into such payments, INSURANCE *COMPANIES averaging out expected lifetimes.

antecedent.   **1** *Log.* In the conditional statement 'if X then Y,' X is the antecedent and Y the CONSEQUENT. See AFFIRM THE ANTECEDENT. **2** *Law* Prior in time.

antenuptial agreement.   A CONTRACT prior to marriage to determine division of PROPERTY after divorce or death of one of the spouses. This normally must be in writing to be enforceable. *Syn.* prenuptial agreement.

anthropology.   The science of human origins and CULTURE. Cultural anthropology intersects with ECONOMICS in economic anthropology, the study of the influence of culture on economies and vice versa. In a FREE MARKET, cultural expression is VOLUNTARY, whereas with INTERVENTION, cultural rules are IMPOSED on unwilling minorities, thus skewing CONSUMPTION and PRODUCTION from what free AGENTS (1) would choose. Institutional economists (INSTITUTIONAL ECONOMICS) pay attention to culture, and some Austrians (AUSTRIAN

ECONOMICS) also do so or favor doing so. Among anthropologists doing economic analysis is Spencer MacCallum, who has written on PROPRIETARY COMMUNITIES and their financing. A basic premise of social science, that human beings form one species, is derived from anthropological theory.

anti-combines legislation. Canadian ANTITRUST law.

anti-dumping law. A legal minimum PRICE for imported (IMPORT) GOODS, preventing imports below the normal production price.

anti-poverty programs. POLICY and GOVERNMENT funds intended to alleviate POVERTY with WELFARE (2) transfers, or possibly reduce poverty. Typically, such programs treat the effects and not the underlying causes, such as TAXATION and legal RESTRICTIONS which limit ENTERPRISE and thus EMPLOYMENT and after-tax WAGES.

anti-trust. Alternative spelling of ANTITRUST.

anticipated inflation. Expected PRICE INFLATION.

antinomian. *Gk.* One who desires to be exempt from social customs and GOVERNMENT law, other than the most basic norms, but who also does not engage in revolutions to overturn the laws.

antique. An old object no longer being made, often a COLLECTIBLE. By extension, antiques are any goods no longer in production.

antitrust. The POLICY of breaking up large FIRMS, AMALGAMATED COMPANIES, and CARTELS, allegedly to enhance COMPETITION and reduce firms' MARKET POWER. The policy also can include the prohibition of practices such as PRICE DISCRIMINATION and exclusive CONTRACTS. Many FREE-MARKET economists view antitrust policy as misguided, since there is global RIVALRY among firms in a domestically concentrated (CONCENTRATION) INDUSTRY (2), large firms can reduce per-unit costs and fund more research, potential entry limits monopoly power, and the policy can be excessive or politically influenced. Ironically, GOVERNMENT itself is the source of much monopoly power, whether with enterprises such as postal service, or in protecting labor union monopolies, protecting domestic industry from foreign competition, and in monopolistic government itself, that is limiting competitive governance, for example by limiting DECENTRALIZATION of government or access to elections by minor political parties.

apartheid.   Intervention enforcing the separation of races, with some placed in inferior status, particularly as was practiced in South Africa until 1992.

apathy.   Without feeling, hence lacking either SYMPATHY or antipathy towards something. Since sympathy motivates benevolent (BENEVOLENCE) acts as well as participation in the POLITICAL process, a society with a large degree of political apathy will have a low level of VOTING, and one having social apathy will have few DONATIONS. The prevalence of apathy when great EVILS occur helps perpetuate those evils. Apathy complements GREED and IGNORANCE to create and maintain SOCIAL PROBLEMS. See also SYMPATHY.

APC.   Average propensity to consume.

apodictic.   Provable as TRUE with certainty, because LOGIC makes it so. For example, if B is a subset of A, then the existence of B must imply that of A. AXIOMATIC-DEDUCTIVE *THEORY is apodictically true if the premises must be true, such as when their negation involves some logical contradiction. LUDWIG VON MISES held that propositions of PRAXEOLOGY are apodictic.

appearance and reality.   ECONOMICS delves beneath the superficial appearance of phenomena (PHENOMENON) to elucidate the underlying reality. A simple example is the difference between NOMINAL and REAL INTEREST rates. KARL MARX thought his THEORY involved this process, but all economic theory attempts to do so. Followers of HENRY GEORGE call the discovery of the underlying reality 'seeing the CAT.'

application lag.   The time interval between enacting POLICY and actually (ACTUAL) implementing the policy. This is one of several lags which can make even desirable policy ineffective when conditions change.

applied economics.   The application of general ECONOMIC *THEORY to specific events or topics.

appraise.   To estimate the MARKET PRICE of an item. See also assess.

appreciation.   An increase in the value of an ASSET. ACCOUNTING practice typically does not recognize unrealized appreciation, although from an economic viewpoint maybe it should.

apprenticeship.   Learning a craft under supervision of a FIRM or person engaged in it. This practice has been undermined with laws mandating schooling until the late teens, prohibiting the EMPLOYMENT of youth, mandating

MINIMUM WAGES, and subsidizing (SUBSIDY) formal and college EDUCATION. See also ADOLESCENCE.

appropriate technology. Technology suitable for local conditions, particularly in ECONOMIC DEVELOPMENT. GOVERNMENT-sponsored development, often with foreign governmental aid, is sometimes inappropriate, if not damaging. The MARKET PROCESS selects what is appropriate, since PROFIT-making AGENTS (1) generally ECONOMIZE.

approval voting. An election system in which the electors vote (VOTING) for those options they approve of, and the one with the highest votes is the winner. This method avoids the PARADOX OF VOTING that plagues simple MAJORITY-RULE systems. See also BORDA COUNT.

approvals. COLLECTIBLES sent on request to a collector, who then selects those items he desires, and returns the rest. This is also referred to as 'on approval.'

APR. Annual percentage rate.

apriorism. The doctrine that there is A PRIORI knowledge, that is KNOWLEDGE that is prior to experience.

aquatic rights. RIGHTS to use the sea and other waters, and to soil beneath the waters.

arable land. LAND fit for plowing and growing crops.

arbitrage. The purchase of an asset where it is relatively cheap and its sale where it is higher priced, thus the practice eventually leveling out the PRICES and tending to keep them uniform. In ISRAEL KIRZNER's concept of the ENTREPRENEUR, arbitrage plays a key role.

arbitrary. 1 Discretionary, based on whim or personal, SUBJECTIVE desire. 2 Not based on RATIONALITY (2), but on the desires and interests of those with power. Hence, arbitrary law is interventionist (INTERVENTION), since it is not based on NATURAL LAW or on principles that enhance an ECONOMY. Randomness, however, is not necessarily arbitrary, such as when the situation calls for a random choice (for example toss of a coin).

arbitration. The binding resolution of a dispute at the request of the parties, an alternative to more costly litigation.

archism.   The opposite of ANARCHISM, hence the belief that a STATE and IMPOSED *GOVERNMENT is necessary for social harmony. See also ANARCHISM, MINARCHISM.

archy.   A society with a ruler; the practice of ARCHISM.

area.   **1** An amount of TERRITORY. **2** A topic or scope.

argument.   Statements in support of a conclusion.

argument from intimidation.   A concept of AYN RAND, a method of squashing real debate with psychological pressure, such as claiming that it is immoral to hold the opposite view.

argumentum a contrario.   *Lat.* Arguing the contrary to make the opposite point.

aristocracy.   In Greek thought this meant rule by the best, but in practice it has been rule by a small elite which typically owns most of the LAND. Traditionally, the aristocracy was also the nobility.

Aristotle (384–322 BC).   Greek philosopher of great influence, who also wrote on ECONOMICS. He distinguished between use and exchange value. He defended PRIVATE (1) PROPERTY, but opposed the use of INTEREST, not understanding its meaning.

arm's length.   Without financial link between contracting parties.

arms, right to bear.   A RIGHT guaranteed by the Second Amendment of the US Constitution, said to be a needed defense against tyranny, hence a protector also of a FREE MARKET.

Arrow, Kenneth (1921–).   American economist famous for his IMPOSSIBILITY THEOREM. He won the economics Nobel prize in 1972, jointly with Sir John Hicks. He and Debreu showed in 1954 that multimarket EQUILIBRIUM requires forward markets. His *Social Choice and Individual Values* (1951, 1966) presented the PROPOSITION that it is impossible to have a social ranking that is consistent with individual rankings. By undermining imposed COLLECTIVISM, Arrow, though favoring welfare INTERVENTION, is a contributor to FREE-MARKET thought.

artificial. Not due to the natural ECONOMY, that is, a FREE MARKET and VOLUNTARY action, but to INTERVENTION.

artificial persons. Organizations such as CORPORATIONS treated by law as PERSONS, in contrast to natural persons.

arts policy. Subsidy and protection of arts by government, which involves evaluations that are necessarily ARBITRARY, given the subjectivity (SUBJECTIVE) of tastes. Protection from foreign art is advocated to protect national culture, contrary to the CHOICES of the CONSUMERS. See also AESTHETICS AND ECONOMICS.

AS. AGGREGATE SUPPLY.

as is. Of GOODS for which the seller offers no warranty other than honesty.

as much as the market will bear. See BEAR, WHAT THE MARKET WILL.

ask. A seller's offering PRICE, in contrast to the buyer's BID.

assault. A willful attempt or threat to use unlawful FORCE to injure another person.

assay mark. A mark placed on a bar of PRECIOUS METAL to indicate the weight.

assertion. **1** A PROPOSITION. **2** A proposition lacking WARRANTS.

assessed value. The value of REAL ESTATE according to the ASSESSMENT, which can be a certain fraction of market value.

assessment. **1** Appraisal (APPRAISE) of property such as REAL ESTATE by a governing AGENCY, often multiplied by some fraction less than one, to establish the ASSESSED VALUE. **2** A payment by a PROPERTY owner (OWNERSHIP) based on an assessment (1) to pay for the cost of common SERVICES, for example in a CONDOMINIUM or RESIDENTIAL ASSOCIATION. See SPECIAL ASSESSMENTS.

asset. **1** An owned item that is valuable. These are divided into REAL ASSETS and FINANCIAL ASSETS. Other distinctions are between current and fixed assets, and CAPITAL GOODS and LAND, and tangible versus intangible assets. **2** An entry on one side of a balance sheet, indicating a resource owned; the other side shows liabilities and net worth. **3** A valued attribute, such as good looks.

asset allocation decision.   In modern portfolio theory, the division of investment funds into various types of ASSETS (1) to achieve the highest return relative to the chosen level of RISK (2).

asset specificity.   The lack of alternative uses for an ASSET (1), making the owner (OWNERSHIP) vulnerable to another party, hence inducing the ownership of the asset within the FIRM using it.

asset tax.   Also called a 'wealth tax,' it is an AD VALOREM TAX on all ASSETS (1) owned. One variant is a VOLUNTARY tax in exchange for recognition and protection of title. Even when IMPOSED, an asset tax has a lower EXCESS BURDEN than an INCOME or SALES TAX, but a tax only on fixed assets has an even lower burden.

association.   **1** A VOLUNTARY organization whose aim is to BENEFIT its members in the pursuit of some interest or commonality. *Syn.* CLUB. **2** A group of persons joined by some legal or biological tie, for example families. **3** An unincorporated organization.

assurance.   INSURANCE against a known occurrence with an unknown time, for example death.

asymmetric information.   Unequal information held by parties of a CONTRACT or TRANSACTION. Remedies include information sources, warranties, price adjustments, and contractual provisions. Some asymmetry, however, is unavoidable as a fact of life.

at or better.   An order to sell at some price or higher, or to buy at some price or lower. One tells the broker, for example, to buy at $10 or better.

at the market.   Buying or selling at whatever the market price is, or the best price currently available, rather than AT OR BETTER. *Syn.* market order.

Atlas Economic Research Foundation.   An organization based in Virginia, it helps to create and develop independent public policy research organizations internationally by providing intellectual ENTREPRENEURS with advice, financial support, workshops, and access to a network of leaders who share a commitment to achieving a free society. It presents annually the Sir Antony Fisher International Memorial Award for the most worthy books.

Atlas Shrugged.   The title of a landmark novel by AYN RAND. It influenced many libertarians (LIBERTARIANISM) and Objectivists (OBJECTIVISM) towards FREE-

MARKET ideas. In a discussion of SACRIFICE, a character asks another about the mythical Atlas, 'who carried the world on his shoulders', and the other says, 'I'd tell him to shrug'. Rand has the people who 'carry the world' on their shoulders – entrepreneurs, inventors, engineers, creators generally – go on 'strike' against a society which doesn't value their role in it – shrugging, so to speak.

atomism. The concept of society as basically composed of interacting individuals or families. This is AHISTORICAL, since human beings have lived in organized groups, though not necessarily under an IMPOSED *GOVERNMENT. Hence, PUBLIC-GOODS theory that treats society as atomistic is unrealistic. ENTREPRENEURS who wish to provide some works can deal with the community governance without having to contract with every individual.

atomistic competition. A market structure with so many FIRMS and no large ones, all making a uniform product, that collusion is infeasible. Each firm is therefore a price taker, having no MARKET POWER. See also PERFECT COMPETITION, COMMODITY EXCHANGE.

auction. A public sale of property to the highest bidders (BID), thus also establishing market values. In the 'English auction,' the bidding starts with a low price. In a second-price auction, the highest bidder takes the good at the price of the second-highest bidder. In a sealed-bid auction, bidders do not know the prices bid by the others. See also DUTCH AUCTION.

auction market. A market which operates as though in an organized AUCTION with continuous competitive bidding (BID) and offering. The concept is used in equilibrium theory.

audit. Examination of accounting records, such as by a taxing agency or by internal or external experts, and verifying them. The taxation of transactions such as income or sales requires audits, but the ASSESSMENT (2) of publicly evident ASSETS (1) such as land does not.

augmented GDP. The official GDP plus items not included but which are additions to or subtractions from economic WELL-BEING. Home production, for example, would be added, and environmental DEGRADATION subtracted as a type of DEPRECIATION (1).

aurophobia. Fear of the GOLD STANDARD that there would not be enough gold or that it would be too rigid or that it would be bad to deprive GOVERNMENT of the control of MONEY.

Australian stock exchange.   The National Stock Exchange of Australia, abbreviated ASX, with exchanges in several cities.

Austrian economics.   A school of economic thought originating in Vienna, Austria having the following key methodological features: i) AXIOMATIC-DEDUCTIVE reasoning for the basic, UNIVERSAL theory; ii) marginal ANALYSIS; iii) METHODOLOGICAL INDIVIDUALISM and PURPOSEFUL human action; iv) an emphasis on discrete goods and disaggregated, heterogenous variables; v) the use of interpretive understanding (*Verstehen*); vi) an emphasis on SUBJECTIVE VALUES. Major topics of interest among Austrians include entrepreneurship (ENTREPRENEUR); money and banking, especially critiques of central banking (CENTRAL BANK), with alternatives such as FREE BANKING; CAPITAL THEORY, including the structure of roundabout CAPITAL GOODS and production; the MARKET PROCESS and SPONTANEOUS ORDER; a critique of German historicism; a critique of socialist CENTRAL PLANNING as well as INTERVENTION; GOVERNANCE and the evolution of RULES; the analysis of TIME and INTEREST RATES; decentralized knowledge; UNCERTAINTY; and learning. Austrians have also criticized Marxism, Keynesianism, and the neoclassical emphasis on mathematical formalism (see Boettke, 1996). With its critique of intervention and interest in market processes, Austrian economists tend to be FREE-MARKET-oriented.

The school was founded with the publication of CARL MENGER'S *Principles of Economics* (1871, 1976). Other key Austrians include FRIEDRICH VON WIESER, EUGEN VON BÖHM BAWERK, LUDWIG VON MISES, FRIEDRICH HAYEK, JOSEPH SCHUMPETER, Gottfried Haberler, Fritz Machlup, Ludwig Lachmann, MURRAY ROTHBARD, and ISRAEL KIRZNER. Centers of Austrian thought include George Mason University, Auburn University, New York University, and California State University at Hayward, particularly institutes at these universities.

Austrian theory of business cycles.   The Austrian (AUSTRIAN ECONOMICS) school theory of BUSINESS CYCLES is financial and also based on its CAPITAL THEORY. An injection of MONEY by the monetary authority artificially lowers interest rates, inducing MALINVESTMENTS in more roundabout capital goods (ROUNDABOUTNESS) than is warranted by the market demand for consumer goods. When interest rates and other costs rise, investment slows and the expansion halts, turning into a contraction. See also the GEO-AUSTRIAN SYNTHESIS.

autarky.   A deliberately self-sufficient economic policy, imposing a lower standard of living by foregoing trade.

authoritarian.   Governed by the whims of an AUTHORITY (2), rather than by the consent of the governed. Hence economically, authoritarian production and consumption are chosen by authorities rather than the free choices of investors and consumers.

authority. 1 A person with recognized competence and knowledge about a topic, or power and position agreed to by the parties. 2 An AGENT (1) who authorizes or CLAIMS (2) legitimacy for GOVERNANCE, law, and doctrine based on its power and prestige and on unwarranted beliefs rather than truth or voluntary acceptance.

autochthonous. Indigenous and aboriginal.

automatic fiscal stabilizers. Government spending and taxation that counteract the BUSINESS CYCLE without any change in policy. Taxes decrease and spending increases during a depression because income is lower and welfare applications higher. However, if the extra expenditure comes from domestic borrowing, and funds would have otherwise been invested, then the effect is largely one of substitution of government for private spending rather than stabilization. Taxes or CHARGES (1) on LAND RENT are fiscal stabilizers by reducing speculative real-estate purchases, holdings, and construction that would otherwise be malinvestments and choke off further investment due to high prices for land for current use.

automatic stabilizers. Processes which maintain ECONOMY-wide equilibrium. For example, with GOLD as international money, an excess of exports results in an importation of gold, increasing the prices of exports, hence bringing trade into balance.

automation. Technology that replicates what LABOR does, hence replaces labor. Automation increases productivity unless its main motive is to escape legally imposed ARBITRARY costs. The term was coined by D.S. Harder of General Motors in 1935. In an ECONOMY without barriers, the displaced labor can find alternative employment, although obsolete CAPITAL GOODS may be scrapped. See also CREATIVE DESTRUCTION.

autonomous (expenditure). Expenditure independent of current income. In Keynesian thought (JOHN MAYNARD KEYNES), investment is largely autonomous.

autonomy. Self-governing, whether of a person, group, or territory. In a FREE-MARKET *ECONOMY, individuals are autonomous, forming VOLUNTARY associations of free persons.

avarice.   The seeking of ever more wealth. It is sometimes used as a synonym for GREED, but it is useful to distinguish wanting riches from obtaining riches by immoral means. Avarice may not be noble, but as a motivator for production and entrepreneurship, it can result in social benefit. See GREED.

average annual returns.   The annually compounded returns were they constant during the period.

average down.   To reduce the average price paid for an investment by purchasing more at lower prices.

average propensity to consume.   Total expenditure for consumption divided by total income. This is an important concept in Keynesian economics, since Keynes thought that this average decreased with income, but studies show that in the long run, it does not.

average propensity to save.   One minus the AVERAGE PROPENSITY TO CONSUME, since income is either saved or consumed.

average rate of tax.   Total TAX payments (for all taxes or particular ones) as a proportion of gross income (revenue minus costs).

Averch–Johnson effect.   The skewing of production towards a greater CAPITAL-GOOD intensity in regulated industries that have a set rate of return.

avoidable tax.   A TAX that one need not pay if one creates the tax shelters that escape it or one adopts an alternative way of handling an item, which is not taxed. Of course one can avoid sales taxes by not purchasing items, and income taxes by not generating income, but genuine avoidance occurs when one achieves the result one desires without paying the tax penalty.

avoidance.   Escaping a tax by legal means, illegal ones being EVASION.

axiom.   A PROPOSITION that is a premise for other propositions but is itself not derived from other propositions, hence is foundational to some body of theory.

axiom of dominance.   The AXIOM that more is better; the desires of people for goods is unlimited.

axiomatic.   Having axioms.

axiomatic–deductive.   Regarding theory deduced from axioms, and the METH-ODOLOGY of deriving PURE THEORY from universally applicable AXIOMS. See also DEDUCTIVE METHOD.

B

back. *Ec.* To exchange at a fixed rate on demand, as for example gold backs BANKNOTES when they can be so converted to gold.

backdoor financing. A government agency's borrowing from the US treasury as a substitute to appropriations from Congress. When Congress cancels the debt, it retroactively appropriates the funds.

bad. *N.* A negative GOOD, generating disutility. Since people do not voluntarily (VOLUNTARY) obtain bads (unless a good turns bad), these are often EXTERNALITIES due to the failure of government to recognize property rights by which the victims could obtain COMPENSATION (1), or also policies and products of government that some disfavor. Often, one person's good is another's bad.

Bagehot, Walter (1826–77). Editor of *The Economist*, among his writings was his *Postulates of English Political ECONOMY*, which sought to list the premises from which CLASSICAL ECONOMICS is derived.

bailout. *Ec.* An AD HOC subsidy by government to cover the debts of an agency such as a city government or a bank.

Bakunin, Mikhail (1814–76). Russian anarchist (ANARCHISM) who advocated a federation of independent collectivist associations with rights to secession. But he also helped associate the term 'anarchism' with violence due to his advocacy of revolution, methods which influenced the Bolshevik cause.

balance of payments. An accounting of all EXPORTS and IMPORTS in foreign trade. The two basic categories are the current and the CAPITAL ACCOUNT. Generally, exports, borrowing, and the sale of ASSETS (1) pay for imports so the payments, along with currency movements, balance to zero. Exports of goods and imports of financial capital are indicated as positive (+), hence a deficit in goods is balanced out with a surplus in financial capital from abroad.

balance of trade. A misleading term, since what is meant is only the balance in merchandize trade, excluding SERVICES and financial capital flows.

If exports of goods exceed imports, the balance is said to be 'favorable,' a throwback to mercantilist thought (MERCANTILISM).

balance sheet.   An ACCOUNTING report of the ASSETS (2), LIABILITIES, and net worth (equity) of an organization at some moment in time.

balanced budget.   A BUDGET in which expected current income equals current planned expenditure. Note that when the budget is divided into a current and a CAPITAL ACCOUNT, funds borrowed for CAPITAL-GOODS investments do not unbalance the budget, as they are offset by expected future benefits from the investment.

bank.   Generally, a financial intermediary, but specifically, one with a specific government charter. Banks accept deposits and loan or invest the funds, and can affect the MONEY SUPPLY. Other institutions such as CREDIT UNIONS also have deposits and make loans, but they are chartered under a different agency and have restricted powers. Banks issue checks which depositors use to transfer funds, while credit unions and money-market funds issue share drafts payable through a bank.

In many countries, banks must be tied to the government CENTRAL BANK, for example be members of the FEDERAL RESERVE SYSTEM in the USA, and they are subject to restrictions in their branch locations and other operations. In addition, the government mandates that banks use the government currency rather than issue their own private bank notes. The ABILITY to expand the money supply is regulated by the central bank, that is in the USA, banks have a required reserve ratio, and the Federal Reserve System affects bank reserves by its expansion of the money supply.

bank note.   See BANKNOTE.

Bank of England.   The British central bank. Established in 1694, it gained monetary policy independence on May 6, 1997. Its nickname is the 'Old Lady of Threadneedle Street.'

bank reserves.   See RESERVES.

Bank Secrecy Act.   A US Federal Act of 1970, the 'Currency and Foreign Transactions Reporting Act,' 31 USCA § 1015+. It requires financial institutions to report to the internal Revenue Service cash transactions of over $10,000. The Act also requires the reporting of large cash movements to or from abroad, as well as reporting on foreign bank accounts and possibly other transactions.

banking. Generally, the institutions and system of holding savings and making loans. Banking is lumped together with money to form the category of 'money and banking' for applied analysis and teaching.

banking principle. A proposition of the BANKING SCHOOL that the banking system will not overissue notes convertible into gold.

banking school. A school of thought about MONEY and BANKING that debated the currency school in Great Britain in the 1800s. It argued against regulation of banknotes, since with conversion of notes into gold, the market would supply the funds according to demand for notes for near-term transactions.

banknote. A currency note, or paper currency, issued by a BANK. These are bearer notes, hence money substitutes. Banknotes in excess of RESERVES are called fiduciary media.

bankruptcy. A legal declaration of insolvency, permitting the orderly resolution of debts, but also typically voiding some of the debt. This latter INTERVENTION permits the abuse of borrowing funds without having to repay, thus making personal loans more risky. Besides reducing the availability of credit, this reduces interest earned and increases interest paid on debt. In the USA, under Chapter 11, a bankrupt enterprise is reorganized, while under Chapter 7, the enterprise is liquidated.

bar admission. Legally, the bar consists of all the members of the legal profession, and admission to the bar is a license to practice law within some jurisdiction. Complex laws, drawn by lawyers, and requiring the assistance of lawyers, thus create a privilege to those holding the license required in order to do legal work for others, providing lucrative gains in a litigious society.

Barclays index. An index of major stocks on the New Zealand Stock Exchange.

bare. 1 Naked; without any covering or furnishings. Bare LAND, for example, is without improvements. 2 Minimal, for example a bare living.

bargain. 1 A contract. 2 To negotiate an agreement. 3 A purchase at a lower than normal price.

barrel of oil. Unit of oil volume, equal to 159 liters or 42 US gallons.

barrier. An obstruction to a flow or ACTIVITY. GOVERNMENT-erected barriers impede enterprise, reducing employment and INVESTMENT. Barriers include TAXATION, REGULATION, prohibition, and license to impose costs on other parties. SUBSIDIES are also barriers, aside from their funding, since they place those not obtaining the subsidy in an unfavorable relative position.

barriers to entry. BARRIERS that make it more costly for new firms to enter an INDUSTRY (2). Some are generated by markets, such as economies of scale which necessitate a large investment. Others, such as licensing, are due to intervention by government. Whether barriers due to patents and copyrights are interventions or enhance the market process is debated by free-market economists.

Barro, Robert J. (1944–). Professor of Economics at Harvard University, previously at the University of Chicago and the University of Rochester. A new-classical FREE-MARKET economist, he is known for his Ricardian equivalence theorem, which posits that there is no future tax burden from debt financing if taxpayers increase savings to fund future tax liabilities.

Among Barro's books are *Black Monday and the Future of Financial Markets* (1989), *A Cross-country Study of Growth, Savings, and Government* (1989), *New Classicals and Keynesians, or the Good Guys and the Bad Guys* (1989), *World Interest Rates and Investment* (1991), *Macroeconomics* (1993), *Democracy and Growth* (1994), *Economic Growth* (with Xavier Savier-i-Martin) (1995), *Inflation and Growth* (1995), *Getting it Right: Markets and Choices in a Free Society* (1996), *Reflections on Ricardian Equivalence* (1996), and *Determinants of Economic Growth: A Cross-country Empirical Study* (1997).

base money. Also called the 'monetary base,' it is the final means of MONEY payments. At the present time, base money consists of CURRENCY and bank reserves. Under a GOLD STANDARD, the base money is gold, while other purchasing media such as BANKNOTES are base-money substitutes. An increase in the monetary base can be multiplied into a several times greater expansion of the money supply.

basis point. A one-hundredth of a percent (.01%). The term is used for changes in INTEREST RATES.

basket. Group, such as a basket of COMMODITIES or of currencies, in which each item has a fixed quantity. MONEY can be backed by such baskets.

Bastiat, Frédéric (1801–50). French *LAISSEZ-FAIRE* economist and legal philosopher *par excellence*. He used fable and satire to argue against INTERVEN-

TION and for FREE TRADE, saying, for example, that if protection from foreign trade is desirable, we should be protected from free imports of sunlight. A major insight of his is 'what is seen and what is not seen,' that is that government benefits and protections are visible and evident, while the costs, though they be much greater overall, are invisible and not evident without some ANALYSIS. See APPEARANCE AND REALITY. His major work was *The Law*, in which Bastiat wrote that LIBERTY precedes legislation, and that lawful plunder is unlawful law that perverts the true law.

battery. *Leg.* The unlawful application of force.

Bauer, Peter (1915–). Economist, at the London School of Economics 1960–83, who criticizes foreign aid and espouses markets for ECONOMIC DEVELOPMENT.

bear. 1 To bring forth, have, or support; pay interest. 2 Named after the animal, a person who expects the prices of COMMODITIES or securities to fall, for example short sellers (SHORT SALE). Such persons are described as bearish. The contrary is a BULL.

bear market. A continuing decline amounting to 20 percent or more in a stock market average.

bear, what the market will. The highest price that an item will fetch or BEAR (1) in an auction-type market for NORMAL (1) ARM'S-LENGTH buyers.

Becker, Gary Stanley (1930–). Professor of Economics and Sociology at Chicago and member of the MONT PELERIN SOCIETY, Becker has described himself as a 'FREE-MARKET person' who believes that 'individuals responding to incentives can do very well.' He has extended economic analysis such as utility maximization and cost–benefit to social areas such as CRIME, discrimination as a preference, education, economics of the family, and HUMAN CAPITAL. His doctoral dissertation, written under the supervision of MILTON FRIEDMAN, published as *The Economics of Discrimination* (1957, 1971), asked how much people are willing to give up to avoid interaction with others, with the implication that public policy can discourage discrimination by raising the price of it. In 1983, the Sociology Department at Chicago offered him a joint appointment.

In 1992 he received the Nobel prize for Economics for 'having extended the domain of economic theory to disciplines such as sociology, demography and criminology' and for showing that rational economic incentives influence decision making in 'areas where researchers formerly assumed that behaviour is habitual and often downright irrational.' In 1997, he was appointed a member of the Pontifical Academy of Sciences by Pope John Paul II.

Among his positions, he served as President and Vice-President of the AMERICAN ECONOMIC ASSOCIATION, and is an associate member of the Institute of Fiscal and Monetary Policy of the Ministry of Finance in Japan. He has also been writing a column for *Business Week* since 1985.

Recent books by and about Becker include *The Economics of Life*, with Guity Nashat Becker (1996); *Gary Becker in Prague* (1996); *Accounting for Tastes* (1996); *Essence of Becker* (1996).

beg the question.   To assume an issue that is in dispute. An example is the issue of whether economic theory can apply to nonhuman animals; arguing that ECONOMICS only pertains to human beings, since animals cannot reason, begs the key question under discussion, whether some animals can reason.

beggar thy neighbor.   Policy to increase domestic output by POLICY that negatively affects other countries, such as by currency devaluation or tariffs. Such effects are typically temporary, with long-term damage, as markets adjust and other countries retaliate.

behavior.   The manner in which a person or some variable ACTS (2).

behavioral assumption.   The premises about the BEHAVIOR of AGENTS (1), from which a theorem is derived, for example profit or utility maximization. The basic behavioral postulate in economics is that of economizing. Narrow self-interest should be an assumption for theory conditional on that premise, rather than a behavioral CLAIM (3) about human beings.

below the line.   1 Figures not included in an ACCOUNTING total. 2 Deductions and exemptions from gross income. 3 Promotion expenses other than advertising (ADVERTISE).

beltway.   A freeway circling a city; specifically, the one around Washington, DC, the inside said to be dominated by the federal government and its spend/control mentality, while the 'American side' (outside the beltway) represents the feelings and thoughts of ordinary citizens, who generally disfavor TRANSFER SEEKING.

beneficiary.   One who inherits property according to a will or specification in a contract. *Syn.* DEVISEE.

benefit. An increase in well-being, from the viewpoint of a knowledgeable recipient.

benefit principle. In PUBLIC FINANCE, a *quid pro quo* between a TAX or fee and the service it pays for. A benefit tax is justified by the corresponding BENEFIT received by a taxpayer, even if he does not voluntarily pay the tax. The benefit can be an increase in ASSET (1) value due to a service rather than the direct use of a service. Examples are a bridge toll or an ASSESSMENT (2) based on site rent to pay for local streets, the latter based on the CAPITALIZATION of the benefit into land rent and land value. The alternative rationale for taxation is ABILITY TO PAY. The benefit principle is more efficient and less distorting of market outcomes. USER FEES adhere to the benefit principle.

benefit societies. Also known as 'friendly societies' and 'fraternal societies,' organizations engaged in mutual aid, such as pooling funds for insurance and lending. These were common during the 19th century, before they were displaced with government programs and restrictions (Mixon, 1996).

benevolence. The desire and practice of voluntarily (VOLUNTARY) acting for the BENEFIT of others, whether from ALTRUISM or from SYMPATHY.

best as enemy of the good. The attitude that if one cannot obtain perfection, one should not obtain the item at all, even though it in fact is better than not obtaining it.

best economic system. The system which generates the greatest efficiency, or else the greatest justice and LIBERTY, or both. FREE-MARKETEERS generally posit a harmony between efficiency and equity, so that there is no trade-off, that is private property is just and more efficient than government controls.

beta. *Fin., Gk.* **1** From the Greek letter, beta is a measure of the volatility of a stock or MUTUAL FUND compared to a market average (S&P 500). If a stock tends to move in the same direction as the market, the beta is positive. A beta greater than one means the item is more volatile than average. See also ALPHA. **2** Letter commonly used as a coefficient of an independent variable in a regression equation.

between reason and instinct. A concept of F.A. HAYEK that the basic institutions and rules of society have not been designed, nor are they a result of human instinct, but are 'between' them, having developed via SOCIAL EVOLUTION.

bid.   An offer of payment by one wishing to buy an item. See also AUCTION.

big bang.   A sudden implementation of some policy, usually liberalization, such as setting prices free. In the UK, a big bang occurred in 1986 with the deregulation of the CAPITAL MARKET. See also SHOCK THERAPY.

big brother.   Pejorative term for BIG GOVERNMENT that watches and controls activity, from George Orwell's novel *1984*.

big business.   Large companies have great impact on an ECONOMY, the term often used pejoratively.

big government.   GOVERNMENT that has a large share of GDP and interferes excessively with business and private life. The term is often used pejoratively.

big labor.   Large unions (UNIONS, LABOR) that can affect the ECONOMY, for example with strikes and wage negotiations, the term often used pejoratively.

big landowners.   Landowners owning a large proportion of the LAND value and obtaining much of an ECONOMY's rent; often pejorative.

bigger fool.   The person to whom one hopes to sells a speculative item before the BUBBLE (1) bursts.

bill of rights.   A declaration of constitutional RIGHTS, especially as intended to correspond with and derive from NATURAL RIGHTS. The concept goes back to the Magna Carta of 1215. Prime examples include the English Bill of Rights of 1689; the constitution of the State of Virginia in 1776, with its bill of rights authored by George Mason; the French *Declaration of the Rights of Man and of the Citizen*, 1789; the Bill of Rights in the first ten amendments to the US Constitution; and the United Nations' declaration of human rights, which includes alleged welfare rights along with natural rights.

bioeconomics.   The intersection of biology and economics.

black economy.   The BLACK MARKET, though sometimes referring only to the evasion of TAXATION.

black market.   The market for illegal voluntary items, legal items at illegal prices and quantities, or otherwise legal items that are produced, traded, and consumed while evading (EVASION) REGULATION and TAXATION, as well as the GDP. *Syn.* underground ECONOMY, informal economy. The greater the interventions, the greater the black market, in some cases making up half the economy. A FREE MARKET has no black market because it does not limit ENTERPRISE.

blacklist. A list of persons shunned because they violated rules.

blight. Urban areas that have decayed; ugly slums with run-down buildings, high unemployment, and CRIME. This is typically a result of TAX *POLICY that penalizes improvements and employment, a culture that disparages work and education, lack of law enforcement against violence, and prohibitions of substances that stimulate illegal provision and turf wars.

blind trust. A TRUST in which the owner has no knowledge of the ASSETS (1); government officials set these up to avoid conflict of interest.

blue chip. Stocks of large, sound, growing companies; after poker chips, blue ones being more valuable.

blue economy. The ECONOMY other than crime or the BLACK MARKET, that is the legal economy, called so in the UK from the publication of the national income accounts, known as the Blue Book.

blue laws. Laws prohibiting work or entertainment on Sundays.

blue sky laws. Laws prohibiting the sale of what the seller does not own, for example the sky.

board of directors. A group of persons elected by and representing the shareholders or unit owners of a CORPORATION or association. They are responsible for the POLICY and operation of the organization, and delegating the operation to hired managers. Members of a board are individually liable for the performance.

Böhm-Bawerk, Eugen von (1851–1914). A member of the Austrian school (AUSTRIAN ECONOMICS) and minister of finance of Austria, Böhm-Bawerk held the Chair of Economics at Vienna after VON WIESER. Extending the foundation MENGER laid out, Böhm-Bawerk developed the core of Austrian theory, which helped establish Austrian economics as a distinct school. He laid out a theory of roundabout production (ROUNDABOUTNESS), the period of production, the structure of CAPITAL GOODS, and a theory of INTEREST RATES. His theory of interest is based on TIME PREFERENCE, and influenced subsequent neoclassical theory; SENIOR also had a time-preference theory, which Böhm-Bawerk criticized. He also stated that land and labor are the original factors of production from which capital goods are produced. He also employed the wages-fund concept and CIRCULATING CAPITAL in the determination of interest rates, as distinct from the time-preference origin.

In the Austrian theory of capital goods that he developed, following Menger, there is a structure of higher- and lower-order capital goods, the higher-order ones being more roundabout and requiring more time for the payoff. Higher interest rates flatten the capital-goods structure; in equilibrium, productivity is geared to the rate of interest. Böhm-Bawerk's major theoretical works have been collected in *Capital and Interest* (1921, 1959).

KNUT WICKSELL as the 'Swedish Austrian' based his theory of interest on Böhm-Bawerk's, expressing it in an improved and clearer fashion. However, this capital and interest theory has not penetrated into the mainstream. MASON GAFFNEY, however, has been integrating Austrian capital theory with GEO-ECONOMIC theory, for a unified theory involving both land and capital goods, including the 'PERIOD OF PRODUCTION.'

Böhm-Bawerk in *Karl Marx and the Close of his System* (1898) also established the Austrian tradition of critiquing Marxism, thus also SOCIALISM and INTERVENTION in general. MISES and HAYEK would later carry out the critique of CENTRAL PLANNING, with contemporary Austrians such as Peter Boettke investigating the Soviet system and the transition from socialism.

bond. A debt instrument with periodic payments of INTEREST, usually at a fixed rate, but possibly indexed to INFLATION. The principal is paid when the bond matures, unless it is a CONSOL. A debenture bond is one for which no security is set for the repayment of principal. A junk bond is a low-quality bond. A zero-coupon bond rather than paying cash interest is bought at a discount and redeemed at maturity at the full face value. Bonds are rated by companies such as Moody's and Standard & Poor's, the riskier bonds having a higher yield, that is a risk premium. The market value of a bond is directly proportional to its risk-adjusted yield and inversely proportional to the long-term interest rate. In economic theory, bonds are used as a generalization of interest-bearing instruments.

book value. A corporation's balance-sheet equity divided by the number of shares. Market value differs because it is based on expectations, and book value may not reflect ASSET (1) market values.

boom. The part of an expansion phase of a BUSINESS CYCLE in which output is growing at a high rate, with much INVESTMENT. SPECULATION in stocks and REAL ESTATE typically sets in. Booms often end in busts because much of the impetus was due to subsidies rather than pure market processes. Key artificial stimuli include the expansion of money by CENTRAL BANKS, artificially lowering interest rates, and the expansion of public works paid for by the taxation of productive effort, which becomes capitalized (CAPITALIZED VALUE) into higher land values, anticipation of which sets off a speculative real-estate boom fueled by the credit expansion. When prices begin to rise, especially real estate and interest rates, the rate of growth of investment slows, eventually leading to the bust. The Japanese boom of the 1980s and bust of the 1990s is an example.

Borda count.   A method of VOTING, proposed by J.C. Borda in 1781, that overcomes the paradox of voting. For *n* choices, a voter gives *n* points to the top choice, *n–1* points to the next best, and so on down to 1 point for the lowest choice. The alternative with the most points wins. See also APPROVAL VOTING.

borrow.   To obtain an item from another person, with the promise to return it, and typically to pay interest as COMPENSATION (1) for the use of it.

bottom.   1 The lowest prices of an investment vehicle. 2 The smallest level of governance. 3 The trough of a CYCLE.

bottom line.   The net income or PROFIT when all is said and done. Also a metaphor for the most important aspect of a deal.

bottom-up investing.   Placing the primary investment criterion on the quality of a corporation, rather than the overall direction of the market.

bottom-up voting.   A multilevel method of VOTING in which people elect a neighborhood council, groups of neighborhood councils elect a higher-level district council, these councils in turn elect a higher-level regional council, and so on to the highest level.

bounded cognition.   The proposition that cognitive ABILITY to process information is limited, so people simplify the task with decision rules and habits. This economizing is fully consistent with RATIONALITY.

bounded rationality.   See BOUNDED COGNITION. What is bounded is not really RATIONALITY but cognitive ABILITY.

bourgeoisie.   *Fr.* The property-owning middle-class, as it developed during the Industrial Revolution, and its culture emphasizing family, work, and ORDER. The class is distinct from the clergy, the aristocracy, and the propertyless proletariat. Such class distinctions are important in Marxist thought.

Bourne, Randolph (1886–1918).   He wrote articles for *The Seven Arts* opposing America's participation in World War I, an unpopular stance. Bourne was arrested, and a trunk full of his manuscripts was stolen. A poem by John Dos Passos (1932, p. 106) has Bourne's ghost crying out, *'War is the health of the state'* (italics in the original), which he wrote in an unpublished manuscript, *The State*.

bourse.   A stock market, commonly called so in Europe.

boycott.   Targeting a firm or product with a refusal to make purchases or associate with it.

bracket creep.   An increase in tax rates under a graduated income tax due to INFLATION's increasing nominal income. Indexing solves this.

branch banking.   A BANK having multiple offices and banking locations. This has been restricted in some US states and by the federal government across states. Restrictions on branch banking led to small, unstable 'wildcat' banks in the USA during the early 1800s. The Scottish FREE-BANKING system pioneered branch banking.

Bretton Woods.   The New Hampshire resort where an international monetary conference took place and designed a global monetary system named after the site. The result was fixed exchange rates for CURRENCIES, with the dollar tied to GOLD at $35 per ounce. The IMF and World Bank were also created to make international loans. The dollar standard based on $35 gold became unrealistic as the dollar was inflated and gold flowed out of the USA. The system was terminated in 1971, after which a managed float system was adopted for the major currencies. Volatile currencies have been costly for enterprises and have created macroeconomic instability, problems that would be avoided with a global GOLD STANDARD combined with FREE BANKING.

broadcast spectrum.   The electromagnetic spectrum bands used to broadcast radio and television transmissions. This is a type of ECONOMIC *LAND. One FREE-MARKET approach to the spectrum is for government to lease spectrum frequencies to users at market rates, and place no restrictions on the ownership and contents of the broadcasts. Currently the opposite is done; the owners pay no fees for using the spectrum, ownership is licensed, and the contents of broadcasts is restricted.

broken joint.   A metaphor for the dysfunctional working of MONEY as alleged by Keynesian economists. See LOOSE JOINT, TIGHT JOINT.

broker. An AGENT (2) who buys or sells property for a client.

Brown effect. Named after HARRY GUNNISON BROWN by NICOLAUS TIDEMAN, the effect of increasing the current use of LAND due to a decrease in speculative (SPECULATION) holding when LAND RENT is taxed. This is due to different EXPECTATIONS about the future price of land, since if everyone had the same expectation, there would be no speculation.

Brown, Harry Gunnison (1880–1975). He was the leading follower of HENRY GEORGE among professional economists of his day. Brown studied under Irving Fisher at Yale and later taught at the University of Missouri. His book *The Economics of Taxation* (1924, 1979) is a classic in tax INCIDENCE theory. Topics of his writings include land and RENT, TAXATION (especially of land value), financial capital and interest, monetary economics (as an adherent of Fisher's monetary approach), pricing theory, and international trade. He also wrote a textbook, *Basic Principles of Economics* (1942 and various other editions). Brown's work is described and analyzed in Ryan (1987). See also GEO-ECONOMICS.

bubble. 1 A speculative BOOM with a great increase in the market prices of a class of items, far beyond that warranted by usual historic values or cost fundamentals. Prices then collapse, just as an expanding soap bubble eventually bursts. Stock, COMMODITY, and REAL-ESTATE markets are prone to bubbles, which may involve CYCLES. 2 A fraudulent investment operation.

Buber, Martin (1878–1965). Jewish religious philosopher and advocate of decentralized 'socialism of spontaneity.' He proposed an economic solution in 1921 ('A Proposed Resolution on the Arab Question') to multiethnic conflict, specifically for then Palestine, based on commonly owned land, self-governing small COMMUNITIES, and equally sovereign nations within a confederation (Buber, 1983). He called this an 'intra-national' approach which would replace politics with economics. This resolution of ethnic conflict over land, with the added geo-economic concept that title holders pay RENT, is one market-compatible approach to the problem of ethnic conflict, notwithstanding Buber's socialist self-label.

Buchanan, James M. (1919–). Nobel prizewinner of 1986 and a member of the MONT PELERIN SOCIETY, Buchanan founded and is a leading economist of the VIRGINIA SCHOOL OF POLITICAL ECONOMY, having made contributions in PUBLIC-CHOICE theory and CONSTITUTIONAL ECONOMICS. The school originated at the Thomas Jefferson Center in the University of Virginia at Charlotte, moved to Virginia Polytechnic Institute and State University at Blacksburg, and finally settled at George Mason University, where he has directed its Center for Study of Public Choice. Buchanan also has been a leading contributor to the theory of CLUBS, contractarianism, optimality, LIBERTY, and SUBJECTIVE COSTS, the latter topic challenging traditional marginal-cost pricing. Buchanan along with Gordon Tullock founded the Public Choice Society in 1962, and its journal, *Public Choice*.

Buchanan studied at the University of Tennessee and obtained his Ph.D. at the University of Chicago. He was highly influenced by the theories of FRANK KNIGHT and KNUT WICKSELL as well as Italian 19th-century PUBLIC FINANCE. The Italians, like Wicksell, presented public finance as an agreement by citizens to pay taxes and submit to government authority in exchange for services. Buchanan's economic approach treats public choice as a political market, with self-interested, utility-maximizing AGENTS (1). *The Calculus of Consent* (1962, 1965), co-authored by Gordon Tullock, has been highly influential in public choice, examining how constitutional rules are chosen and which rules can preserve the social contract. Buchanan's numerous books and articles, often with co-authors, examine many facets of public economics.

budget.   An accounting of planned expenditure and expected income, normally for one year. It is sound practice to have a current budget for consumption and a CAPITAL BUDGET for major INVESTMENTS that take place or have payouts of greater than one year.

budget deficit.   Current expenditures that exceed current income. Some governments deliberately have a deficit in order to stimulate the ECONOMY (particularly if the borrowing is from abroad). Deficits also occur because expenditure has strong constituents, taxation is unpopular, and the constitutional system permits and induces shifting the costs to future generations in the form of either higher taxes and interest payments or else the repudiation of the debt.

budget surplus.   Current expenditures that are less than current income. The surplus, which is savings, can be used to reduce debt or to build an endowment for future use.

building cycle.   See REAL-ESTATE CYCLE.

building society.   A mutual-aid financial institution, similar to CREDIT UNIONS, specializing in loans for real estate.

bull.   A person who expects market values to increase. Such persons are described as bullish. The contrary is a BEAR.

bull market.   A market in which average share prices have a sustained and substantial increase in value.

bullion.   GOLD, SILVER, and platinum ingots or bars.

bureaucracy.   Rule by bureaus, or administrative offices and departments. The bureaucracy consists of a hierarchy of departments and agencies of a large organization, which administer policy using complex rules, procedures, and specifications, imposing depersonalized and laborious processes on affected parties. Theories of bureaucracies presented by MISES, Niskannen, Weber, and others involve the tendency of the bureaucrats to maximize their budgets and to pursue their AGENDA as well as that of the organization. Private bureaucracies in for-profit corporations tend to avoid extreme waste because of competition, but such constraint does not apply to government, especially to states. DECENTRALIZATION, demonopolization, and PRIVATIZATION are antidotes to excessive government bureaucracy.

Buridan's ass.   An illustration by Aristotle, later associated with the philosopher Jean Buridan (1295–1356), of an ass faced with two equally desirable bales of hay and starving because it could not decide between them. Critiques of indifference curves assert that pure indifference implies such an impossibility to choose, when in fact one does choose. However, one could decide randomly, for example by tossing a coin.

business.   **1** Commercial enterprise and trade engaged in for gain and livelihood. **2** An organization which conducts business (1).

business cycle.   Also called the trade cycle. A repeating pattern of expansion and contraction of output in an ECONOMY. There are cycles of varying type and duration, including seasons within a year, short inventory or political cycles of about four years, medium (Juglar) cycles of about 9–10 years, major cycles of about 18–20 years (see REAL-ESTATE CYCLE), and possibly 'long wave' KONDRATIEFF cycles of about 60 years.

The expansion is also called the upswing and, in the latter stages, the BOOM. The contraction is also called downswing, recession, and BUST. The bottom of the cycle is called the trough or depression. The top is called the peak, or, in some cases, a crisis, when a panic or crash quickly turns the boom into a bust. The points of inflection occur when the second derivative switches signs, that is during the expansion, the change of the rate of growth turns negative, and during a contraction, the change of the rate of contraction turns positive. The decrease in the rate of growth eventually halts the growth and then leads to a decline. Hence, the seeds of the depression are sown at the height of a boom, when rate of growth begins to decline.

Explanations of the cycle, particularly of the downturn, are generally divided into financial and real theories. The key variable is INVESTMENT. The Austrian-school theory (AUSTRIAN ECONOMICS) is financial, based on credit expansion that creates higher-level investments that turn out to be unprofitable. The GEO-ECONOMIC theory is real, based on the REAL-ESTATE CYCLE. Neoclassical real business cycle theory centers on clusters of innovations. Neoclassical theory also posits random shocks which create fluctuations. The regular repeated pattern of major depressions since the early 1800s seems to cast doubt on random shocks or innovations as the main determining cause of the cycles.

business ethics. The code of conduct that governs an enterprise, such as honest dealing and equal treatment of employees. Also the study of such.

business risk. Risk due to the type of business engaged in.

bust. The downturn of an ECONOMY, ending in depression.

butterfly effect. That small changes in the inputs of a function can have a large effect on the dependent variable, a principle of 'CHAOS' or TURBULENCE theory. To the degree that this exists, it makes POLICY ineffective, since the effects cannot be predicted.

buy. To obtain an item by exchanging something else, usually money, for it. A 'good buy' is something which one got at a low price.

buyers' market. Excess supply, leading to buyer's ABILITY to set terms.

by-product. A product other than the main ones intended in the production process, generally of low or negative value.

bylaws. The rules governing an association, based on its charter, articles of association, or master deed.

C

C. Symbol for CONSUMPTION in MACROECONOMIC equations. In Keynesian economics, consumption is first recognized as a function of income, but then by moving all of Y to the left side of the equation, income becomes a function of autonomous consumption. See CONSUMPTION FUNCTION.

cadastral survey. A survey and recording of land titles, boundaries, and values.

calculation. See ECONOMIC CALCULATION.

calculus. Higher mathematics dealing with derivatives, the slopes of curves (hence the maxima and minima of functions), and integration, areas under a curve, much used in modern neoclassical economics, its applications and methods criticized by some schools of thought (see Boettke, 1996). Calculus is also a more general term for calculating values, as in the book *The Calculus of Consent* (Buchanan and Tullock, 1962, 1965). Also, the basic concepts of a first derivative, indicating the rate of change (or slope) of a variable, and the second derivative, indicating the change in the slope, are useful even if not expressed mathematically; for example see BUSINESS CYCLE.

call option. An option to buy an ASSET (1) at a certain price during some period of time. The opposite is a PUT OPTION.

cambist. One who BUYS and sells foreign currencies.

Cambridge school, modern. A successor to schools of thought centered in Cambridge, England, starting with Marshall, Robertson, and Pigou, then highly influenced by J.M. KEYNES along with RICARDO and MARX. The school after World War II, also called post-Keynesian, became critical of neoclassical theory, using instead a macroeconomic approach. The adherents tend to favor mixed and socialist economies. Among the economists associated with the school were Robinson, Kaldor, and Sraffa.

canons of taxation. Criteria for judging a TAX system. The two famous canons are by ADAM SMITH and HENRY GEORGE. Smith's criteria in the *WEALTH OF NATIONS* (1776, 1976) were equality, certainty (clear manner and quantity), convenience, and economy in collection. George's criteria in PROGRESS AND POVERTY (1879, 1975) were minimal excess burden, economy in collection, certainty (least opportunity for corruption and evasion), and equality. George showed how a tax on LAND RENT satisfies the canons best.

Cantillon effect.   When the MONEY SUPPLY is expanded, PRICES do not all rise at the same rate, but at differing rates depending on the areas of the money injection as it flows and spreads, hence an increase in the money supply alters the structure of prices. This perhaps reduces the explanatory power of the EQUATION OF EXCHANGE.

Cantillon, Richard (*c.* 1680–1734).   Irish-born French economist who analyzed ENTREPRENEURS, economic systems, and economic processes. His thought on entrepreneurship included uncertainty and arbitrage. His work on money and banking included the CANTILLON EFFECT. His great work was his *Essay on the Nature of Commerce in General* (1755).

cap.   CAPITALIZATION (market value) of a company. A small cap is a company with a market value of about $1 billion or less. A large cap is a company with a market value of $1 billion or more. A mid cap is a company with a market value of $400 million to $7 billion. A mini cap is a company with a market value of less than $100 million.

capital.   FINANCIAL CAPITAL or CAPITAL GOODS, that is both or either. Capital is also divided into fixed capital (long-term capital goods) and CIRCULATING CAPITAL (financial capital and inventory). Also, a metaphor for human skills and knowledge, which one can invest in as with capital goods.

capital account.   In the BALANCE OF PAYMENTS, the account of major purchases and sales of long-term ASSETS (1).

capital accumulation.   See CAPITAL FORMATION.

capital asset pricing model.   In modern portfolio theory, the pricing of returns in a diversified portfolio as based on their BETA (1) VOLATILITY, more volatile securities warranting higher yields. Investing using this model thus uses volatility-adjusted criteria. See WILLIAM SHARPE.

capital budget.   The section of a BUDGET that allocates expenditure for investment in capital goods.

capital consumption.   The DEPRECIATION (1) or CONSUMPTION of CAPITAL GOODS.

capital decumulation. See CAPITAL CONSUMPTION.

capital deepening. Increasing the CAPITAL-LABOR RATIO.

capital flight. The escape of financial capital from a country due to its high taxes and policy of CONFISCATION.

capital formation. Additions to the CAPITAL STOCK.

capital gain. For realized gains, the selling price minus the purchase price, and for unrealized gains, the current market price minus the purchase price. For the real gain or income, the nominal gain due to INFLATION is subtracted. A negative gain is a capital loss.

capital gains tax. A TAX on CAPITAL GAINS, usually realized gains. When NOMINAL capital gains taxes include inflationary gains, the tax taxes the CAPITAL as well as any income. Hence, to only tax the income, the capital gains tax must be indexed to INFLATION (as it is in the UK), and DEPRECIATION (1) must also be indexed, since otherwise CAPITAL GOODS are overtaxed. A tax only on realized capital gains tends to lock in the asset, to avoid the tax penalty, whereas a tax also on unrealized gains makes the gain tax neutral with respect to timing the sales. The limitation on the deductibility of capital losses further skews the tax with respect to risk; risky projects are tax punished either way. A pure free-market ECONOMY would have no gains tax, avoiding the lock-in problem, other than, in a geocracy, possibly a CHARGE (1) on unrealized gains in land value to supplement charges on LAND RENT.

capital goods. The FACTOR OF PRODUCTION consisting of produced goods. Neoclassicals, Marxists and some Austrians (AUSTRIAN ECONOMICS) lump LAND in with capital goods, while classical and GEO-ECONOMIC theory makes land a distinct factor as not produced by human effort. Capital goods are also distinct from FINANCIAL CAPITAL. INCOME from capital goods is a CAPITAL RETURN; it is misleading to call this 'INTEREST.' Shares of stock are titles to assets that are part financial and part real.

Capital goods are not just physical items, but are embedded with knowledge. Capital goods can also be intangible, such as a recipe or a computer program, as distinct from the media on which they are imprinted. Moreover, Austrian theory treats capital goods as heterogenous; higher-order capital goods are more roundabout (ROUNDABOUTNESS). A lower interest rate makes the structure higher, inducing more roundaboutness, while higher interest rates flatten the structure (see BUSINESS CYCLE). Capital goods also have a PERIOD OF PRODUCTION, which is the time it takes for the payback of the investment, unlike land, which has no period, since it is not produced. *Syn.* REAL CAPITAL. See also INTEREST.

capital intensive.   Production with a high ratio of CAPITAL GOODS to LABOR.

capital–labor ratio.   The ratio of CAPITAL GOODS to LABOR, or the average amount of capital goods used per worker. This can be measured by the value of CAPITAL RETURNS to WAGES, or the value of the CAPITAL STOCK divided by the number of workers.

capital markets.   The market for CAPITAL GOODS, land, and long-term financial assets. As pointed out by LUDWIG VON MISES, these are of great importance in a market ECONOMY, hence their absence is a major source of failure in a centrally planned ECONOMY, since it lacks rational ECONOMIC CALCULATION.

capital–output ratio.   The ratio of the CAPITAL STOCK to output.

capital reswitching.   Normally, given some investment demand, a greater quantity of investment is made at lower INTEREST RATES. However it is possible that due to the heterogeneity of CAPITAL GOODS, at some lower rate, firms switch back to less CAPITAL-INTENSIVE methods, so that investment then falls as the interest rate falls. This is contrary to neoclassical (NEOCLASSICAL ECONOMICS) and Austrian theory (AUSTRIAN ECONOMICS), but one can question its empirical importance.

capital return.   The return on the ownership of CAPITAL GOODS. It is antiquated and inaccurate to call this 'INTEREST.' The capital return is made up of DEPRECIATION (1) plus interest on the non-depreciated ASSET.

capital stock.   The aggregate of CAPITAL GOODS, measured for example by its market value, that is the present value of capital returns.

capital structure.   1 In Austrian (AUSTRIAN ECONOMICS) CAPITAL THEORY, a pyramid-like arrangement of CAPITAL GOODS according to their ROUNDABOUTNESS. The lowest level of goods is consumer goods. The second level is goods that produce the consumer goods, the third level being goods that produce the second level, and so on. The structure is functional rather than referring to specific goods, which can be used in various ways, for example an automobile can sometimes be a consumer good and other times (such as when used as a taxi) be a capital good. 2 The various types of a company's shares of stock and debt.

capital tax. ASSET TAX.

capital theoretic approach. Thus called, an approach that treats all factors of production as CAPITAL GOODS generating income, the capital valued at the net present value of the future yields.

capital theory. Theory about CAPITAL GOODS and their yields.

capital widening. Increasing the amount of CAPITAL GOODS while keeping the CAPITAL-LABOR ratio constant, hence not CAPITAL-DEEPENING.

capitalism. (The OED cites the earliest use by Thackeray in 1854. The term was popularized by Marxist writers.) **1** A label for industrialized mixed ECONOMIES. **2** PRIVATE ENTERPRISE using MONEY, with the private ownership of CAPITAL GOODS and land and their yields. **3** For Marxists, a system in which workers do not own the capital goods with which they work. By Marxist doctrine, the property-owning class, the capitalists, are able to extract the surplus value from the exploited propertyless working class, the proletariat, due to the army of the unemployed that drives the WAGE LEVEL to SUBSISTENCE.

The term 'capitalism' is used for polemics and propaganda. Critics of markets use the term with shifts of meanings, so that in one passage it is (1) a label for the MIXED ECONOMY that has social problems such as unemployment and poverty, then the meaning shifts to (2) as private enterprise is blamed for causing the problems, and finally the meaning shifts to (3) as an unwarranted conclusion.

Clearer synonyms for (2) are market economy or free enterprise, while a clearer meaning for (1) is a mixed or interventionist economy. As for (3), excess profits in capital goods would increase the supply and drive down the profits, so only a rent on a non-expandable resource, rather than CAPITAL, could have a surplus value, and even then, barriers to enterprise are needed to prevent the unemployed from becoming self-employed.

capitalist. (The OED cites the first use of the term by A. Young in 1792 for 'moneyed men.') **1** An owner of CAPITAL. **2** A person engaged in BUSINESS and has capital with which to employ others. **3** Regarding CAPITALISM.

capitalization. **1** *Ec.* The conversion of a stream (of INCOME or cost) into an ASSET value. The PRESENT VALUE of an asset equals the expected net yields divided by a DISCOUNT or INTEREST rate. **2** *Fin.* The value of the net assets of a company. See CAP.

capitalized value.   The discounted PRESENT VALUE of a stream of income. For fixed perpetual income and a fixed interest rate, the capitalized value equals the annual yield divided by the interest rate. If the asset has an AD VALOREM TAX, then one divides by the sum of the interest and tax rates, that is $p = y / (i + t)$ where p is the price, y the annual yield, i the interest rate, and t the tax rate.

capitation tax.   A HEAD TAX.

capture theory.   The capture or taking over of a regulatory agency by the INDUSTRY (2) being regulated, so that policy will favor the industry, or perhaps protect it from new competitors. Since those in the industry have expertise in it, they are appointed to regulatory positions, and the industry can also exert political influence. This theory was developed especially by GEORGE STIGLER.

carbon tax.   A TAX on fossil fuels, either on the amount of carbon dioxide or the value of the product, intended to reduce carbon dioxide emission. Whether the carbon tax would make much difference in the amount of carbon dioxide is disputed, since practices such as burning the rain forests may dominate. A general pollution CHARGE (1) may be sufficient for environmental protection.

cardinal.   *Ec.* Reporting how many, as with numbers used in counting.

cardinal utility.   A quantitative approach to utility (UTILITY, MARGINAL), in which the intervals between utility levels are scalable, though not measurable with specific numbers. For example, given goods X and Y, one could say, cardinally, that X is only slightly preferred to Y or else greatly preferred. With ordinal utility, one can only say that X is preferred to Y. Most economists think of utility as ordinal, yet when marginal utility is compared to a price, it seems that cardinality may be silently snuck in through the back door.

Carlyle, Thomas (1795–1881).   Scottish writer who in 1849 in his *Latter-day Pamphlets*, 'No. 1, The Present Time,' described economics as 'what we may call, by way of eminence, the *dismal science*,' because of the pessimistic Malthusian scenario that population growth outruns the growth of production (August, 1971). Technology has forestalled the dismal scenario of DIMINISH-ING RETURNS, but economists joke that PUBLIC-CHOICE theory, showing how MASS DEMOCRACY degenerates into TRANSFER-SEEKING by interest groups, has made economics a dismal science all over again.

carrying charge.   The cost of owning property, such as taxes, insurance, and storage; usually the OPPORTUNITY COSTS are not included.

cartel. An agreement among firms, including government-owned oil producers as with OPEC, in an oligopolistic (OLIGOPOLY) market to act together as a monopolist (MONOPOLISTIC), setting a common price or quantity. Cartels are unstable, since it profits a member to lower its price a bit to increase its sales. Also, new firms outside the cartel arise when the economic profit is high, and high prices encourage the development of SUBSTITUTES.

case study. A study of an example of some theory or application.

cash. Liquid, transferable PURCHASING MEDIA, namely CURRENCY and, more broadly, DEMAND DEPOSITS. When GOLD is MONEY, cash consists of monetary gold plus MONEY SUBSTITUTES, that is BANK NOTES and demand deposits.

cash basis. ACCOUNTING based on actually paid or received funds rather than those which only ACCRUE.

cash flow. Retained earnings plus the provision for DEPRECIATION (1). As the source of internally generated funds, it is a measure of the viability and future prospects of a firm. Dividends are a skewed measure of performance, since companies may prefer to minimize dividends' payments due to their DOUBLE TAXATION. If there are net expenses, then there is negative cash flow.

cash ratio. The ratio of the cash banks hold and their LIABILITIES.

Cassel, Gustav (1866–1945). Swedish economist. In *The Nature and Necessity of Interest* (1903), Cassel posited that the human lifespan creates a 2 to 3 percent floor on interest rates. His *Theory of Social Economy* (1918) described a simplified version of Walrasian GENERAL EQUILIBRIUM theory. In *The World's Monetary Problems* (1921), he presented the purchasing power parity theory of international exchange rates. During the 1930s, Cassel, a CLASSICAL LIBERAL, was a critic of Keynesian COUNTERCYCLICAL policy as well as Soviet CENTRAL PLANNING. See Carlson (1994).

casual employment. Employment which is uncertain, irregular, temporary, or incidental, and usually without fringe benefits.

cat. From the GEORGIST expression, 'seeing the cat.' A Georgist was looking at a jumbled drawing which was supposed to contain a picture. After sensing some of the parts, suddenly the picture was clear: it was a cat. He then realized that an ECONOMY is like the drawing, a confusing jumble unless one realizes the underlying PRINCIPLES, when one sees the cat. Once one sees the cat, the drawing is never again a jumble.

catallactics.   Economic EXCHANGE and other market phenomena, theory thereof, and an alternative term for 'ECONOMICS' proposed by HAYEK and used by MISES.

catallaxy.   An EXCHANGE *ECONOMY.

catastrophe theory.   Theory regarding discontinuity in various contexts, including economics, in which sudden changes (catastrophes) are caused (CAUSE (1)) by gradual changes that suddenly reach a critical point and cause a rapid discontinuity, such as an earthquake. A financial panic or a market crash are caused by prior structural and behavioral patterns and events that may not be noticed until the catastrophe happens.

categorical imperative.   From Kant, an unconditional and objective moral injunction, such as 'do not coerce others.' The FREE MARKET is based on such an imperative, delineating the domain of market-compatible ACTS from market-violating acts.

cats and dogs.   Highly speculative securities.

causal principle.   A FOUNDATIONAL *PRINCIPLE of science that all events and effects have CAUSES (1).

causality.   The fact that effects and events have CAUSES. MISES regards causality as a category or necessary element of HUMAN ACTION.

cause.   1 An origination of a phenomenon, as an AGENT (1) producing the outcome, such that if that origination did not exist, the same phenomenon would not occur. A cause of a cause is also a cause of the effect. See also CAUSALITY. 2 A reason for the existence of a phenomenon. 3 A social or political movement or IDEOLOGY.

caveat emptor.   *Lat.* Let the buyer beware. The policy that the buyer, assuming the risk, has the responsibility to check on the worthiness of an item he buys. In a FREE MARKET, the buyer has the responsibility of assuming risks, once they are disclosed.

caveat venditor.   *Lat.* Let the seller beware. The seller has the responsibility of ensuring the quality and integrity of the product sold. In a FREE MARKET, the seller has the responsibility to avoid FRAUD and to disclose the harmful CHARACTERISTICS of what he sells.

CCR. Community collection of rent.

censorship. As a restriction of expression, censorship is also an economic INTERVENTION in the ENTERPRISE of providing ideas and images, both on the provider and CONSUMER.

Center for Market Processes. An organization, based in Virginia at GEORGE MASON UNIVERSITY, which supports studies in AUSTRIAN ECONOMICS.

Center for Study of Public Choice. An organization at GEORGE MASON UNIVERSITY which studies and supports PUBLIC CHOICE theory, using the approach of the VIRGINIA SCHOOL OF POLITICAL ECONOMY. See JAMES BUCHANAN.

central bank. A BANK for all other banks in a jurisdiction, and the bank for the GOVERNMENT, providing clearing and lending services, as well as the major AGENT (2) implementing a country's MONETARY policy. Typically, a central bank provides the national CURRENCY as an ABSOLUTE MONOPOLY and regulates (REGULATION) the banks. The BANK OF ENGLAND is the central bank in the UK, and the FEDERAL RESERVE SYSTEM in the USA. Sweden's Riksbank is the oldest. Countries where the central bank is more independent of political influence tend to have more monetary stability and less INFLATION. Some countries have CURRENCY boards rather than central banks, and historically, economies with FREE BANKING, such as Scotland, had no central banks. A pure FREE-MARKET *ECONOMY would either have no central bank or else confine it to VOLUNTARY services. See FREE BANKING.

Central Europe. Countries between the Commonwealth of Independent States (former Soviet republics) and Western Europe, such as Poland, Czechia, Slovakia, Hungary, and Slovenia. Germany and Austria could also be considered to be in Central Europe, though they were in the Western side of the Iron Curtain. People in the Baltic countries, not part of the CIS, also consider themselves to be Central Europeans, while Ukraine and Belorussia are in Eastern Europe and the CIS. The countries of Central Europe have achieved a transition to MIXED ECONOMIES and are striving to join the EUROPEAN UNION and NATO.

central government. The highest-level GOVERNMENT, normally the government of the state, in contrast to the governments of the subdivisions or the states of a federation. Historically, government power has tended to become concentrated (CONCENTRATION) in the central government, leaving the public with less access and influence. An antidote may be a change in the voting system to COMMUNITARIAN DEMOCRACY, devolving (DEVOLUTION) power to small local jurisdictions.

central planning.   The totalitarian control over the substantial elements of an ECONOMY by a planning bureau that treats the economy as one large firm. This was practiced by the Soviet Union, China, and the other Soviet-style countries, a practice now abandoned by all except North Korea. However, market economies as well as countries that retain large government sectors, such as Cuba, have some central planning, such as central banking controls over the currency. LUDWIG VON MISES in his work *Socialism* (1922) showed how central planning is inefficient due to its lack of CAPITAL MARKETS and poor ABILITY to perform ECONOMIC CALCULATION.

centralization.   The CONCENTRATION of political and economic power in the CENTRAL GOVERNMENT, contrary to FEDERALISM and DECENTRALIZATION. Decentralization creates COMPETITION among political jurisdictions, leading to less WASTE and control, but local governments can be oppressive as well. Thus, to ensure LIBERTY, decentralization needs to be carried to its logical conclusion, individual CHOICE in governance.

certainty.   KNOWLEDGE without any doubt or puzzle. Also, precision and accuracy rather than vagueness and ambiguity. Certainty is relative and conditional. I am quite certain of my name, but it is possible that my mind has been fooled. I am certain, given that I have not been fooled or that my memory is not playing tricks.

EMPIRICAL *PROPOSITIONS are always subject to UNCERTAINTY, because no observation can be certain, other than one's own existence. Some logical DEDUCTIONS (2) are certain.

certainty equivalents.   The rate of return of a volatile (VOLATILITY) asset relative to that of a certain return that makes an investor indifferent among them, since the risk premium makes the risk-adjusted returns equivalent.

change in demand or supply.   A shift of the DEMAND or SUPPLY schedule, so that for example greater quantities are demanded or supplied at all prices.

change in quantity demanded or supplied.   A movement along a DEMAND or SUPPLY curve or schedule, quantity being a function of price.

chaos.   Disorder, utter confusion, and lack of form or structure beyond any probability measurement, like a wild mob. See also TURBULENCE, with which it should not be confused, and ORDER. MARKETS can be turbulent at times, but they have a SPONTANEOUS ORDER.

chaos theory. TURBULENCE THEORY.

characteristics. The approach and theory developed by K. Lancaster for consumer DEMAND, that what is demanded are the characteristics of goods rather than the physical goods. The concept was extended to PUBLIC and PRIVATE GOODS by Auld and Eden (1990) and Foldvary (1994b). Distinguishing goods that are public or private according to characteristics overcomes the problem of physical goods which are mixed, that is those that have both private and public characteristics.

charge. 1 A payment, such as a price, fee, or tax, or to request or impose such. 2 Credit.

charity. 1 Voluntary DONATIONS to other persons and organizations that are engaged in benevolent ACTIVITIES. 2 An organization that receives charity (1) other than for its own members. 3 See CHARITY, PRINCIPLE OF.

INCOME TAXES usually allow deductions for charity if expenses are itemized, and organizations need to qualify in order for donations to be tax-deductible and for the income of the charity to be tax-exempt. Some NONPROFIT ORGANIZATIONS, such as churches, are implicitly subsidized by government by making them exempt from property taxes, while they consume tax-paid services.

In a FREE MARKET, DONATIONS to charities fill the gap of activities that commercial enterprise normally does not fund, as well as helping those in unfortunate circumstances. Moreover, since in theory, POVERTY and unemployment are minimal if not eliminated by a free market, charity would normally be sufficient for such needs. See also SYMPATHY.

charity, principle of. In reasoning (REASON), the principle of charity prescribes that one interprets an opposing view in its best light, so as to soundly defeat it rather than beat a straw man.

charta de foresta. *Lat.* 'Laws of the forest,' allegedly part of the Magna Carta, granted by Henry III in 1217.

chartae libertatum. *Lat.* The two English charters of liberty, the Magna Carta and the *charta de foresta*.

chartist. One who studies graphs of stock, bond, or COMMODITY prices and volumes to do technical analysis, that is, find patterns (such as previous highs and lows, and moving averages) that predict future prices.

chattel. Movable property.

chattel slavery. The ownership of other human beings. Some NATURAL-LAW theorists hold that a CONTRACT to make oneself a chattel slave is morally unenforceable, since NATURAL RIGHTS are inalienable. See Locke (1690, 1947), *Second Treatise*, paragraph 23.

cheap money. Low INTEREST RATES, which as POLICY stimulating INVESTMENT in the short run, only to create MALINVESTMENTS, INFLATION, and a SLUMP later.

Cheung, Steven N. S. An economist who, like RONALD COASE, has worked on the theory of firms and social cost (SOCIAL COSTS AND BENEFITS). Cheung emphasizes lower transaction costs as the reason for firms. His books include *The Theory of Share Tenancy; with Special Application to Asian Agriculture and the First Phase of Taiwan Land Reform* (1969), *The Myth of Social Cost* (1978, 1980), and *Will China go 'Capitalist'?: An Economic Analysis of Property Rights and Institutional Change* (1982).

Chicago school. A school of thought originating and centered at the University of Chicago. The School's principles include value-free economics, neoclassical price theory, free-market allocation of resources as efficient, and monetarism. Adherents include giants such as FRANK KNIGHT, Jacob Viner, MILTON FRIEDMAN, Henry Simons, RONALD COASE, GARY BECKER, and GEORGE STIGLER. Its public-choice approach differs from that of the VIRGINIA SCHOOL, which disputes the efficiency of political markets (Rowley and Vachris, 1996).

children. Human beings below the legal age of maturity and fetuses above the legal age of personhood. In a FREE MARKET, children have the right to perform suitable work, the right to receive care and protection, and rights to PROPERTY. While their freedom over their actions may be limited, they have the right to pursue their own future goals. JOHN LOCKE discussed the rights and upbringing of children in his works, something quite rare for his time (Yolton, 1993, p. 37). A.S. Neill's book *Summerhill: A Radical Approach to Child Rearing* (1960) presents an approach to education without compulsion.

Chodorov, Frank (1887–1966). A leading GEORGIST libertarian (LIBERTARIANISM) like his friend ALBERT J. NOCK, Chodorov was an opponent of war and imperialism. He was the founding editor of *The Freeman*, associate editor of *Human Events*, and author of *The Economics of Society, Government and State* (1946), *One is a Crowd* (1952), *The Rise and Fall of Society* (1959), *The Income Tax: Root of All Evil* (1954), and *Out of Step: The Autobiography of an Individualist* (1962). Some of his essays are collected in *Fugitive Essays* (Liberty Press, 1980).

While living in Chicago, Chodorov read a friend's copy of *Progress and Poverty* (1879, 1975) by HENRY GEORGE, which gave him his life cause: liberty with economic justice. In 1937, he became the director of the HENRY GEORGE SCHOOL of Social Science at New York City, serving until 1942. Chodorov was a major influence on the post-war old-Right conservative (small government) and libertarian movements, including William F. Buckley and MURRAY N. ROTHBARD. He published the journal *Analysis*, which then merged with *Human Events*. Chodorov also helped found the Intercollegiate Society of Individualists. Some of his Georgist libertarian friends founded the journal *Fragments*, which still carries on Chodorov's libertarian, individualist Georgism.

choice.   A purposeful selection from known OPTIONS. Choice can be private, confined to the chooser, or public, selected for others as well as oneself. PUBLIC-CHOICE theory studies the latter.

chronic unemployment.   UNEMPLOYMENT that persists even during prosperous times and is not due to structural changes. The leading CAUSE (1) is BARRIERS to enterprise that leave behind the less able and less determined, along with inadequate schooling.

circulating capital.   CAPITAL GOODS with a relatively rapid turnover, for example up to one year, such as inventory and goods in the process of being produced. When available funds are invested in fixed capital, less is available for circulating capital, which is the near-term source of revenues. If there is a wages fund, it is circulating capital, providing the means to pay for inputs. Hence, intervention that artificially increases fixed capital is a source of later diminution of circulating capital and production, a malinvestment as in geo-Austrian cycle theory (GEO-AUSTRIAN SYNTHESIS). MASON GAFFNEY has done work in this area.

circulation credit.   Credit created by new banknotes and demand deposit not taken from existing funds, as is COMMODITY credit.

citizen.   An officially recognized member of a country. In a democratic country, a citizen is an equal co-owner of the country and its assets, having one vote; in effect, the country is a cooperative owned by the citizens. Citizens in many countries have economic legal rights not assigned to other residents.

citizen dividend.   A payment to a citizen (or perhaps also to other residents) as one's share of the returns on commonly owned assets such as natural resources, as practiced, for example, in Alaska for oil royalties. Some GEOISTS advocate the payment of equal citizen dividends as a supplement or even instead of using the collected land rent (LAND-RENT TAX) for government expenditures, leaving the decision of the allocation of expenditures to individual citizens.

Citizens for a Sound Economy Foundation.   A nonprofit educational institution with headquarters in Washington, DC, which conducts research and publishes analyses on sound economic policy. The CSE Foundation is affiliated with Citizens for a Sound Economy, a public-interest advocacy group with a membership of 250,000. CSE promotes initiatives which reduce INTERVENTION and promote growth.

civic.   Regarding COMMUNITIES, especially urban ones, and citizens.

civic association.   A VOLUNTARY organization that provides COMMUNITY services to its members. The members can be residential as well as commercial. Examples include condominiums, residential associations, and cooperative housing.

Civic Education Project.   A privately funded organization headquartered in Yale University, connected with the Soros foundations, that has sent college teachers to Eastern Europe and other countries to teach social science, as a part of a broader effort to restore democracy and open societies in those countries.

civic goods.   Collective goods provided for a COMMUNITY, such as streets, parks, and security.

civil.   Regarding CITIZENS and citizenship, distinct from religious, military, and criminal affairs. CIVIL LAW, derived from Roman law rather than common law, pertains to individual relations. A civil action is a non-criminal court case against a person or company. In a free society, civil action is conducted by individuals against individuals, not government against individuals, which should be in the domain of criminal law, subject to constitutional rights.

civil asset forfeiture.   The CONFISCATION of ASSETS (1) by government as a non-criminal action, not subject to the legal rights of persons accused of crimes. The victim need not be convicted or even accused of a crime, and the perpetrator of the civil offense is regarded to be the property and not the owner. See *DEODAND*. (See Reed, 1992).

civil disobedience.   Deliberate violation of laws thought to be unjust, in order to change them or at least avoid the tyranny or evil of conforming to them. The term originated with Henry David Thoreau in his essay *On the Duty of Civil Disobedience*; he also practiced it by going to jail rather than pay taxes during the war with Mexico. Civil disobedience was practiced by Mahatma Gandhi in India and by Martin Luther King's civil rights movement. Civil disobedience offers a way to peacefully challenge laws that violate LIBERTY and to promote liberty, including FREE MARKETS.

civil law.   The law concerning CONTRACT and tort, applying PERSON to person rather than state to person, as with crimimal law, although in modern times civil law is being applied or misapplied as state to person.

civil liberties.   Personal liberties, such as free speech, freedom of religion, freedom of peaceful lifestyles, and freedom of association. Civil liberty is tied to economic liberty, since the means are economic, for example to have a free press, one must be free to obtain and use a press.

civil rights.   The legal rights of citizenship, such as voting and becoming a candidate for elected positions.

civil service.   Non-military government employees, ideally appointed and selected on merit according to uniform rules.

civil society.   Voluntary associations and COMMERCE, the rule of law, and an equality of rights. The transition from socialist central planning is towards civil society as congruent with MARKET ECONOMIES.

civilization.   Social order, culture, capital goods, and amenities, all of which are in jeopardy by various forces as identified by those warning of the 'decline of civilization.'

civitas.   *Lat.* In Roman law, an independent union of citizens, such as were the Greek city states. LOCKE stated that the English equivalent is a COMMON-WEALTH.

claim.   1 A potential exertion of effective DEMAND. Hence, money is a claim on WEALTH, since it is readily accepted within an ECONOMY in exchange for wealth. 2 To request what one is entitled to. 3 To assert a PROPOSITION.

Clarke tax.   A tax related to DEMAND REVELATION in collective choice, developed by Edward Clarke. Clarke (1971) proposed a tax that CHARGES (1) the voter the net marginal cost to others of including his preference in the decision.

class. 1 A group of students and a teacher. 2 A subset of society with common economic characteristics, with a relationship of superiority and subordination between classes, hence a class struggle. In Marxist (KARL MARX) thought, the two classes are the PROLETARIAT and the CAPITALISTS, while OPPENHEIMER viewed them as landed conquerors, the conquered losing their lands. In a libertarian (LIBERTARIANISM) view of classes, the ruling class consists of those with governing POWER, who extract wealth from those producing it, and who impose their values on others.

classical. Referring to CLASSICAL ECONOMICS.

classical dichotomy. The split between the real and the financial sides of an ECONOMY. CLASSICAL ECONOMICS states that the determination of the PRICE LEVEL is separate from the determination of output and relative prices. Given some amount of output, the price level will adjust to the supply of money, that is the money stock times the VELOCITY of money. Output depends on the market for factors and not on the money supply. In the short run, money supply changes can affect output by increasing NOMINAL *DEMAND, but when prices rise, there can be a reversal of demand, and no long-run effect other than from the dislocation of relative prices and of resources wasted on ventures that turn out to be unprofitable. Demand-side theory posits that money changes do affect output when there are idle resources due to price rigidities. Rational expectations theory shows that in the long run, AGENTS (1) anticipate the money manipulation, hence lose their rigidity (see Foldvary and Selgin, 1995).

classical economics. A school of economic thought, especially in the UK, from the mid 1700s to the latter 1800s, emphasizing economic growth, FREE TRADE, and the three FACTORS OF PRODUCTION. Key classical economists were ADAM SMITH, JEAN BAPTISTE SAY, DAVID RICARDO, NASSAU SENIOR, and JOHN STUART MILL. HENRY GEORGE and John Cairnes have been called the 'last of the classicals,' although George was critical of some classical concepts such as Malthusian doctrine. The classical LABOR THEORY OF VALUE was adopted by Marxists (KARL MARX) and then turned against market economics; however, some classical economists, such as SAY and SENIOR, held a SUBJECTIVE VALUE theory. Classical doctrine posits a long-run subsistence wage due to population growth and the diminishing MARGINAL PRODUCT of land, but countered by rising wealth due to growth with free trade. The classicals also held to SUPPLY-SIDE macroeconomics, in contrast to the preceding Mercantilism and its reincarnation with Keynes. GEO-ECONOMICS retains classical elements such as the distinction and importance of the three factors of production and the DISTRIBUTION (1) of income among the factors. In modern times, supply-side economics has been termed the CLASSICAL MODEL. See Sowell (1974).

classical liberal.   Favoring economic and civil LIBERTY; 'liberal' in the 19th-century and European usage. In this philosophy, government should mainly be limited to protection and justice. The lacuna in classical liberalism is PUBLIC FINANCE, since classical liberals weaken liberty if a TAX on peaceful effort is permitted in order to fund even the approved functions of the state. The lacuna can be filled by GEO-ECONOMIC policy or by a LIBERTARIANISM which goes further than classical liberalism in rejecting taxation.

classical model.   A SUPPLY-SIDE model of the determination of OUTPUT and the PRICE LEVEL. The factor markets (for example labor, with capital goods and land held constant) determine the amount of labor at market-clearing wages, which then determines output, hence a fixed (vertical) AGGREGATE SUPPLY in relation to the price level. In demand-side models, some markets do not clear, and there is excess supply, such as of labor or savings, that is stuck. FREE-MARKET policy would remove INTERVENTIONS that lead to such rigidities, rather than treating the effects with more intervention and DEFICIT spending, which in the long run bring INFLATION and distortions.

clean float.   A FLOATING EXCHANGE RATE without INTERVENTION.

clear.   1 To offer just that quantity which is demanded (DEMAND (2)), hence with neither a SHORTAGE nor a GLUT. 2 To present checks for payment among banks. 3 Lucid; readily understandable and unambiguous. 4 To cover expenses, or profit after expenses. 5 Correct and unencumbered, as with clear title.

closed shop.   Legally required union (UNIONS, LABOR) membership in order to work for a FIRM. This provides the union leaders with MONOPOLY *POWER.

club.   An organization providing services to its members. The goods are COLLECTIVE but typically EXCLUDABLE.

club goods.   EXCLUDABLE *COLLECTIVE GOODS, such as provided by CLUBS.

clubhouse goods.   Collective goods that are both excludable and CONGESTIBLE.

clubs, theory of.   Theory of the determination of the optimum (OPTIMAL) amount of COLLECTIVE GOODS and membership size of CLUBS, a key paper being BUCHANAN (1965). Club theory also examines alternative ways of financing the CLUB GOODS, such as with the RENT generated by the club goods (Foldvary, 1994b).

Coase, Ronald H. (1910–).   Coase is famous for his theory of the FIRM and especially his COASE THEOREM in Coase (1960) regarding EXTERNAL EFFECTS, one of the most cited articles in economics. Born in Great Britain, he has taught at the London School of Economics, the University of Virginia, and the University of Chicago, and served as editor of the *Journal of Law and Economics*. His theory of the firm (1937) states that firms exist to minimize TRANSACTION COSTS. His 1974 essay 'The Lighthouse in Economics' is a CASE STUDY of a good that had been assumed to require government funding, but which in Great Britain in fact had been funded by users (thus inspiring the logo of The Independent Institute). Coase won the Nobel Prize in economics in 1991 'for his discovery and clarification of the significance of transaction costs and property rights for the institutional structure and functioning of the economy.' His main themes are in *The Firm, The Market, and The Law* (1988) and *Essays on Economics and Economists* (1995). He also wrote *British Broadcasting: A Study in Monopoly* (1950).

Coase theorem.   A THEOREM presented by COASE (1960), 'The Problem of Social Choice,' which showed how if parties to EXTERNALITIES can bargain without TRANSACTION COSTS, and PROPERTY RIGHTS and boundaries are CLEAR (5), they will attain an OPTIMAL solution regardless of the initial allocation of the property rights: when sparks from a train burn a field, the lesser of the cost of the damage or the cost of preventing the damage will be paid. Since transaction costs are high when many parties are involved, the theorem implies that institutions are needed to cope with the externality, but it also informs that the reciprocal costs need to be taken into account as well as the problem of GOVERNMENT FAILURE.

The article and theorem influenced the subsequent literature on LAW AND ECONOMICS and the economics of property rights.

Cobb–Douglas production function.   A PRODUCTION FUNCTION in which the FACTORS OF PRODUCTION are multiplied together, each factor raised to a power: $Q = A \cdot L^a \cdot K^b \cdot N^c$, where Q is output, A, a, b, c are constants determined by technology and government policy, and $L, K,$ and N are labor, capital, and natural resources. In most applications, c is zero and the other exponents sum to one. Cobb and Douglas (1928) simplified the function to two factors (N usually gets lumped in with K), but stated (p.165) that '... We should ultimately look forward to including the third factor of natural resources in our equations and seeing to what degree this modifies our conclusions and what light it throws upon the theory of rent.' The Cobb–Douglas form is also used for utility (UTILITY, MARGINAL).

cobweb. A dynamic MODEL whose graph looks like a spider's web, where one begins off the MARKET-CLEARING price and hops from the supply to the demand curve horizontally and vertically, either converging to market-clearing or diverging, depending on the ELASTICITIES of the curves. For convergence, the elasticity of the demand curve must be greater than that of the supply curve. Divergence presumes that the agents don't learn from past experience and don't use futures markets. If farmers pre-sell their produce in the futures market over some time interval, they add to supply until the future price is at the cost of production, leading to convergence. Divergent cobwebs do not contradict the principle of EQUILIBRATION, since equilibration is based on known data, and divergence eventually ends.

coerce. To compel someone to do something against his will, or to forcibly prevent someone from doing what he desires to do. The force can include a THREAT of physical FORCE. See also INTERVENTION. LIBERTY is the absence not of coercion but of coercive harm, since one may use coercion in self-defense to prevent the initiation of force. Usually, 'coercion' is used to mean an initiatory coercion.

coercion. The act of coercing (COERCE).

coercive. Using COERCION.

cognition. The capacity (in speed and amount) to perceive, reason, remember, and mentally process information. See BOUNDED COGNITION.

coin. A true coin is an amount of metal with a particular size, shape (usually a flat disk), and recognizable picture. These are then used as CURRENCY, based on the metallic content. Similar disks but with a face value much higher than the metal value are commonly called 'coins' but are actually tokens used as currency.

collapse. A sudden fall or breakdown, such as a fall in the price of one or more stocks, a business failure, or the breakdown of an ECONOMY or GOVERNMENT.

collect. **1** To assess (ASSESSMENT) a CHARGE (1) and receive the funds due. **2** To save and arrange examples of a class of objects in an organized way.

collectible.   A class of attractive physical items that people collect (2). The term particularly applies to items no longer being produced or of limited production, so that if DEMAND increases, the items will increase in value.

collective.   For and by a group, or *(n.)* the group itself.

collective choice.   SOCIAL CHOICE and PUBLIC CHOICE, decisions made on behalf of a group, such as by voters and legislators.

collective goods.   Also called public goods, COLLECTIVE goods are simultaneously used by more than one person, the amount used or available to each person being the whole amount of the good. All other goods are private (PRIVATE GOOD (2)) or severable (SEVERABLE GOOD). Samuelson (1954) laid out the distinction in mathematical form. In the CHARACTERISTICS approach, it is the attributes of goods, their characteristics and properties, which is collective or private, rather than the physical goods.

Other attributes are sometimes assigned to collective goods, such as their being NON-EXCLUDABLE, with CLUB GOODS a third category, but the Samuelson benchmark only distinguishes between collective and severable uses. Also, the conclusions drawn by Samuelson and others that voluntary, market provision is precluded from the very nature of collective goods, that is their vulnerability to free riding (FREE RIDER), is neither logically nor empirically warranted (Foldvary, 1994b).

collectivism.   A family of concepts involving placing POWER and OWNERSHIP in groups rather than in individuals. In forced collectivism, the group has COERCIVE authority over the individual, while in voluntary collectivism, the members willingly delegate decisions to the group.

collectivization, agricultural.   The CONFISCATION of PRIVATE (1) and communal farm lands, forcing the farmers into large government-run farms.

colonialism.   The doctrine and practice of conquering other territories in order to exploit their natural and human resources, as well as for the prestige of expanding the ruler's realm and extending the area of the dominant ethnic group. The term is still applied to regions in which ethnic minorities are ruled and restricted by the dominant ethnic group of a country.

command and control.   REGULATION specifying methods in detail, such as requiring specific ways of handling pollution. This is usually less efficient than levying a CHARGE (1) and letting the firm find its own way to minimize costs.

command economy. An ECONOMY in which the CENTRAL GOVERNMENT plans and operates production. The enterprises are told what to produce and given quotas. The result is often poor quality and a SHORTAGE of usable CONSUMER GOODS. The planning itself often FAILS, and a BLACK MARKET develops not only for consumer goods but also among enterprises to overcome the COORDINATION failures. LUDWIG VON MISES showed why CENTRAL PLANNING fails in his book *Socialism* (1922).

commanding heights. The vital, most important industries in an ECONOMY, such as banking, energy, and transportation. States such as the Soviet Union which sought to control an economy took control over the commanding heights.

commandment. See TEN COMMANDMENTS.

commerce. The exchange of goods and money, associated transportation and communications, and related INSTITUTIONS.

commercial. Regarding for-profit enterprise and COMMERCE.

commercial policy. REGULATION of external trade.

commercial speech. Advertisements (ADVERTISE) and other expressions related to COMMERCE. It had not been accorded the same legal protection as non-commercial speech, despite there being no distinction in the US First Amendment, but more recently has been better protected against INTERVENTION. However, bans on advertising some substances still exist, and some types of expression such as nudity are restricted in commercial and non-commercial speech, as well as in commercial activity such as photography.

commission. The WAGES paid to a salesperson, broker, or AGENT (2), often as a proportion of sales.

commodity. Something produced for sale in a MARKET. More specifically, the 'commodity market' takes place in exchanges that buy and sell items of uniform quality, such as foods (grains, soybeans, coffee, sugar, cattle), metals, other raw materials, currencies, and derivatives such as indexes of stocks and interest rates.

commodity credit. Bank loans based on 100 percent reserves, in contrast to CIRCULATION CREDIT.

commodity exchange.   The solution to the puzzle of how in an atomistic market (ATOMISTIC COMPETITION) the price of a good can change if no firm can affect the price. The answer is in the commodity exchange, a central clearing house of bids and offers for the commodity, in which traders and hedgers buy and sell spot and FUTURES CONTRACTS.

commodity market.   See COMMODITY EXCHANGE.

commodity money.   MONEY in which the unit of account is a certain amount of a COMMODITY. In a GOLD STANDARD, for example, money is gold, and the unit such as a dollar is defined as a certain weight of gold. The money is not backed (BACK) by the commodity; the money *is* the commodity itself. Paper notes are backed by the real money. Commodity money may be a BASKET of commodities, with a fixed amount of each good.

common.   Owned or used by anyone in some DOMAIN. Common OWNERSHIP means anyone may use the PROPERTY, and the benefits either go to the users or are allocated equally to all in the domain. With government ownership, the government acts like a firm and can exclude persons from the property, as it does with military bases. The atmosphere and oceans are commonly owned.

common elements.   The COLLECTIVE GOODS of a CONDOMINIUM, including the outside walls and roof, the gardens and grounds, parking, and AMENITIES such as swimming pools and tennis courts.

common law.   Law that developed from customs and from court decisions rather than statute law and legislation, and also distinct from remedies in equity. Common law is the residual law of countries, states, and provinces of English descent; the California Civil Code specifically provides that English common law is the 'rule of decision' in the courts of the State. (The term 'common law' has different meanings in non-English countries.)

common market.   A CUSTOMS UNION that permits the unrestricted movement of capital and labor among the members. A country without internal trade BARRIERS among its regions is a common market, as is a union of countries such as the European Union. See also ECONOMIC UNION.

common stock.   Shares of stock of a CORPORATION which have voting rights. The other type is preferred stock, which has a prior CLAIM (2) on earnings.

commons.   Lands owned collectively by residents of a COMMUNITY. Parcels may be allocated to certain families, or the usage may be in COMMON, as with a park. The ENCLOSURE movement took commons from villages and transferred them to the aristocracy. See also TRAGEDY OF THE UNMANAGED COMMONS.

commonwealth. The COMMON or PUBLIC welfare. Hence, a GOVERNMENT for all the members rather than a privileged (PRIVILEGE) class or the ruler. JOHN LOCKE in the *Second Treatise* (paragraph 133) defined it as an independent community, what the Romans called *CIVITAS*. The term 'commonwealth' is in the title of four US states, the Commonwealths of Virginia, Kentucky, Pennsylvania, and Massachusetts. It is also invoked in the British Commonwealth of Nations and now the Commonwealth of Independent States in the former Soviet Union.

commune. A COMMUNITY jointly owning and operating REAL ESTATE or an ENTERPRISE. Primal tribes often own territory communally. A modern example is the Israeli kibutzim. Typically, income is also distributed according to need or in an egalitarian way.

communism. 1 The COMMON *OWNERSHIP of PROPERTY. Most families have such ownership. 2 Totalitarian (TOTALITARIANISM) rule and ownership of production by parties calling themselves 'Communist' since, in Marxist thought, communism would follow CAPITALISM (3) and SOCIALISM.

communitarian democracy. Political power centered in small neighborhood COMMUNITIES. Elected neighborhood councils in turn elect representatives to higher-level districts, which in turn elect the next higher level, up to the highest level. This reduces the role of mass media and transfer-seeking, especially when combined with similarly decentralized PUBLIC FINANCE.

communitarianism. Values centered on COMMUNITIES, usually coercively imposed on individuals. However, a market-based communitarianism is also possible, based on CONSENSUAL COMMUNITIES (Foldvary, 1994b).

community. A group of people with some COMMON interest and interaction in its pursuit. Territorial communities have a governing agency that provides the members in the territory with services. They can be government jurisdictions or CONTRACTUAL COMMUNITIES. See also PROPRIETARY COMMUNITY.

community charge. So called, a HEAD TAX imposed in the UK in 1989–90 to replace real-estate taxes. There was popular opposition, and the tax was repealed.

Community Collection of Rent (CCR). The view that LAND RENT properly belongs to a relevant COMMUNITY, whose governing agency collects it from siteholders on behalf of the members. The rent funds can be spent for community services or paid to the members as an equal CITIZEN DIVIDEND. The implementation of CCR by a government is commonly referred to as land-value taxation (LAND-VALUE TAX). The payment by a landholder is called a rent assessment. CCR is called the 'public collection of rent' when the community is large.

commuting. Travel from residence to work and back. INTERVENTIONS creating long and congested (CONGESTION) commuting include a property tax system that induces SPRAWL, the implicit SUBSIDY of automobile use, the lack of congestion pricing, DYSFUNCTIONAL financing of public transit, and restrictions on private transit such as jitneys.

company. A for-profit firm, or more specifically in the UK, a CORPORATION.

comparable worth. Legislation intended to eliminate discrimination (DISCRIMINATE) against women by requiring equal pay for work of comparable value based on qualifications. Besides infringing on the rights of the owners of enterprises, comparable worth is based on the long-rejected LABOR THEORY OF VALUE.

comparative advantage. An advantage in OPPORTUNITY COST, that is having a lower opportunity cost. An example is a doctor who hires a nurse. Even if the doctor can nurse better, the nurse is hired because the doctor has a high opportunity cost in lost earnings if the doctor were to do nurse's work. Similarly, one country may have an ABSOLUTE ADVANTAGE over another in many goods, but if the less productive country has a relative advantage in some goods, trade is worth while. Each worker, firm, or country specializes in those goods for which they have comparative advantage, to mutual gain.

The concept of comparative advantage was discovered by Torrens and others in the early 1800s, and is most commonly associated with David Ricardo. John Stuart Mill added to the theory by including RECIPROCAL DEMAND.

comparative economic systems. The study of ECONOMIC SYSTEMS such as MARKET ECONOMIES, MIXED ECONOMIES, and COMMAND ECONOMIES, contrasting their operation and performance. It may also include theoretical systems not currently implemented.

comparative statics. Coined by OPPENHEIMER (Schumpeter, 1954, 1986, p. 855), it is the comparison of a new and old EQUILIBRIUM after some EXOGENOUS change has altered the old one. For example, a shift in demand will result in a new price and quantity. The alternative method is DYNAMIC analysis.

compensation. **1** Payment received for losses or paid-for benefits. **2** IN-COME. **3** Adjustment for income, as with the compensated demand curve, in which the income effect (extra purchasing power due to a fall in price) is removed, thus holding real income constant.

compensation principle. Well-being is increased if, after some change, any losers are compensated (COMPENSATION (1)) by the gainers to their mutual satisfaction. Nicholas Kaldor elaborated it. It is market-based for actual compensation, rather than hypothetical compensation which does not take place, hence does not really compensate.

compete. To engage in RIVALRY, or to be successful in rivalry, especially by increasing one's relative share of the market.

competition. RIVALRY among economic AGENTS (1), both among those selling and those buying goods. Each buyer or seller is in effect bidding or offering against the others, because buyers cannot all have a SCARCE (1) good and sellers cannot sell their good if others can sell it for less. Competitive markets thus tend to reduce supernormal profits if there is ENTRY into the field, and they allocate resources to the goods most desired by consumers. See also ATOMISTIC COMPETITION, CONCENTRATION.

A related meaning of 'competition' is the degree of MONOPOLY or any monopolistic power, more competitive industries having less monopoly power. Having more competitors reduces the ABILITY of firms to control the price of their products (see PERFECT COMPETITION). However, the presence of MARKET POWER does not imply an absence of rivalry, hence of competition.

competitiveness. The ABILITY to successfully COMPETE with other firms or other economies. For countries, a measure developed by Feenstra and Rose (1997) is the degree to which a country exports new goods earlier than others.

complement. A good that tends to be used in conjunction with another good, like cups and saucers. Technically, complementary goods have a negative CROSS ELASTICITY OF DEMAND. See also PERFECT COMPLEMENT.

compliance cost. The cost of complying with REGULATIONS and TAXES. The annual cost in the USA has been estimated at $677 billion, $6800 per household (Crews, 1996).

compound interest. INTEREST that is periodically paid on the accumulated past interest as well as the principal. The final amount in t years for interest rate i for principal p is p times $(1 + i)^t$. The period can become infinitely small, in which case interest is continuously compounded, with the formula e^{rt}. The time for money to double with continuous compounding is 69 divided by the interest rate.

concentration.   A measure of the number and relative size of the units in a DISTRIBUTION (3), such as firms in an INDUSTRY (2), directly proportional to the INEQUALITY (index) and inversely proportional to the number of units of a DISTRIBUTION (3), hence $C = I / N$ (Foldvary, 1995). Concentration can be measured as various ratios (percentage of the total held by the top n firms), or a measure of the whole distribution. The most common total measure is the HERFINDAHL INDEX (H). A completely concentrated industry is an ABSOLUTE MONOPOLY, with $H = 1$, while a highly unconcentrated, atomistic, industry has a H close to zero. Hall and Tideman (1967) developed an alternative measurement that is related to the GINI COEFFICIENT of inequality. The inverse of concentration is DIVERSIFICATION.

Conventional economists deem high industry concentration to be less competitive, while more free-market-oriented analysts see RIVALRY even with few firms (indeed, the most successful competitors), global competition lowering the effective concentration, and government countermeasures not helpful to consumers. ECONOMIES OF SCALE produce efficiencies as well.

concentration ratio.   The percentage of market share held by the largest n firms, n usually set from 4 to 8. These ratios are published in the *Census of Manufacturers*. While economists typically believe that low concentration ratios indicate more competition, the Austrian (AUSTRIAN ECONOMICS) concept of competition as RIVALRY implies that rivalrous competition can occur with higher ratios, although it is generally agreed that BARRIERS TO ENTRY create social WASTE.

concept.   An idea about some class of items that constructs some mental image of it. For example, a 'firm' is a concept.

conceptual realism.   The treatment of MENTAL CONSTRUCTS or IDEAL TYPES such as 'national income' as having the reality of a CONCRETE EXISTENT, what A.N. Whitehead called the 'fallacy of misplaced concreteness (Greaves, 1974, p. 24).'

concrete existent.   A tangible object, rather than a MENTAL CONSTRUCT. A 'government' is a mental construct, while an apple is a concrete existent. A police officer is a mental construct, while the human being and the uniform are concrete existents. But even concrete existents are theory-laden, that is interpreted with meaning.

conditional right. A moral or legal RIGHT subject to a condition. For example, a license gives one the legal right to drive a car on the condition that one is not intoxicated.

conditional theory. THEORY of the form: if X then Y. The theory does not assert that X is necessarily true, but if X is true, then the theory states that Y is TRUE.

condominium. An ASSOCIATION with individual units of PROPERTY and COMMON ELEMENTS in which each unit is assigned a percentage interest in the common elements, which is also its percentage of the vote and of the ASSESSMENTS (2). Hence, the association itself owns nothing. The economic effect is that the amenities and other common elements generate site RENT, which is then collected (COLLECT) as the assessments, an example of private GEOECONOMIC financing.

Condorcet, marquis de (1743–94). French political theorist who discovered the possibility of majority-rule CYCLING in SOCIAL CHOICE (see IMPOSSIBILITY THEOREM). He also proposed the 'Condorcet' system of pairwise voting, comparing every pair of candidates, but this too can cycle.

confederation. A union of organizations, usually sovereign states, in which each state retains substantial domestic GOVERNANCE. The USA were a confederation prior to the adoption of the Constitution. The PUBLIC FINANCE can either be confederate-wide revenue collection or payments by the states to the confederation.

confiscation. A seizure by a government. It is not a normal TAX that can be anticipated, but a sudden taking of PROPERTY without COMPENSATION (1). Illegal substances are often confiscated, but also governments have confiscated property to nationalize (NATIONALIZATION) it. In the USA, all levels of government confiscate property as civil acts. See CIVIL ASSET FORFEITURE, DEODAND, SEIZURE AND FORFEITURE.

congestible. Of a COLLECTIVE GOOD, having a MARGINAL cost of admitting another person into the DOMAIN. A congestible good is capable of becoming crowded, crowding being a DISUTILITY.

congestion. Crowding. The DISUTILITY of an extra person because it leaves less available space and fewer resources per person. One countermeasure is to CHARGE (1) a USER FEE proportional to the congestion, such as a higher bridge toll at peak use. Greater density in general, however, can also have increasing returns from larger markets and a greater DIVISION OF LABOR.

congestion fee.   A FEE (1) charged to a user of a CONGESTIBLE good. Examples include bridge tolls during rush hour, higher fees for public transport during crowded hours, and higher telephone charges during business hours.

conjecture.   A proposition that seems plausible but has not yet been warranted (WARRANT). See also HYPOTHESIS, SPECULATION, THEOREM.

conscription.   One of the categories tracked in *Economic Freedom of the World 1775–1995* (Gwartney *et al.*, 1996), conscription or a military draft forces people into the military. Besides being involuntary servitude, conscription is a selective TAX with an economic cost of what the conscripts would otherwise produce. An all-volunteer army shifts the cost to the whole population and lets those with lower OPPORTUNITY COSTS enter the service.

consensual community.   A voluntary COMMUNITY, for which membership is VOLUNTARY. These include PROPRIETARY COMMUNITIES and CIVIC ASSOCIATIONS. See CONTRACTUAL COMMUNITY.

consensus.   A general AGREEMENT arrived at not by voting but by discussion until differences are resolved; some may go along without agreeing if judgments are not converging and they believe that some decision is better than none.

consensus facit legem.   *Lat.* CONSENT creates LAW. Hence, contractors create their own private law.

consent.   AGREEMENT with the acts and proposals of others; conjoint will. The point has been made that true consent is actual, or overtly expressed: the alleged tacit consent of law (because one does not move away) is not a true agreement, but can be due to the higher cost of moving, just as a choice between two unpleasant prison cells is not a free choice to be in either. One may consent operationally, relative to the alternative current choice under current constraints, but not constitutionally, given an alternative set of constraints one would prefer. See CONSTITUTIONAL ECONOMICS.

consequences.   The results of a decision or set of rules. See UNINTENDED CONSEQUENCES.

consequent. In the conditional statement 'if X then Y,' X is the antecedent and Y the consequent. See DENY THE CONSEQUENT.

consequentialism. The view, usually utilitarian (UTILITARIANISM), that the proper moral criterion for policy consists of the CONSEQUENCES. An alternative view is DEONTOLOGICAL ETHICS, such as that of NATURAL RIGHTS, that a policy which violates natural rights is wrong regardless of the consequences, and that which does not violate rights should be considered by the respective agents by whatever criteria they choose. A third view is that natural rights themselves are based on consequences, so that a partial and conditional consequentialism is built into the rights' position. A problem with consequentialism is the determination of the consequences, given SUBJECTIVE VALUES, the arbitrariness of the time horizon, and the impossibility of knowing all the intended, let alone the unintended, consequences.

conservation. The act of conserving (CONSERVE).

conservativism. The IDEOLOGY of conserving (CONSERVE) the prevailing CULTURE and POWER relationships. Conservatives as a type typically view their culture as superior or morally correct, hence they wish to restrict other cultures, including religions and expressions. They oppose the egalitarian (EGALITARIANISM (1)) treatment of women or minorities currently in a subordinate power relationship. They favor the power structures of the state, church, and military, and thus promote nationalism and the sanctity symbols of power such as the national flag. Where MARKET ECONOMIES are current, they oppose government INTERVENTION that imposes restrictions on current powers over enterprise and property, but do not favor radical changes such as complete FREE TRADE.

Hence, while often opposing greater economic intervention, conservatism also typically favors substantial government control over expression and opposes enterprise that expresses alternative cultures in sexual expression, clothing and body coverage, religious practices, drug production and use, and non-traditional occupations by males or females. In the USA, the label is confused, since some CLASSICAL LIBERALS are labeled conservative due to their opposition to economic intervention. Thus, Hayek wrote an essay on 'Why I am Not a Conservative' as a postscript to *The Constitution of Liberty* (1960).

conserve. To ECONOMIZE or to keep from damage.

consideration. Something of value paid in exchange for receiving a good or service.

consol.   A BOND that never matures, paying INTEREST until the issuer buys it back. A compounding consol would pay interest in other consols rather than in cash. Originally, a consol was an annuity issued by the British government for the 'consolidated funds,' replacing a variety of bonds and funds.

constant dollars.   When comparing dollar (or other CURRENCY) amounts in different years, adjusting the values for INFLATION using some base year, for example using 1996 dollars, so that one compares REAL (3) amounts of what is measured.

constitution.   The fundamental RULES of an organization, not dependent upon or authorized by other rules. Hence, a constitution consists of the supreme rules, from which all the other rules are derived. Constitutions are also called charters, articles of association, and master deeds.

constitutional economics.   Part of PUBLIC ECONOMICS, it studies the choice of CONSTRAINTS rather than choice within constraints, as defined by JAMES BUCHANAN (1990). At the constitutional level, one freely chooses to join a CONSENSUAL COMMUNITY by accepting its RULES, thus achieving UNANIMITY. The rules then provide for representative and majority rule for the operational level, where it is EFFICIENT. Constitutional economics examines various alternative rules to determine which constraints and empowerments best minimize TRANSFER-SEEKING or inefficiency. The journal *Constitutional Political Economy* is devoted to that field.

constitutional failure.   The violation of CONSTITUTIONS by GOVERNMENTS because the constitutional structures failed (FAIL) to be specific enough or because the constitution failed to provide adequate enforcement structures and processes. When POWER is usurped by a tyrant who ignores the constitution, the constitution is overpowered, rather than a failure. Failure is due to a constitution's own inadequate provisions.

The US Constitution's First Amendment, for example, states that Congress shall pass no law restricting the freedom of speech, yet Congress has restricted expression in broadcasting as well as commercial speech. The Constitutional guarantee against takings is violated by SEIZURE AND FORFEITURE confiscation. The Ninth Amendment recognizing non-enumerated RIGHTS is almost ignored, and the Tenth Amendment limiting federal power is overcome by grants of funds to the states conditional on meeting requirements, and there are mandates to the states despite the dual sovereign powers of the states and the federal government.

constraint. Something that restrains and confines, such as constitutional provisions limiting the powers of GOVERNMENT, or a hard BUDGET line limiting spending. A 'soft' budget constraint can be stretched. Mathematical economic models typically find the optima (OPTIMAL) of variables subject to some constraint.

constructive possession. Having the POWER and intent of control.

consume. To use up economic VALUE. When one consumes food, one uses it up, so there is no value left. When one consumes an automobile, the consumption is the DEPRECIATION (1), or wear and tear, since the car still has value and has not been used up.

consumer. One who purchases CONSUMER GOODS.

consumer durable. A GOOD which is a final good, not used to produce other goods, but is not used up all at once, but over time, hence is durable and is effectively a CAPITAL GOOD providing services over a long duration. Examples include cars, furniture and refrigerators. Their production is related to REAL ESTATE, since a new house or office needs furnishings. In US national accounting, they are classified as CONSUMER GOODS.

consumer goods. GOODS that are final products (not used to produced anything else) and are intended to be consumed (CONSUME). Consumers include individuals, families, organizations, and government.

consumer goodwill. A favorable view of a FIRM by consumers.

consumer price index. An index (INDEXED) of price INFLATION for a typical BASKET of CONSUMER GOODS (there is also a retail price index). Since CONSUMER GOODS are constantly changing, there is no CLEAR (3) way to construct such an index. It has been thought that in the USA, the CPI is too high because it does not take into account improving quality and shifts to lower-priced SUBSTITUTES. See CORE INFLATION RATE.

consumer sovereignty. Freedom of CHOICE in consuming (CONSUME), a fundamental element of a MARKET ECONOMY. In mixed (MIXED ECONOMY) and interventionist economies, consumers do not have full sovereignty, since some products are restricted, prices are skewed, and much of consumption is imposed collectively (COLLECTIVE).

consumer's surplus.   A consumer's purchase price being less than the most he would have willingly paid, hence the difference is his surplus. In graphs, it is the area between the demand curve and the price. There is also a producer's surplus.

consumerism.   A movement to provide more information, honesty, and standards for CONSUMER GOODS. Critics say this creates excessive REGULATION, since the remedy for FRAUD should be via the courts.

consumers' cooperative.   A COOPERATIVE that sells CONSUMER GOODS to its members as well as to the public. They can provide specialized goods, more consumer information, services such as home economists, and can boycott disfavored firms and products. The members share in any profits as dividends in proportion to shares owned or rebates on the amount of their purchases.

consumption.   The act of consuming (CONSUME), or using up economic value. The amount or value of goods consumed.

consumption function.   CONSUMPTION (or purchases of CONSUMER GOODS) as a function of INCOME. KEYNESIAN ECONOMICS posits a linear function that includes a variable for autonomous consumption, the amount that would be consumed even at zero income. Since the slope of the function is less than one, a lower proportion of income is consumed as income rises. EMPIRICAL studies show that in the long run, autonomous consumption is zero, so that consumption is proportional to income. This demolishes the Keynesian model of income determination, which depends on a consumption function crossing the income line, with investment and government riding on top.

consumption tax.   A TAX on income not saved. This can be a SALES TAX or an INCOME TAX with SAVINGS exempt. While income taxes penalize savings, consumption taxes penalize borrowing (BORROW), since one has to borrow extra to also pay the tax, and then pay interest on the extra borrowing. While a sales tax reduces the record-keeping and form-filling burden of individuals, there is otherwise no economic reason to favor consumption taxes over income taxes, since the excess burdens are similar. The burden of taxes on consumption ultimately fall on the factors generating the income, such as wages. To remove disincentives, taxes both on income and on consumption need to be removed.

contestability.   The feasibility of a firm entering an INDUSTRY (2), a perfectly contestable one being no cost BARRIERS at all.

Continental currency.   Paper MONEY issued by the Continental Congress to help pay for the American Revolutionary War. The CURRENCY was so inflated that, as the saying goes, it was 'not worth a continental.'

contingent valuation.   The pricing of items that don't have COMMERCIAL markets by presenting persons with hypothetical choices and asking them how much they would be willing to pay or be paid to obtain them. This is used for environmental COST–BENEFIT ANALYSIS, although it is criticized, since the answers may not be meaningful. An alternative is DEMAND REVELATION.

contract.   A voluntary AGREEMENT creating mutual OBLIGATIONS among competent parties. Correctly completed contracts are enforceable by law. Some agreements, such as a chattel slave (CHATTEL SLAVERY) contract, are legally or morally not enforceable. See also SOCIAL CONTRACT.

contractarianism.   A social philosophy as well as CONSTITUTIONAL ECONOMICS based on a constitutional contract, that is, an agreement on a CONSTITUTION, which forms the basis for further operations. What is right or wrong is whatever the contractors agree to.

contracting out.   The provision of a SERVICE by GOVERNMENT by contracting the PRODUCTION to a PRIVATE (1) firm. This is often more EFFICIENT because the private firms are in COMPETITION and have more flexible labor policies and are less subject to political influences. It privatizes production but not PROVISION.

contractual community.   A proprietary community or a subdivision composed of multiple owners bound by CONTRACT in an ASSOCIATION; either one is a VOLUNTARY association at the constitutional (CONSTITUTION) level of joining the COMMUNITY and agreeing to its basic law.

convertibility.   Of a CURRENCY, the ABILITY to convert it to another currency or to GOLD at MARKET PRICES.

cooperative.   A nonprofit CORPORATION in which the shareholders are members each having one vote. The main types of co-ops are producer, consumer, housing, and financial, for example CREDIT UNIONS. They achieve the socialist (SOCIALISM) aim of workers and consumers owning their means of production and DISTRIBUTION (2), while in a MARKET context. These are outcomes of a cooperative movement that began in Rochdale, England, in 1844, which not only seeks to form cooperatives but to move society towards greater cooperation and less conflict. A motto of cooperatives is 'cooperation among co-operatives.' See also CONSUMER'S COOPERATIVE. The Mondragon workers' cooperatives in the Basque region of Spain is an example of cooperative success. In a housing cooperative, the member owns a share of the whole property and leases his unit from the co-op.

cooperative individualism.   Individuals freely joining ASSOCIATIONS and cooperating with one another rather than achieving ends through conflict. Some advocates such as Edward Dodson also include geocratic (GEOGRACY) principles.

coordination.   Bringing plans and ACTIVITIES into mutually beneficial alignment. The market coordinates individual plans via PRICES and PROFITS.

copyright.   The legal protection of a text from copying. The legal notice is in effect a contract between buyer and seller, saving transaction costs. Copyrights recognize that labor products can be intangible, but as a contract and extension of the author's mind, it would seem that a copyright should expire with the death of the author. Some free-marketeers do not favor copyrights.

Coquelin, Charles and Guillaumin.   Editors of *Dictionnaire de l'Economie Politique* (1853), Coquelin writing the article on political economy.

core.   A set of EQUILIBRIUM prices.

core inflation rate.   The CONSUMER PRICE INDEX excluding volatile prices as with many food and energy products.

Corn Laws.   Laws until 1846 which taxed and prohibited grain imports to prop up the price. CLASSICAL economists recognized that the effect was to increase the price of farmland while hurting consumers, and urged the repeal.

corn model.   A model in CLASSICAL ECONOMICS used by RICARDO and GEORGE to illustrate the determination of WAGES and RENT, using a single product, corn. This model is now ignored in NEOCLASSICAL ECONOMICS and economics textbooks. It is still central to GEO-ECONOMICS. The wage level is set at the rent-free MARGIN OF PRODUCTION, and the corn output of more productive land is rent.

corporate income tax.   A TAX on the profits of CORPORATIONS. In the USA, this is an EXCISE TAX on the PRIVILEGE of operating as a corporation, the tax measured by the PROFITS of the firm. Since DIVIDENDS are subject to tax as well, corporate income in the USA is subject to DOUBLE TAXATION. The UK has an imputation system in which the tax is levied whether or not the profits are distributed as dividends, shareholders getting a TAX CREDIT for the tax paid by the company.

corporation.   Also called a joint stock company or a limited company, a firm with an independent legal status as an artificial PERSON, whose owners usually own tradable shares. The shareholders have LIMITED LIABILITY; only their investment is at risk. A BOARD OF DIRECTORS elected by the shareholders is responsible for the operations. This structure enables corporations to obtain large amounts of funds for investment. PRINCIPAL AND AGENT problems arise, such as weak boards, high salaries for executives, and stock options as delayed costs.

correction.   A decline of 10 percent or more in the price of a stock of stock market average. If the decline continues, then it becomes a BEAR MARKET or, if sudden, a CRASH. A decline supposedly 'corrects' for an increase that was not warranted by the fundamentals of the firm or ECONOMY.

corruption.   A payment to a government official to give the payer some PRIVATE (1) advantage beyond that provided by law. Also, the exercise of POWER and taking of ASSETS by a government official beyond that warranted by law.

corvée.   *Fr.* Forced unpaid labor.

cosmos.   *Gk. Kosmos* The ordered universe. In society, the SPONTANEOUS ORDER, or what Hayek called the extended order (see Chapter 2, Hayek, 1973).

cost.   A loss, or what must be paid in order to obtain something. Economically, a cost is the opportunity that must be foregone in order to obtain something. The true cost of buying something is not the money paid, but the next best thing one could have obtained with the funds. This 'OPPORTUNITY COST' concept, developed by WIESER, includes the time and resources involved in obtaining an item. Costs imposed on others are called EXTERNALITIES, versus costs one bears, which are PRIVATE COSTS. The private costs plus the externalities equal the social costs (SOCIAL COSTS AND BENEFITS). See also HISTORIC COST.

cost–benefit analysis.   A major tool of applied economics, it evaluates the gains and losses of a project to determine the expected net gain. For government projects or the evaluation of projects that impact the public, many of the costs and benefits are difficult to quantify, since they are SUBJECTIVE and do not trade in markets. The appropriate DISCOUNT RATE (1) may also not be CLEAR (3). Politically, the analysis is subject to manipulation. Still, it is often better to do the analysis badly than not to do it at all, since a written report at least provides a focus for debate and may prevent blatantly inefficient practices. One possible measure of the costs and benefits of territorial goods is RENT, since AMENITIES increase the rent and negative EXTERNALITIES decrease it. Thus, a good should be provided at the amount for which the induced marginal rent equals the marginal cost, where the marginal rent is declining.

cost of living. The PRICE LEVEL, measured by an index, of CONSUMER GOODS, including the CONSUMPTION of housing services.

cottage industry. Production for markets that takes place in home residencies, commonly using telecommunications.

council. Representatives elected as legislators or administrators, similar to a BOARD OF DIRECTORS. Also, a group of advisors.

countercyclical. Moving in the opposite direction of the BUSINESS CYCLE, or policy that is intended to counteract the cycle. Such policy that treats effects rather than CAUSES (1) may lead to long-term economic distortions and debt burdens.

country fund. A MUTUAL FUND that invests in shares of a foreign country or region.

coupon. The nominal INTEREST RATE of a security, or a warrant presented for payment of the interest.

covenant. An AGREEMENT, especially in REAL ESTATE. CIVIC ASSOCIATIONS typically have covenants specifying how alterations to the individual and common properties may be done, so as to conform to community standards. The basic covenants can be in the master deed, hence unchangeable, unlike municipal zoning that can be changed. For example, forests can be preserved in perpetuity by a covenant.

crack-up boom. The term used by MISES for the final stage of accelerating INFLATION, in which there is a flight into goods as the MONEY system breaks down.

crash. A decline of 20 percent or more in a market index within a few days, as with the US stock market in 1929.

creative destruction.   The replacement of old products and technology with new ones brought forth by successful ENTREPRENEURS. The term is associated with the Austrian economist JOSEPH SCHUMPETER (1976).

credentialism.   The requirement of degrees for positions for which EDUCATION has little to do with the jobs. Diploma inflation occurs when the supply of credentials increases more than the positions really requiring them, allowing employers to upgrade the standard for qualification. This is rational for employers, since the credentials serve as a proxy for the needed skills, but not for employees, who need to invest too much in education. The excessive time required for job credentials may reflect the SUBSIDY of college education and the resultant cultural (CULTURE) prestige of diplomas.

credible.   Believable policy due to past performance and structures to remedy exploitation of the belief. Constitutional provisions are more credible since they are more difficult to change, unless the government can easily ignore or evade constitutional law. Ultimately it is actual structures (STRUCUTRES OF GOVERNMENT) and performance rather than promises and texts that provide credibility.

credit.   1 A loan of funds or goods, or the ABILITY to readily obtain a loan. 2 An accounting entry on the right side of a double-entry account. 3 An increase in the amount of funds, hence a TAX CREDIT offsets a tax liability, and crediting an account adds value to it. 4 The ability of borrowers to pay back their loans, thus the availability of ready loans.

credit creation.   The expansion of the MONEY SUPPLY by a BANKING system using fractional reserves (FRACTIONAL RESERVE BANKING) by loaning out funds in excess of the original deposits. Funds lent are redeposited into the banking system and loaned out again, minus a reserve, hence it multiplies into new money according to the CREDIT MULTIPLIER. With FREE BANKING, or competitive note issue and redemption of notes into BASE MONEY, the expansion is limited by the public DEMAND FOR MONEY. For CENTRAL BANK *MONOPOLY (1) money, there is no limit to the credit and money creation.

credit money.   BANKNOTES and bank deposits.

credit multiplier.   The ratio of CREDIT CREATION to an increase in the RESERVE assets (or a decrease). It is basically $1/(c + r)$, where c is the ratio of cash to bank deposits, and r is the banking reserve ratio.

credit squeeze.   A reduction in the rate of increase in the MONEY SUPPLY by the MONETARY authority, raising INTEREST RATES and reducing CREDIT (1) for investment, thus slowing growth or inducing a RECESSION. It can also take the form of restrictions imposed by government on lending.

credit transfer. A transfer of funds from one AGENT'S (1) account to another's. Giro (GIRO SYSTEM) banks and the LETS system operate this way without checks.

credit union. A COOPERATIVE which pools members' savings and lends only to its members. They are often formed from a group with some common interest. The aim is better service for the members, especially those with modest accounts.

crime. An ACT (1) contrary to law. Organized crime is committed by organizations who often commit extortion and monopolize some industries and territories for some legal as well as illegal products. In some economies, organized crime dominates many sectors in conjunction with a corrupt government, forming a KLEPTOCRACY. Morally, government commits crime when it acts contrary to NATURAL LAW.

The 'economics of crime' applies theory to crime, including concepts such as criminals' decisions based on the costs/benefits of crime. The economic analysis of law enforcement and crime reduction is another field.

crimes without victims. Also called 'victimless crimes,' the prohibition of ACTS (1) which do not coercively (COERCIVE) harm others. The criminalization of victimless acts is also an economic INTERVENTION, since they restrict and prohibit associated enterprise, which then flourishes in the underground ECONOMY.

cross-elasticity of demand. The responsiveness of the quantity sold of a good when the price of another good changes, measured as the percentage change in quantity divided by the percentage change in price.

crowding out. A decrease in private INVESTMENT (1) due to government borrowing which raises INTEREST RATES or to TAXATION that reduces funds available for investment as well as the INCENTIVE to invest.

crown lands. In Canada and England, lands belonging either to the sovereign (monarch) or to the government or the nation.

cui bono. *Lat.* For whose good. In analyzing ACTUAL policy, the investigation of who is benefitting, or which interest groups would benefit.

culture. The cultivation of the mind, hence the totality of the human discoveries and creations (beliefs, attitudes, practices, institutions, and artifacts), of a people that have a common history. Culture co-determines economic activity along with purely economic (incentive) elements. Some cultural elements are enforced by governments, intervening (INTERVENTION) in dissenting subcultures.

culture of poverty. The CULTURE of some poor people whose attitudes, beliefs, and habits contribute to the BARRIERS that keep them in POVERTY. Regulatory and tax barriers combined with disincentives of the welfare system reinforce the cultural barriers.

cumulative voting. A voting system in which each voter has a number of votes and may allocate them to any one or more of the candidates. This measures the intensity of PREFERENCE. This method is often used for shareholders of corporations.

currency. The circulating CASH of a particular country. Currency appreciation is the rise in value of a currency relative to others. Currency DEPRECIATION (2) is the contrary. Currency devaluation is a reduction in the exchange rate when it is fixed by government. The increase in the fixed value is a currency revaluation. A currency reform replaces a currency which has been inflated, often with many zeros in the denominations, with a new, sounder currency, sometimes with a change of name. Currency risk is the possibility of changes in the value of a foreign currency which then affects the profit of an investment.

currency principle. The PROPOSITION of the CURRENCY SCHOOL that MONETARY stability is best achieved by controlling the amount of CURRENCY using an automatic RULE system, mainly by the amount of GOLD.

currency school. A 19th-century British school of thought regarding money and banking which advocated the CURRENCY PRINCIPLE in opposition to the BANKING SCHOOL.

current account. **1** The ACCOUNTING of income and expenditure for CONSUMPTION, operations, and short-term items, rather than the long-term major investments that are entered into the CAPITAL ACCOUNT. Normally, it is good practice to fund current expenses from current income unless one really wishes to reduce future consumption in order to finance current consumption. **2** A British checking account paying no interest.

current charges. USER FEES.

current dollars. Dollar (or other CURRENCY) measurements not adjusted for price INFLATION, hence NOMINAL rather than REAL (3) comparisons. Adjusted dollars are CONSTANT DOLLARS.

custom. Traditional practice and belief, some of which is formalized and made compulsory by law.

customer. One who buys goods. Because he has MONEY, which is generally accepted, and the seller has GOODS that he needs to sell, the customer is normally in a better bargaining (BARGAIN) (2) position, hence is catered to by the seller ('the customer is always right').

customs duties. TARIFFS.

customs union. A trading bloc of countries such as the European Union, in which trade BARRIERS among members are eliminated and a common set of trade barriers are imposed on countries outside the bloc. See also COMMON MARKET, ECONOMIC COMMUNITY, FREE-TRADE AREA. While increasing trade within the bloc, the union can divert EFFICIENT trade from outside the bloc to the inside, where production is less efficient but the price is lower due to the absence of TARIFFS.

cyber. Concerning media created by computers and the internet system, including communications, data, and institutions such as gopher and the world wide web. These are also referred to as 'virtual,' since the objects are not the tangible equipment but the intangible data, relationships, and other MENTAL CONSTRUCTS.

cybergovernance. Self-governance in virtual or cyber communities. Coined by Richard MacKinnon.

cyberlaw. Law regarding CYBER or virtual COMMUNITIES.

cybernation. The increased use of computers and electronic communication and data, often with substitution of such CAPITAL GOODS for LABOR.

cycle. A similarly repeating series of fluctuations. The main ones in economies are seasonal cycles, agricultural cycles, and BUSINESS CYCLES, also called trade cycles.

cycling. Any system of voting on several issues that has no determined solution, given individual PREFERENCES. See IMPOSSIBILITY THEOREM.

D

Darwinism. See EVOLUTION.

Davenant, Charles (1656–1714). A writer of economic pamphlets and disciple of Sir William Petty. He stated that restrictions on trade serve special interests rather than the public interest. Other insights of his were that a bill of exchange becomes a money substitute and that the final incidence of taxes (INCIDENCE OF TAXATION) rests on LAND.

Davenport, Herbert J. (1861–1931). An institutionalist (INSTITUTIONAL ECONOMICS) who developed some Austrian-type (AUSTRIAN ECONOMICS) concepts regarding value, cost, and CAPITAL THEORY (Gunning 1997a, 1997b). He also wrote on PUBLIC FINANCE, including arguments against HENRY GEORGE'S SINGLE TAX, although he sympathized with its aim of deriving public revenue from income not due to effort. His works include *Value and Distribution* (1908) and *Economics of Enterprise* (1914).

David Hume Institute. A research institute in Edinburgh founded in 1985. Sir Alan Peacock was its first executive director. Its research, publications, conferences and other events have been primarily concerned with MARKET approaches to public policy, and it has attracted support from Nobel laureates in economics such as Professors JAMES BUCHANAN, James Meade and GEORGE STIGLER.

de minimis non curat lex. *Lat.* The law does not concern itself with trivialities. Hence, trivial negative EXTERNALITIES are not actionable (ACTION) in a MARKET ECONOMY.

deadweight debt. DEBT not covered by any ASSET, as is the case with most national debts.

deadweight loss. A loss of producer's or CONSUMER'S SURPLUS stemming from the price of a good being higher than MARGINAL cost or to a TAX that increases the cost. A lower quantity is purchased than would be the case without a tax or under ideal conditions, such as the elimination of artificial BARRIERS to entry. However, if this loss is based on an unrealistic comparison with 'PERFECT' COMPETITION, it is no real loss, since one cannot lose what one cannot gain.

death tax.   A TAX on the PROPERTY of a PERSON who dies or its transfer, hence an inheritance or ESTATE TAX. Since the INCOME and WEALTH were already taxed when obtained, the death tax is a form of DOUBLE TAXATION. However, in the USA, CAPITAL GAINS escapes taxation upon death, since inheritors receive it on a stepped-up basis, although the asset may be taxed as a whole. (See STEP UP OF BASIS.)

debenture.   A BOND backed by the general CREDIT (4) of the company rather than its specific property.

debit.   *Acc.* The left side of a double-entry ACCOUNT (2). The right side is a credit.

Debreu, Gerard (1921–).   French-born American economist, professor at Chicago, Yale, and Berkeley, and winner of the 1983 Nobel prize in economics for his mathematical proof of the existence of GENERAL EQUILIBRIUM. With ARROW he confirmed Walrasian (LEON WALRAS) equilibrium prices with the use of set theory and topology, and he showed how a competitive (COMPETITIVENESS) MARKET ensures a stable allocative EFFICIENCY. His major book is *The Theory of Value, an Axiomatic Analysis of Economic Equilibrium* (1959, 1971). While Austrian (AUSTRIAN ECONOMICS) and other economists question the relevance of the general equilibrium construction, the demonstration of the theoretical soundness of an ECONOMY-wide market even under unrealistic assumptions nevertheless is a bulwark against accusations of CHAOS by critics of the market.

debt.   The net amount of assets borrowed (BORROW), which one is obligated to repay. When public revenues are based on LAND RENT, then the debt becomes capitalized (CAPITALIZATION) into lower land values, since it is a liability on future rents. This would create an incentive to avoid unproductive debt.

decentralization.   The shift of government bureaus and operations from the CENTRAL GOVERNMENT to the lower levels of government, bringing them under more direct and local control. This increases flexibility, incorporates decentralized KNOWLEDGE, and reduces the BUREAUCRACY and political influences of the central government.

decision lag.   The time interval between the recognition that some policy action is desired, and the policy decision.

decision theory.   The theory of rational decision making. Some companies use such theory in their planning process. A related field is GAME THEORY. One common decision-making method is to list the weighted benefits and costs of the decision. Another technique is a determination tree, starting with the major options, and then, successively, for each subordinate option, setting down the subsequent options and their likelihoods. A branch of decision making involves group decisions, which can weed out error, but can also tend to conformity, especially with the leader. Intuition – subconscious reasoning – is part of the decision-making process used by successful ENTREPRENEURS. See also RATIONALITY.

deconstruction. **1** The disassembly of a theory by breaking it into parts and mercilessly examining each part. Two key questions in this process are 'what does this mean' and 'how do they know.' Texts which superficially seem reasonable can often be revealed as meaningless, contradictory, and/or un-warranted. **2** A philosophy and movement developed by the French postmodern philosopher Derrida that we cannot obtain KNOWLEDGE of reality, hence we can only comment on the texts of ideas, but in that case, the deconstruction (2) is itself also an unwarranted and meaningless text.

decriminalization. Legislation which makes ACTS (2) that were formerly CRIMES subsequently non-criminal.

deduction. **1** A subtraction, such as from taxable income. INCOME TAXES skew expenses and outlays towards those that are tax deductible. **2** A logical conclusion.

deductive method. The methodology of deriving PROPOSITIONS, hence THEORY, from premises. In a field of science, universally applicable theory is derived from general AXIOMATIC propositions. CLASSICAL, neoclassical (NEOCLASSICAL ECONOMICS), microeconomic, Austrian (AUSTRIAN ECONOMICS), GEO-ECONOMIC, and other schools and bodies of economic theory use axiomatic-deductive methodology for their PURE THEORY, though not to the exclusion of specific empirical studies. See FOUNDATIONAL, PRAXEOLOGY.

deed. A written agreement, especially to convey title to REAL ESTATE.

deed fee. A USER FEE paid to a COMMUNITY in return for holding a TITLE to LAND.

defamation. Libel or slander. As a deliberately deceptive ruining of anoth-er's reputation, it is a type of FRAUD, although some libertarians (LIBERTARIAN-ISM) would not prohibit it.

deficit. The excess of expenditures over income (budget deficit) or imports of goods exceeding exports (trade deficit). Whereas it is normally sound economic practice to avoid budget deficits on CURRENT ACCOUNTS, DEMAND-SIDE advocates have claimed that government budget deficits provide beneficial economic stimulation. Aside from creating a political bias towards deficits even during BOOM times, the policy can lead to long-term distortions and instability, and also does not confront the causes of DEPRESSION. See Buchanan *et al.*, *Deficits* (1986).

definist fallacy. Defining a CONCEPT with a different word for the same concept or in a manner biased towards one's ARGUMENT, so that the conclusion is true by faulty DEFINITION. For example, if a critic of markets defines 'capitalism' as coercive exploitation, then his conclusion that capitalism is bad because it exploits people commits the definist fallacy.

definition. A brief set of statements which provides the meaning of a term and possibly some background. Sound theory begins with clear definitions for the key terms. The question 'what do you mean?' seeks to clear semantical ambiguities prior to the substantive question, 'how do you know?'

deflation. A continuing decrease in the PRICE LEVEL. A decrease in the MONEY SUPPLY relative to desired money holdings can be caused by an absolute decrease in the money stock or by productivity gains manifested in decreasing prices. A gradual deflation of prices relative to wages is normal with COMMODITY MONEY, but a sudden contraction of the money supply can be destabilizing and can lead to a DEPRESSION. The term also refers to the adjustment of a PRICE INDEX for INFLATION, that is using a deflator.

degradation (environmental). The destruction of the habitat for wildlife as well as human life, including POLLUTION, the destruction of forests and wildlife, and the destruction of protective features such as the ozone layer. These are effects of the failure by governments to establish PROPERTY RIGHTS throughout the earth so that the invasion of the property is subject to payments for the damages.

demand. 1 A schedule of quantities purchased at various prices. There are three types of demand: individual, market, and aggregate. Individual demand is the quantities of a good which someone desires at various prices at some moment or duration in time. Market demand is the sum of individual demands, while AGGREGATE DEMAND for all goods is the relationship between a PRICE LEVEL and expenditure for output (since at lower prices, a given money stock will buy more goods). Another taxonomy is notional demand, which is just desire, and effective demand, the willingness plus the ABILITY to pay. See also LAW OF DEMAND. **2** To purchase something. The quantity demanded of a good is the amount purchased at a particular price – this is a different meaning from demand (1), since (2) does not refer to the entire schedule. An increase in demand (1) means a shift of the entire demand schedule at all prices, in contrast to a change in the quantity demanded (2) when the price changes. **3** To request payment. Payable on demand means whenever requested.

demand deposit.   Funds in banks, against which checks can be written, and which can be withdrawn on the DEMAND (3) of the depositor.

demand for money.   The DEMAND (1) to hold cash. The PRICE LEVEL rises if the MONEY SUPPLY increases beyond the demand for money.

demand revelation.   A TAX that discloses the DEMAND (1) for a COLLECTIVE GOOD by charging the MARGINAL cost of changing the outcome (Tideman and Tullock, 1976). See also CLARKE TAX.

demand-side.   Theory and policy stating that a shift in AGGREGATE DEMAND can alter total output. This would be because the AGGREGATE SUPPLY curve is upward-sloping, due to idle resources such as labor at too high prices which are stuck. RATIONAL EXPECTATIONS and NEW-CLASSICAL theory point out that when expansionary policy is expected, prices will rise in anticipation, making the policy ineffective. Austrian (AUSTRIAN ECONOMICS), GEO-ECONOMIC, and Virginian public-choice theory (VIRGINIA SCHOOL OF POLITICAL ECONOMY) point to various INTERVENTIONS which cause rigidities, in which case the effective remedy is clear.

democracy.   Rule by the people. In direct democracy, the members vote on policy options, while in representative democracy, the members vote for representatives who then make the PUBLIC CHOICE on policy. Majoritarian democracy imposes majority rule on unwilling minorities, whereas under unanimous democracy, all members voluntarily participate at the constitutional level.

Some critics of MARKETS advocate ECONOMIC DEMOCRACY in which voters make decisions that are made by private AGENTS (1) in an unhampered MARKET ECONOMY. Actually, 'economic democracy' is practiced in a market setting within corporations and civic associations. Such voting is usually representative and according to the shares of property, but in COOPERATIVES, each member has an equal vote. Such organizations also incorporate the unanimity principle, since the owners voluntarily (VOLUNTARY) join the ASSOCIATIONS.

Public choice theory studies actual and alternative democratic governmental structures and their impact on an economy, while economic philosophy also examines the connection between democratic governance and liberty. The problem of democracy is how to structure it so that the apparatus is not co-opted by SPECIAL INTERESTS. Structural options include COMMUNITARIAN DEMOCRACY, constitutional constraints, federalism and decentralism (DECENTRALIZATION), and a division of powers in separate branches of government. The latter three have not prevented the centralization of power in the USA, however, so a more fundamental structure is required if that is a goal. See also VOTING.

demonstrated preference.   The demonstration of PREFERENCES by the results of choice, a term used by MURRAY ROTHBARD.

Demsetz, Harold (1930–).   Economics professor at Chicago, the Hoover Institution, and (emeritus) UCLA, he developed the theory of economic PROPERTY RIGHTS as a condition for MARKETS (Demsetz, 1964, 1967). He also developed the theory of incomplete CONTRACTS, such as for employment, property rights being influenced by information costs. He has also written on the private production of PUBLIC GOODS (1970) and on CONCENTRATION in INDUSTRY (2). Demsetz is a member of the MONT PELERIN SOCIETY.

denationalization.   Turning over or returning GOVERNMENT enterprises and property to PRIVATE (1) ownership.

denationalized money.   Money provided by private AGENTS (1) such as banks rather than by the state or a CENTRAL BANK. See Hayek (1990).

deny the consequent.   Given the true statement 'if X then Y,' then to deny the consequent is to argue validly that if Y is false, so is X. *Syn. modus tollens.*

deodand.   In old English law, personal property which was the instrument of killing a person, would be forfeited to the crown for distribution in alms. This law became the basis for CIVIL ASSET FORFEITURE, the CONFISCATION of property without conviction and the notion that it is the property that is at fault.

deontological ethics.   MORALITY based on DUTY (1), an OBJECTIVE *ETHIC, and/or moral RIGHTS, rather than directly on CONSEQUENCES, in contrast to TELEOLOGICAL *UTILITARIANISM or CONSEQUENTIALISM. But if the duty is to avoid harmful consequences, then a deontological ethic is not only consequential but also provides a non-arbitrary way to judge consequences, unlike pure consequentalism.

dependency ratio.   The ratio of dependents such as children, the unemployed, and retired persons, to those working. As it increases, especially as the proportion of the aged increases, the burden on workers who pay SOCIAL SECURITY taxes and other forms of welfare increases, and the viability of those transfers (TRANSFER PAYMENTS) becomes more questionable.

deposit insurance.   INSURANCE, now mainly by GOVERNMENT, of the deposits of BANKS and other financial institutions. The wasteful malinvestments of the 1980s in the USA were to some extent made possible by this governmental insurance, which made it superfluous for the depositors to monitor the soundness of the banks and savings and loans. But the bank failures of the 1930s cannot be blamed on deposit insurance, so more fundamental elements led to the savings and loan debacle.

depreciation.   1 A physical reduction of the ABILITY of a CAPITAL GOOD to contribute value to output, reducing the value of the ASSET (1). Besides wear and tear, obsolescence can cause depreciation; a reduction in market value in itself is not depreciation, because it is not physical. Hence, land is not depreciated. LABOR could in principle be depreciated; the write-offs of capital goods but not labor biases TAXATION against labor. The CONSUMPTION of capital goods is an expense allocated over the life of the asset. US tax rules, however, do not index depreciation for INFLATION, therefore in the later years, the true value is not deducted, in effect taxing the capital good, a problem remedied to some extent by the ACCELERATED COST RECOVERY SYSTEM. 2 A fall in the value of a CURRENCY relative to others.

depression.   Also called a slump, a bottom, and the trough of a BUSINESS CYCLE, a depression follows a RECESSION, and is a lengthy time of low output, high UNEMPLOYMENT, and generally hard times. Historically, the major depressions have coincided with the bottoms of the REAL-ESTATE CYCLE.

deregulation.   The removal of ARBITRARY restrictions and controls on ENTERPRISE. This SUPPLY-SIDE policy reduces costs, increasing output while reducing prices. Supply-side policy also involves DETAXATION.

derivative.   1 The instantaneous change in a dependent variable when an independent variable changes. The first derivative provides the slope of a curve, or the rate of change; economically, it provides the MARGINAL function (for example of cost, revenue) when the curve is of the total function. The maxima and minima of curves are found where the derivative or slope is zero. The second derivative provides the rate of change of the first derivative, hence the change in the slope. See BUSINESS CYCLE. **2** A financial instrument or resource derived from an underlying security, commodity, or FACTOR. For example, a FUTURES CONTRACT in corn is derived from the spot or physical market for corn and its expected price in the future. OPTIONS are another common derivative.

design.   A non-random structure. Specifically, a plan for a political or ECO-NOMIC SYSTEM.

despotism.   Unconstrained and tyrannical government POWER held by one person.

detaxation.   The removal or reduction of TAXES, just as DEREGULATION reduces REGULATION.

determined.   Having a known or derivable outcome.

determinist.   THEORY that predicts an outcome to a historical process, as with determinist Marxist (MARXIST ECONOMICS) theory that predicts the overthrow of MARKET ECONOMIES. See also NONDETERMINIST.

devaluation.   A reduction in the value of a CURRENCY whose value is fixed by government. It lowers the price of EXPORTS while it increases the price of IMPORTS, a mixed blessing, if that.

development.   See ECONOMIC DEVELOPMENT.

devisee.   Beneficiary of a will.

devolution.   DECENTRALIZATION and the transfer of political power to subordinate jurisdictions, such as transferring the responsibility for WELFARE (2) assistance from the federal to the state government in the USA, or transferring some authority from the British parliament to a Scottish legislature. Legally, devolution is any transfer of property or office from one person to another.

differential rent.   The origin of the RENT of LAND, namely the difference between the PRODUCTIVITY of a plot of land relative to land at the rent-free MARGIN (1). The theory of differential rent was developed by JAMES ANDERSON, DAVID RICARDO and HENRY GEORGE. In the CLASSICAL-ECONOMICS agricultural model, land differs in fertility and locational advantages, and as the MARGIN OF PRODUCTION moves to less productive land, rent increase in the more productive land, since all the product after paying for labor and capital goods goes to rent. George extended the concept to all land, and also developed the theory that the WAGE LEVEL is set at the margin of production. Thus he developed a marginal productivity theory of wage determination and its relationship to rent. The concept of differential rent is congruent with that of the MARGINAL PRODUCT of land. Ricardo, George, and others drew the logical conclusion that the rent which arises from the differential unrelated to the efforts of the landowner could be taxed without any EXCESS BURDEN.

HENRY GEORGE took the theory of rent further, finding that rent arises not only from the movement of the margin of production to less productive land, but also due to the increasing productivity of land with increasing commerce and technology. But this rent in urban and industrial land is also a differential.

differentiated goods.　See PRODUCT DIFFERENTIATION.

diffusion.　The spreading of INNOVATIONS among FIRMS.

Dillon's rule.　A ruling in 1911 by US Judge Dillon by which any doubt concerning municipal power is resolved by the courts against the municipal corporation. This helped tilt political power away from local government in favor of state government. See HOME RULE.

Dilthy, Wilhelm (1833–1911).　A German social philosopher, he was a developer of the concept of *Verstehen*, the understanding of the meaning of HUMAN ACTION and expression, and of history, a METHODOLOGY of the human but not the physical sciences.

diminishing marginal utility.　In neoclassical (NEOCLASSICAL ECONOMICS) theory, the diminution of the extra utility (UTILITY, MARGINAL) a person obtains with increasing amounts of a good. In Austrian (AUSTRIAN ECONOMICS) utility theory, ends are ranked in decreasing order of importance, and a good serving those ends will diminish in utility as it is applied to ends of ever lower importance.

diminishing returns.　See LAW OF DIMINISHING RETURNS.

direct taxes.　TAXES levied on the AGENT who explicitly pays the tax rather than collecting it from some other ultimate payer. A direct tax is not levied on any activity of an agent, but directly on the agent and his income or property. Economically, direct taxes include head (poll), property, death, and income

taxes, while sales taxes are indirect, since a seller pays it but collects the tax from the buyer, who actually pays it. The distinction between direct and indirect taxes is not that of the INCIDENCE or burden, but concerns the explicit payer and the object of taxation.

The US Constitution distinguishes between direct and indirect taxes, direct ones requiring apportionment by the population of the States. The federal tax on corporate income is thus not legally a direct tax on profits but an indirect excise tax on the PRIVILEGE of operating as a corporation. The 16th Amendment to the US Constitution has been interpreted by the Supreme Court as placing the personal income tax in the category of an indirect, excise tax, thus not subject to the enumeration clause. The US income tax is thus on the activity of earning income, measured by the amount of income. This legal ruling originated in the Hylton case of the 1790s, when a tax on carriages was ruled to be indirect, since Congress did not apportion the tax by population.

Director's law.   Aaron Director's HYPOTHESIS that income REDISTRIBUTION in a DEMOCRACY favors the middle class, since the median voter is of that class.

dirigisme.   *Fr.* The control of an ECONOMY by GOVERNMENT, as the French kings did during the 1600s. The term is used as a label for state INTERVENTION.

dirty float.   Floating EXCHANGE RATES, usually set by supply and demand, but with INTERVENTION by CENTRAL BANKS to affect the rates.

dirty public goods.   COLLECTIVE GOODS which benefit the population in general but not those living near them. A noisy airport, for example, leaves an 'EXTERNALITY footprint' in the vicinity. If the local BAD is already there, the market has adjusted by capitalizing (CAPITALIZATION) down the price of local sites. In a market context, site rights and COVENANTS could include quiet enjoyment, which could be rented by a firm that wished to create the bad, if the price was right.

disabilities.   A lack of normal functions; handicaps such as not being able to see or hear, or having to use a wheelchair. The Americans With Disabilities Act of 1990 began with the good intentions to help the physically handicapped, but the law has been extended to behavioral problems, and the requirement to install expensive structures that are not cost effective. See O'Quinn (1991).

discoordinating.   While MARKETS coordinate (COORDINATION) plans and activities, INNOVATIONS make previous operations less profitable, hence alter plans. The term 'discoordinating' is used for this, but it is not really a lack of coordination, but an alteration of coordinates.

discount rate.   1 The rate at which future items are discounted in value, either by individuals or by markets. The market discount rate is the same as the INTEREST RATE (actually, a family of rates). See TIME PREFERENCE. 2 The interest rate charged (CHARGE (1)) on loans by the Federal Reserve system to private banks.

discourse.   A continuing conversation among many parties with respect to some issue or policy. Some conceptions of MORALITY and of DEMOCRACY are connected with the ABILITY to engage in social discourse.

discretionary policy.   Government FISCAL and MONETARY policy which does not follow fixed rules, but lets policy makers change the policy according to how they judge the circumstances. While this provides flexibility, it also opens the door to manipulation, political influences, and also can fail due to the KNOWLEDGE PROBLEM. Market alternatives, for example FREE BANKING, can provide flexibility without the POLITICS.

discriminate.   To distinguish among persons other than on merit. In decisions on employment, renting or selling housing, entrance to colleges, and so on, those who discriminate select applicants on the basis of elements not related to qualifications. Sex/gender, race, ethnicity, nationality, religion, cultural practices, appearance, marital status, sexual orientation, and age, when unrelated to the qualifications, are common characteristics of discrimination. Minority ethnic groups are commonly discriminated against by government in many countries, if not persecuted and oppressed. 'Statistical discrimination' occurs when someone is not personally biased against some characteristic but associates it with the probability of success, hence uses such discrimination as a rule of thumb. The economics of discrimination are analyzed in BECKER (1971).

Discrimination is illegal in many contexts in the USA and other countries. In a pure market ECONOMY, government is obligated not to discriminate, but private agents may discriminate as an exercise of their PROPERTY RIGHTS and personal LIBERTY. A strong market for labor and the absence of subsidies (for example for college students) would tend to minimize negative discrimination, since it would be costly for employers to reject qualified workers, and the price system would ration entrance to colleges. The elimination of BARRIERS to SELF-EMPLOYMENT would further reduce the injuries of discrimination. So long as barriers maintain high UNEMPLOYMENT, employers will be able to discriminate despite contrary law. See also PRICE DISCRIMINATION.

diseconomies of agglomeration. DISECONOMIES caused by urban growth and DYSFUNCTIONAL policy, such as CONGESTION and POLLUTION.

diseconomy. A reduction in PRODUCTIVITY with increasing size.

disequilibrium. A situation in which GAINS FROM TRADE have not yet been exhausted (EXHAUSTION OF GAINS FROM TRADE), hence there is movement towards such exhaustion unless there are DISCOORDINATING counterforces, such as INNOVATION or a diverging COBWEB, which upset previously equilibrating action and open up new paths towards equilibration. Disequilibrium at the microeconomic level can consist of temporary GLUTS and SHORTAGES of a product, where the market is not clearing (CLEAR (1)).

disincentive. A reduction in the INCENTIVE for gain by imposing COSTS (such as taxes) and RESTRICTIONS that reduce the gain.

disincentive taxation. TAXATION which reduces incentives. See also INCENTIVE TAXATION.

dismal science. See THOMAS CARLYLE.

displacement effect. The historical tendency of national government expenditures to rise during a war or crisis, and then not fall to its previous level, hence the long-term trend towards ever larger proportions of government expenditures.

distortion. WASTE and inefficiency, thus loss of WELL-BEING, caused by policy such as ARBITRARY *REGULATION and the TAXATION of productive activity. Prices and profits become skewed (SKEWED MARKET), hence distorted, from what they would be in a FREE MARKET.

distribution. 1 Functional distribution, the allocation of income and created wealth to the owners of the FACTORS producing it, for example according to their MARGINAL PRODUCTS or monopoly gains. 2 The physical delivery of goods to intermediaries and consumers. 3 The elements of a set and their respective shares of the total, such as the distribution of market shares in an INDUSTRY (2) among firms or the distribution of income among classes of population. In statistics, a set of values and their relative frequency. A normal distribution and its mean and variance forms the basis of probability theory and much of econometrics. See also REDISTRIBUTION.

distributive justice. The fairness or justice of the DISTRIBUTION (1, 3) of income and wealth in an ECONOMY. The ETHIC used in such normative analysis can be based on an outcome or on the PROCESS. Ethical views based on outcomes are typically egalitarian (EGALITARIANISM (2)) or posit merit goods (MERIT GOODS AND BADS), distributions to the poor to prevent deprivation; such policies typically treat effects without remedying the causes. Ethical views based on process view an outcome as just, if the process of generating income is just. FREE-MARKET analysis generally considers any VOLUNTARY arrangement to be a just process. However, this leaves open the question of the original ownership or endowment of NATURAL RESOURCES.

The GEORGIST or GEO-ECONOMIC ethical premise is that since SELF-OWNERSHIP does not extend to NATURE, the RENT of these resources is properly COMMON and can be collected as revenue for governance and COLLECTIVE GOODS, whereas ALLODIAL free-marketeers view homesteading or the *status quo* TITLES as proper, except possibly for cases such as the *latifundia* inherited from the Spanish conquest in Latin America. Taiwan is an example of an ECONOMY which developed while maintaining a relatively equal DISTRIBUTION (3) of income, in part because of its LAND REFORM and taxation of LAND RENT and land gains.

distributive socialism. A variant of SOCIALISM in which income is redistributed (REDISTRIBUTION) according to an egalitarian (EGALITARIANISM (2)) criterion. Even if production is in private hands, if productive effort is taxed to redistribute, it is still to that extent socialized, with the resultant DISINCENTIVES.

disutility. Negative utility (UTILITY, MARGINAL) caused by a BAD. See also EXTERNALITY. A good can turn into a bad good if there is too much. LABOR is considered to have disutility in typical neoclassical theory (NEOCLASSICAL ECONOMICS), but work can also be satisfying.

diversification. Divergence in a DISTRIBUTION (3), the inverse of CONCENTRATION. Diversification is directly proportional to the number of units (the range of items) and inversely to the INEQUALITY (index) of the units of a distribution (3) (more inequality yields less diversification), hence the formula $D = N/I$ (Foldvary, 1995). Applications include the number of products a company produces, the number and proportions of different types of investments in a portfolio, the variety of industries in an ECONOMY, and the diversity of students or workers.

dividend. A payment to a shareholder as a return on his INVESTMENT (2). In the USA, dividend income is taxed as well as corporate profits, resulting in DOUBLE TAXATION for taxable incomes. The UK avoids this with a TAX CREDIT to shareholders to offset the tax due. See also CITIZEN DIVIDEND.

divisia money index. An index of the MONEY SUPPLY, being a weighted combination of various moneys, measuring it more effectively than the usual M1, M2, and other direct measures.

division of labor. The specialization of LABOR, increasing PRODUCTIVITY as workers become more specialized according to their COMPARATIVE ADVANTAGE, and also increasing the range of products, since more labor is available to produce other goods. The concept can be generalized to the division of CAPITAL GOODS and the division of LAND, and the DIVISION OF RESOURCES in general, but ADAM SMITH focused the discussion on labor in his *WEALTH OF NATIONS* (1776, 1976).

division of resources. The specialization of input resources into particular uses and applications, such as specialized labor, tools, and lands. The most commonly discussed type is the DIVISION OF LABOR.

doctrine. A set of related PROPOSITIONS, especially of religious, political and economic thought. Movements and schools of thought have doctrines which, if warranted (WARRANT), are THEORIES.

dogma. 1 The official creed of an organization, upheld by its authority. 2 By extension from (1), beliefs of persons who refuse to engage in dialogue with those who question these beliefs.

dollar. A name for the UNIT OF ACCOUNT of many English-speaking countries, for example the USA, Canada, Australia, New Zealand, Singapore, and Hong Kong. Until 1934 the US dollar was defined as .048379 ounce of GOLD ($20.67 per ounce), and from 1934 to 1971, $35 could be exchanged for an ounce of gold internationally. Now the US dollar, along with other CURRENCIES, is FIAT MONEY. After World War II, with the BRETTON WOODS Agreement, the US dollar became an international reserve currency and is still the most important global currency.

dollar voting. As an analogy with political voting, a consumer votes for goods with dollars or other currency. This private choosing allocates goods more efficiently (EFFICIENT) than political choosing ('Dollar vote,' Block and Walter, 1989).

domain. 1 A field of thought, rights, territory, or action. One's domain can consist of one's PROPERTY, including one's PERSON. Mathematically, a domain consists of the values a variable can take. 2 The ultimate, paramount, ownership of land, normally as the sovereign power claimed by states as in EMINENT DOMAIN.

domestic labor. See HOME PRODUCTION.

donation. A GIFT to a charity or other benevolent (BENEVOLENCE) or mutual organization or cause.

double-entry bookkeeping. The accounting system in which every TRANS-ACTION has two entries, a CREDIT (2) and a DEBIT. Credits record the source of funds, and debits the expenditures. The debits and credits must necessarily balance.

double taxation. Economically, the TAXATION of the same item in the same tax period (year) more than once, such as corporation dividends when income is taxed as corporate income and by personal income in the USA. (Interest and dividend income are not taxed twice just because they come from the principal that was taxed, since the principal generates new income.) Double taxation also occurs when income is taxed by two jurisdictions, and there is no TAX CREDIT or deduction. Legally, however, double taxation means taxing the same item of the same owner in the same year twice by the same governing body, which is why economic double taxation is not illegal.

doubt policy of liberty. The POLICY principle that when in doubt do not intervene (INTERVENTION). Err on the side of not restricting.

downsizing. A firm becoming more EFFICIENT by reducing its less productive (PRODUCTIVITY) employees and operations.

droit–droit. *Fr.* A double RIGHT, of possession and of the property, hence its yield. In ancient law, these rights were distinct, and this phrase indicated the union of the two. The possession of LAND was thus recognized as distinct from its OWNERSHIP and right to its RENT.

duarchy. GOVERNMENT with two joint rulers, as with spouses.

dues. Periodic payments members pay to a club.

dumping. Selling a good at a price below the cost of production other than brief promotional sales. Firms are accused of doing this to drive out the competitors, and then raise the price. Though illegal in many cases, it is not evident that dumping is generally successful. If the dumper later makes

ECONOMIC PROFITS, this will invite COMPETITION again. A permanent dumping by foreigners due to a SUBSIDY benefits the domestic consumers. Nevertheless, there can be instances where local production is demolished and cannot be restored on the old basis, but market-based remedies such as covenants could protect the traditional arrangements if that is desired.

durable good.   A major long-lasting good, providing services over a number of years. Economically, it is an INVESTMENT (1), although some are counted as CONSUMER GOODS. See CONSUMER DURABLE.

Dutch auction.   An AUCTION in which the starting price is above the normal expected value.

Dutch disease.   The example of The Netherlands, which has had natural gas and used this wealth to pay high salaries and enact expensive welfare legislation which the country can subsequently not afford. The Pacific island country of Nauru is another example.

duty.   1 A moral or legal OBLIGATION or requirement, usually to do something rather than avoid doing something. It is considered wrong if one does not do it. 2 A TAX, especially on sales and the customs duty on IMPORTS. Goods not subject to the tax are then 'duty-free.'

dynamic.   Taking place over a duration of time, hence ANALYSIS of a PROCESS, DISEQUILIBRIUM, and/or intertemporal phenomena. In contrast, a STATIC analysis examines a phenomenon at a moment in time.

dysfunctional.   Of INSTITUTIONS, laws, and policies, which have harmful CONSEQUENCES, unwelcomed by most in society, often unintended by the original policy makers. Government welfare programs, for example, are dysfunctional if they induce family break-up and keep the poor trapped in POVERTY. See IATROGENIC.

dysnomy.   Harmful legislation.

dystopia.   A negative UTOPIA, such as Orwell's *1984.*

E

E-money. ELECTRONIC MONEY.

earmarking. Raising revenues for particular EXPENDITURES rather than the budget in general. A gasoline tax used for road maintenance is an often used example. This is also called 'hypothecation.'

earned income. Economically, income from LABOR and the products of labor, including INTEREST payments originating from WAGES and CAPITAL RETURNS. GIFTS deriving from earned income are not earned by the recipient but are broadly earned since they are earned income whose TITLE is transferred. MONOPOLY PROFITS are unearned, as are rents from NATURAL RESOURCES. Legally and in tax law, earned income is usually confined to wages, and in some cases is given preferential treatment, and in other cases, worse treatment, for example subjected to social security taxes.

earnings per share. The net profits of a CORPORATION divided by the number of shares. This is a key indicator of the performance of a corporation.

easement. A right to use PROPERTY whose TITLE is held by another person. Access, preservation, and other aims often sought by legislation such as zoning and land-use laws can be achieved by MARKET PROCESSES through COVENANTS and easements.

easy money. The expansion of the MONEY SUPPLY to lower INTEREST RATES and provide more CREDIT (1) than warranted (WARRANT) by current SAVINGS. The term can also refer to the reduction in restrictions on lending.

economic. **1** Regarding ECONOMICS and ECONOMIES. **2** Indicating that the term is used with a particular meaning in economics, as in ECONOMIC RENT. **3** Of minimal or low COST.

economic calculation. The market pricing of ASSETS (1), reflecting SUBJECTIVE VALUES and scarcity (SCARCE). A key deficiency of CENTRAL PLANNING is its inability to conduct economic calculation.

economic community.   A union of countries without any TARIFFS among them, and a common external tariff. See also COMMON MARKET, CUSTOMS UNION, FREE-TRADE AREA.

economic cost.   See OPPORTUNITY COST.

economic democracy.   Control over economic decisions, micro as well as macro, by voters who are not investors. Besides a taking of property from the owners, this type of intervention would most likely result in inefficient outcomes, lacking the cost–benefit approach (COST–BENEFIT ANALYSIS) of private enterprise. The logical conclusion of unlimited economic democracy is socialized production. Limited forms of economic democracy exist when city councils, state legislatures, and national officials determine and influence which enterprises are set up and what and how they produce.

economic development.   A change in the structure of an ECONOMY towards more powerful TECHNOLOGY, and the conversion of TERRITORY to more intensive use. This usually changes traditional societies into more commercial cultures. Development raises average income, but whether it raises the standard of living of the lowest-income people depends on the forces affecting the inequality of the DISTRIBUTION (3) of income. Studies (Gwartney *et al.*, 1996) provide evidence for the theoretical proposition that economies with more ECONOMIC FREEDOM experience more growth and development.

economic disturbances.   Sudden shifts in AGGREGATE SUPPLY and AGGREGATE DEMAND, changing OUTPUT or the PRICE LEVEL. See SHOCK.

economic freedom.   The degree of legal FREEDOM for economic AGENTS (1). See Gwartney *et al.* (1996).

economic good.   A GOOD that is SCARCE (1).

economic growth.   An increase in OUTPUT or per-capita output due to an increase in inputs or to more PRODUCTIVITY, that is, ECONOMIC DEVELOPMENT.

economic history.   The ECONOMIC (1) aspects of the past, as a field of economics, as well as the application of theory to examine and understand past economic phenomena. More broadly, economic history includes any EMPIRICAL information and study, including statistics and contemporary economies and events. All historical facts are theory-laden; their understanding necessarily is via theory. Historical studies, in turn, can help improve and revise theory.

economic justice.   ECONOMIC POLICY consistent with an ETHIC. See DISTRIBU-
TIVE JUSTICE.

economic land.   LAND, hence NATURAL RESOURCES.

economic liberalism.   The theory that INTERVENTIONS reduce GROWTH and
PROSPERITY, therefore FREE MARKETS will have the outcomes that most people
want. The state's role is to provide the legal framework, the prohibition of
private intervention (force and fraud) and a court system for the ultimate
resolution of crime and disputes. This is a subset of the CLASSICAL-LIBERAL
view, with the question of public finance similarly left open.

economic man.   See *HOMO ECONOMICUS, HOMO CUPIDITUS*.

economic means.   Using VOLUNTARY, market-based methods of obtaining a
good, rather than the POLITICAL MEANS of taking it by legal force. The distinction was made by OPPENHEIMER and NOCK.

economic philosophy.   Topics such as the relationship between ETHICS and
ECONOMICS, the role of GOVERNMENT in an ECONOMY, the meaning of 'economics,' and the evaluation of WELL-BEING.

economic planning.   Designing an economic PROCESS and estimating the
outcome before engaging in the process of achieving it. Private agents have
the feedback of PROFIT and loss in measuring the success of their planning,
whereas government planners seldom have and usually do not need this
corrective. Government 'imperative plans,' or CENTRAL PLANNING, encompass
most economic activity, whereas 'indicative planning' leaves enterprise nomi-
nally in private hands, but influences output via fiscal and monetary policy,
regulation, and industrial policy geared to centrally determined targets. The
Soviet Union attempted imperative planning, and France after World War II
is a major example of indicative planning.

economic policy.   Government's law, TAX STRUCTURE and tax rates, regulatory processes, and conduct as it affects the ECONOMY under its jurisdiction.
Policy can be MARKET ENHANCING or MARKET HAMPERING.

economic profit.   ACCOUNTING PROFIT above normal returns to FACTORS. Economic profit can consist of MONOPOLY PROFIT or ENTREPRENEURIAL PROFIT.

economic rent.   A payment to a FACTOR beyond what is needed to put that factor
into use. LAND RENT, beyond what is needed to maintain a market for land, is

economic rent, and economic rents are also earned by movie, sports, and music stars whose second best alternative would be a lower earning. MONOPOLY PROFIT is economic rent as well. Economic rent can be taxed without any EXCESS BURDEN.

economic rights. Moral or legal RIGHTS to receive property from others, rights of POSSESSION, and rights to the yield of property possessed. Aside from CHILDREN, FREE-MARKET thought generally holds that there is no rightful claim on the property of others, although some classical liberals make exceptions for welfare rights of the indigent or emergency cases. Rights of possession stem from the right of SELF-OWNERSHIP and voluntary exchange and transfer. Allodial free-marketeers hold to a homesteading theory of rights to NATURAL RESOURCES, and to a default for *status quo* rights, whereas geoist (GEOIST ETHIC) free-marketeers hold to the COMMON ownership by humanity of resources not based on self-ownership. Some free-market theorists hold that there are no objective moral or NATURAL RIGHTS, rather basing their policy views on utilitarian, consequentialist (CONSEQUENTIALISM), contractarian (CONTRACTARIANISM), and other philosophies.

economic sanctions. Restrictions and penalties on trading with certain parties, usually foreign countries which are enemies or that have policies that are morally objected to.

economic system. The private and governmental structures of an ECONOMY. Private structures include the relationship between banking and manufacturing, the interconnections between major enterprises, and the types of ownership, and LAND TENURE. Governmental structures include planning and control of INDUSTRY (2), the degree of government ownership and REDISTRIBUTION, and MONETARY and FISCAL policy. Systems include PRIMAL ECONOMIES, traditional economies, MARKET ECONOMIES, SOCIALISM (COMMAND ECONOMIES), and mixed (MIXED ECONOMY) systems, the latter now dominant. The two paradigms of pure market systems are the ALLODIAL and the geoist (GEOIST ETHIC). The three major mixed systems are the export-oriented East-Asian, with government direction but moderate government sectors; the American, with regulation, income taxation and redistribution; and the European, with large welfare programs, employment restrictions, and value-added taxes. See also BEST ECONOMIC SYSTEM.

economic union. A CUSTOMS UNION that to some degree has a unified FISCAL and MONETARY policy and INSTITUTIONS. The EUROPEAN UNION has been moving towards such a union.

economic welfare. Well-being due to the CONSUMPTION of goods, studied by WELFARE ECONOMICS. It is usually measured by GDP, which many economists recognize as incomplete, and more complete measurements have been proposed. Such alternatives are even more imprecise, hence there is a trade-off between completeness and accuracy of measurement.

economics. There is no generally accepted DEFINITION of the field. The CLASSICAL definition is the science of wealth. A typical contemporary definition is the allocation of SCARCE (1) resources among alternative uses. Other definitions include the study of an ECONOMY, a particular view of human behavior, the science of HUMAN ACTION, the science of how people coordinate their wants, social provisioning, and the science of EXCHANGE. The science of utility (UTILITY, MARGINAL) is perhaps the most general definition which does not overlap other fields.

economics of law. See LAW AND ECONOMICS.

economies. Increasing per-unit output (or decreasing per-unit costs) due to an increase in some variable such as size.

economies of agglomeration. Increased PRODUCTIVITY due to density, such as greater population per unit of surface area, or enterprises locating near one another, that is, a cluster of stores that make it attract more shoppers. Such economies make feasible a greater DIVISION OF LABOR and more EFFICIENT transport and INFRASTRUCTURE. These economies induce a higher RENT and thus become capitalized in higher land value in that location, hence the benefits may largely be shifted to the recipients of the site rents. See also DISECONOMIES OF AGGLOMERATION.

economies of density. Increases of output and increased variety of products due to greater density, saving on transportation costs, making available a greater local market.

economies of scale. ECONOMIES due to more output. See also EXTERNAL ECONOMIES OF SCALE.

economies of scope. ECONOMIES due to the expansion of the scope of activities, such as the joint production of several related goods by a firm.

economies of size. ECONOMIES due to the size of a firm, farm, or factory.

economist. A specialist in the fields of ECONOMIC (1) *THEORY and its applications, economic history, and/or economic POLICY. Good economists usually are also knowledgeable about philosophy, law, history, political science, and mathematics.

economize. To minimize COSTS given some OUTPUT or BENEFIT, or to maximize benefits given some cost. A FOUNDATIONAL *AXIOMATIC premise of economics is that all persons economize.

economizing man. PERSONS *QUA economizers (ECONOMIZE).

economy. 1 The totality of PRODUCTION, EXCHANGE, and CONSUMPTION within some territorial DOMAIN. 2 Economizing (ECONOMIZE).

ecu. European Currency Unit, a unit of account created by the EUROPEAN UNION. It is based on a BASKET of European CURRENCIES. It is being replaced in 1999 by the EURO currency.

education. The acquisition of knowledge, skills, and culture. Often the term refers to the schooling of youths. The industry of educating CHILDREN is largely a government enterprise worldwide, except for some private, often religious, schools, as well as much private supplementation. Private schooling was common prior to the middle of the 1800s.

FREE-MARKET proposals for children's education include voucher systems or tax credits for tuition to provide equal choice, and, ultimately, the privatization of the provision as well as the funding of education. A radically free-market college could consist of students hiring instructors, who would then contract with universities for classrooms and facilities. While there are external benefits to educating a child, it is not evident that these are necessarily relevant EXTERNAL EFFECTS, and local communities could well provide the desired supplement to parents' provision.

effective demand. Desire plus cash. Notional demand and the resources with which to obtain goods. DEMAND (1) is normally thought of as effective demand.

efficiency. 1 Technical or productive efficiency: output per unit of input. 2 Economic efficiency: an ECONOMY in which no one can be made better off without making a person worse off. Allocative efficiency concerns the mix of resources used in production, and distributional efficiency concerns the mix of consumer goods. Real-world economic efficiency needs to include TRANSACTION costs.

efficient. Having more EFFICIENCY than other PROCESSES, or having the greatest possible efficiency. An ECONOMY is efficient when WASTE is minimized, that is, when processes minimize costs and resources are allocated to where they are most desired. Markets create EFFICIENCY (1) through COMPETITION, while

CENTRAL PLANNING and INTERVENTION create social waste due to the KNOWLEDGE problem, political influences, and lack of INCENTIVES.

efficient market.   **1** In stock and commodity markets, the proposition that, because of widespread information and COMPETITION, it is normally unlikely for an individual to consistently outperform financial market averages. **2** In a competitive INDUSTRY (2), the proposition that firms in the long run will not earn economic profits.

efficient portfolio.   A portfolio that for a given level of volatility risk, maximizes the return, or for a given level of return, minimizes the volatility risk. This is accomplished by a DIVERSIFICATION in relatively uncorrelated investment types.

effluent fee.   A CHARGE (1) proportional to the amount of POLLUTION created. It has been implemented in Germany and some other countries. When it compensates for the damage caused, and the fee is not greater than the MARGINAL costs of pollution, the fee is market enhancing, since it internalizes the pollution costs, avoiding the EXTERNAL EFFECT. See also CARBON TAX, COASE THEOREM.

eftpos.   Electronic funds transfer at point of sale.

egalitarianism.   **1** The philosophy that human beings are of equal moral worth, applied as the concept of EQUALITY before the law. This moral equality, recognized by NATURAL-LAW philosophers such as JOHN LOCKE and inscribed in the US Declaration of Independence, is a premise of classical liberalism (CLASSICAL LIBERAL) and FREE-MARKET thought. Geoist (GEOIST ETHIC) thought goes further and ascribes to humanity an equal share of the natural endowment, LAND. **2** The philosophy that people are entitled to equal WELL-BEING, a key premise of redistribution as well as the ABILITY-TO-PAY doctrine of TAXATION. See DISTRIBUTIVE JUSTICE.

elastic.   The percentage change of one variable such as quantity being rather responsive to a percentage change in the price, the ratio being greater than one.

elasticity.   The responsiveness of one variable to a change in another. Elasticity is measured by the percentage change in the responding variable divided by the percentage change in the other variable, for small changes.

electromagnetic spectrum.   Radio, television, and other broadcast frequencies and wavelengths. As a natural resource, it is a type of ECONOMIC LAND. See also BROADCAST SPECTRUM.

electronic funds.   MONEY conveyed by wire, such as the US Fedwire or via computer connections or at a point of sale. Most of the value of US payments is conducted with electronic funds.

electronic money.   See ELECTRONIC FUNDS.

elegant.   Complete and correct, and with graceful simplicity. An elegant THEOREM or derivation is strikingly EFFICIENT in its presentation.

élite.   A small group of people who have most of the WEALTH and POWER, such as due to government-protected PRIVILEGES.

embodied knowledge.   The concept that CAPITAL GOODS contain technological KNOWLEDGE. Some capital goods such as computer software are pure knowledge (Baetjer, 1993).

eminent domain.   The ultimate ownership by GOVERNMENT of LAND, giving it the POWER to take it, with compensation, for uses beneficial to the public. This principle, even if sound, is in practice violated by TAKINGS that benefit special and private interests. Eminent domain has been regarded as proper by some ethical philosophers, such as Grotius and Pufendorf, and is inscribed in the US Constitution. Some libertarians (LIBERTARIANISM) and other FREE-MARKETEERS oppose eminent domain, holding that rights of POSSESSION should be totally PRIVATE (1), without the state as co-owner. Lack of eminent domain powers have not prevented large developments such as Walt Disney World and many RESIDENTIAL ASSOCIATIONS. See also DOMAIN.

emission charge.   EFFLUENT FEE.

emphyteusis.   In Roman and civil law, a long-term or perpetual contract for land tenancy subject to maintaining it (for example not depleting its fertility) and the payment of periodic rent.

empirical.   Of observations, facts, and data. Empirical studies examine actual, real-world phenomena, rather than hypothetical models or THEORY conditional on premises which have never taken place.

empirical policy.   Policy implemented as an experiment to determine the effect. If the policy is effective, then it is assumed that it was the appropriate remedy for the problem. The concept is similar to empirical therapy in medical science.

employee. A person who is employed (EMPLOYMENT) under the direction of another person or organization, which then pays the worker a wage. The term has more legal than economic meaning, since the line between a contractor and an employee is not sharp, which creates disputes for TAXATION.

Employee Stock Ownership Plan. Various methods in the USA and UK whereby EMPLOYEES collectively (COLLECTIVE) obtain shares of stock in their employers' company. The most common plan is an ESOP, a trust with which the pension plan borrows money and buys newly issued stock. The aim is to increase employee ownership, hence increase the ownership in shares by the population, giving the people as a whole a greater share in the returns on CORPORATIONS and a greater equity stake in the economy's capital goods and land. Payments by the company to support an ESOP are tax-deductible.

employment. The application of a FACTOR, especially LABOR, in the PRODUCTION of WEALTH. See also FULL EMPLOYMENT, SELF-EMPLOYMENT.

enclosures. Converting commons, or communally owned lands, into ESTATES (1) owned by an aristocracy. This occurred in Great Britain after the Middle Ages, reducing the availability of land for small farmers, reducing incomes, and creating a class of landless workers who provided labor for industrialization. The abundance of cheap labor induced low wages, long hours, and harsh conditions, but critics misleadingly blamed private enterprise rather than the state-protected enclosures.

endogenous. From within a SYSTEM.

ends. What people ultimately want, rather than means to what they fundamentally want. An AXIOMATIC premise of economics is that persons have ends which they can rank in ordinal order. The economizing (ECONOMIZE) premise then states that they will pursue their highest ends first, relative to the costs.

energy. The generation of heat, light, and movement. Energy EFFICIENCY (1) conserves and minimizes the use of materials such as oil, natural gas, and coal, which generate energy.

English tort system. Having the loser of lawsuits pay the legal costs of the winner, so that if one is wrongfully sued, one does not have to bear one's legal expense. In the AMERICAN RULE, the loser usually bears his legal costs, thus imposing a tax on losers of lawsuits initiated by others. A FREE MARKET uses the English system.

Enlightenment.   The era in Europe and America during the 1700s when thinkers valued REASON in science, ethics, religion, and government, rather than blindly obeying authority and tradition. NATURAL-RIGHTS and NATURAL-LAW philosophy flourished, and toleration was advocated for cultural and religious differences. Key Enlightenment figures include JOHN LOCKE, Voltaire, and Immanuel Kant, along with economists such as the French Physiocrats and ADAM SMITH. The SCOTTISH ENLIGHTENMENT was especially influential. American figures include Benjamin Franklin, Thomas Jefferson, James Madison, George Mason, and THOMAS PAINE. In France, the *Encyclopédie* embodied the humanist thought of the era, which was regarded to have ended with the French Revolution. In America, however, the US Constitution, despite its imperfections, is a lasting legacy of the Enlightenment, and the philosophy lives on in CLASSICAL-LIBERAL thought and institutions.

entail.   To limit inheritance to a specific class of heirs.

enterprise.   An undertaking or productive activity, or a firm (or a set of firms under common ownership) that engages in it. See also FREE ENTERPRISE.

enterprise zones.   Districts in which TAXES and REGULATIONS are reduced. The SUPPLY-SIDE effect may be limited if site RENTS rise to equalize the normal returns inside and outside the zones. But the fact that such zones are being proposed and implemented shows the acceptance of supply-side POLICIES, and the existence of political barriers preventing their implementation economy-wide.

enthymeme.   An argument in which some premises or conclusions are implied but not explicitly stated.

entrepreneur.   The role or IDEAL TYPE that organizes the FACTORS OF PRODUCTION to new uses, methods, and markets. Entrepreneurship is a type of LABOR, but its earnings are not based on its MARGINAL PRODUCT, or contribution to the value of output, as with ordinary labor, but on ENTREPRENEURIAL PROFIT due to successfully anticipating and shaping the market DEMAND for a product. Some economists classify entrepreneurship as a fourth factor of production, in effect splitting human exertion into two categories.

   What an entrepreneur confronts is not 'RISK' but UNCERTAINTY (see FRANK KNIGHT), which cannot be insured against: an entrepreneur is 'acting man exclusively seen from the aspect of the uncertainty inherent in every action' (Mises, 1944, 1966: 253). Entrepreneurs are not a set of specific persons but persons who take on that role. Though entrepreneurial profit is based on uncertainty, it is not a return on uncertainty, but on the human exertion (hence labor) that attempts to exploit (EXPLOITATION) (1) perceived opportunities in exchange for an uncertain gain.

Entrepreneurs are the 'drivers' of an ECONOMY, introducing INNOVATIONS and conducting ARBITRAGE. Key economists who have written on entrepreneurship include CANTILLON, Casson, KIRZNER, Knight, Mises, and SCHUMPETER. Austrian economists (AUSTRIAN ECONOMICS) have been in the forefront of research on entrepreneurship.

entrepreneurial failure.   The failure (FAIL) of ENTREPRENEURS to take advantage of an available profitable opportunity. This contrasts with MARKET FAILURE, which is a systematic, long-term failure of the MARKET PROCESS to provide demanded goods or to do so at MARGINAL COST.

entrepreneurial profit.   ECONOMIC PROFITS earned by ENTREPRENEURS, consisting of revenues minus the costs of FACTOR inputs, including the entrepreneur's OPPORTUNITY COSTS. Such profits tend to become reduced over time as others copy the products and methods of the innovating (INNOVATIONS) entrepreneur.

entropy.   The increasing disorder and unusable energy of a closed system. A correct application to economics is that capital goods, including infrastructure, are subject to entropy, wearing out unless investment is applied to maintain them. The crackpot application is that entire economies wear out; it is false because the earth obtains ever new ENERGY from the sun, and there has been no lack of innovation.

entry.   Initiating affiliation in an organization, or starting operations in some field such as an INDUSTRY (2), or the option of doing so. In competitive industry, BARRIERS to entry (the formation of new firms) are low.

entry monopoly.   A fixed amount of a resource, so that a new firm must obtain some of the resource from an existing firm rather than expand the supply. The fixed resource thus commands a monopoly price. An example is taxi medallions that are fixed in number, or land within some economic region. CLASSICAL economists often referred to such monopolies.

envalued.   Having moral or other values, as with envalued theory that includes a moral dimension. *Syn.* value free.

environment.   The natural and produced surroundings and habitat. The natural environment includes the atmosphere, oceans and other waters, soil, wildlife, and audial as well as visual effects. The environment is a COLLECTIVE GOOD, and many environmental AMENITIES (1) have been destroyed due to a lack of PROPERTY RIGHTS – a TRAGEDY OF THE UNMANAGED COMMONS. The assignment of enforced rights and charging users for the costs of use would lead to the preservation of the environment. However, an open question is the rights of future generations, who cannot vote or make purchases. It is generally recognized that the preservation of renewable resources is a wise policy for both the present day and for posterity.

environmental charge.   Charges compensating for environmental destruction, as with EFFLUENT FEES. These are also referred to as 'green taxes.' See also ENVIRONMENTALISM.

environmentalism.   A movement and body of thought which places high importance on maintaining the natural ENVIRONMENT and ecology. FREE-MARKET environmentalism maintains that MARKETS offer the best protection. Much of government environmental policy does not use COST–BENEFIT ANALYSIS, and many governments, especially in command economies such as the former Soviet Union, have been among the worst polluters. Among many market-oriented books are Panayotou (1993) and Anderson and Leal (1991).

epistemics.   The study of KNOWLEDGE, and emphasis on the role of knowledge, as with the Austrian school (AUSTRIAN ECONOMICS).

equal opportunity.   1 The absence of legal PRIVILEGES, a cornerstone of classical liberalism (CLASSICAL LIBERAL). 2 EQUALITY with respect to NATURAL OPPORTUNITIES, as claimed by GEOISM. 3 Legally mandated equal treatment of persons in sexual, racial, and other categories, which FREE-MARKETEERS hold violates private PROPERTY and the freedom of contracting (CONTRACT).

equal pay.   See COMPARABLE WORTH.

equal sacrifice.   The criterion for TAXATION that all taxpayers should suffer the same loss of MARGINAL or absolute utility, hence to base taxation on the ABILITY TO PAY. The alternative is the no-sacrifice approach of benefit taxation or charges (BENEFIT PRINCIPLE), which is a quid pro quo. The subjectivity and unmeasurability of utility makes equal sacrifice dubious, and the benefit principle makes such sacrifice redundant.

equality.   The situation in which nobody is or has greater or less than the others. There are various levels and types of equality, such as of opportunity, wealth, and moral worth. The basis of CLASSICAL-LIBERAL and FREE-MARKET *ETHICS is equality before the law, based on equal moral worth. Equal LIBERTY provides equal legal OPPORTUNITIES. Equal outcomes, such as income or wealth, is inconsistent with equal opportunity, since some will not have the opportunity to advance in wealth, and it contradicts equal liberty, since some are held back by FORCE. The most fundamental equality, of moral worth, thus endows humanity with equal NATURAL RIGHTS, but not of any claims to egalitarian income or wealth. GEORGIST or geoist (GEOIST ETHIC) thought would go further and endow human beings with an equal claim to the RENT of ECONOMIC LAND, since equal SELF-OWNERSHIP does not extend to natural resources. See also INEQUALITY.

equation of exchange. The equation $MV = PT$, where M is the MONEY SUPPLY, V the VELOCITY of MONEY, P the PRICE LEVEL, and T the amount of TRANSACTIONS or OUTPUT in REAL (3) terms. If V and T do not change, then an increase in M leads to an increase in P. Some Austrian (AUSTRIAN ECONOMICS) economists such as MISES have considered the equation a holistic concept that does not really explain the purchasing power of money (Greaves, 1974, p. 41). See CANTILLON EFFECT.

equation of inequality. Inequality equals CONCENTRATION times number (Foldvary, 1995): $I = CN$.

equilibration. Exhausting gains from trade (EXHAUSTATION OF GAINS FROM TRADE). An exchange reduces the MARGINAL UTILITY of the next item of a type, thus as exchange proceeds, gains are reduced until they are exhausted. Market exchanges are thus equilibrating, but INNOVATIONS provide new OPPORTUNITIES to GAIN FROM TRADE, and shifting SUPPLY and DEMAND also create ever new opportunities.

equilibrium. The EXHAUSTION OF GAINS FROM TRADE, the result of EQUILIBRATION. At exhaustion the MOMENTUM of the relevant variables is constant, though not necessarily zero (stationary). This implies MARKET CLEARING, the harmony of plans, and the cessation of economic action (price or quantity movements). Markets equilibrate as GAINS FROM TRADE are exploited, hence markets move towards equilibrium, but they do not reach equilibrium as the market agents continuously shift their DEMANDS and SUPPLIES. See also the EVENLY ROTATING ECONOMY, which has an equilibrium of constant momentum.

equity. 1 MORAL (1) JUSTICE. An ECONOMIC (1) PROCESS or outcome can be judged for its EFFICIENCY (1) and for its equity. Judging equity presumes a moral standard to judge by, which would be a UNIVERSAL ETHIC independent of any particular CULTURE or ARBITRARY personal view. It is generally agreed that the basis of such an ethic and of equity is the moral EQUALITY of human beings. 2 A firm's ASSETS minus its LIABILITIES, which can be negative. Also called 'net worth.' **3** *Leg.* Justice according to fairness rather than common or statute law.

equity/efficiency trade-off.   An alleged trade-off between EQUITY (1) and EFFICIENCY (1). The allegation is that an ALLODIAL *FREE MARKET is efficient, but INTERVENTION is required for a more egalitarian (EGALITARIANISM) distribution of income, which would reduce efficiency. But a third option is a geocratic (GEOCRACY) free market that is both efficient and more egalitarian than the allodial case.

ERE.   EVENLY ROTATING ECONOMY.

ESOP.   A common type of EMPLOYEE STOCK OWNERSHIP PLAN.

Esperanto.   The most popular international language, constructed by L.L. Zamenhof in 1887, in use by several million persons. With its simple, consistent structure, its universal use would reduce language barriers and translation costs. Nationalist control over EDUCATION may be the main barrier to its adoption. Adherents share an IDEOLOGY of global peace and harmony. Other constructed languages such as Interlingua have their advocates as well.

estate.   **1** A large landholding. **2** The ASSETS of a deceased person.

estate tax.   A DEATH TAX, on the value of ESTATES (2). An inheritance tax is levied on an inheritor, while an estate tax is on the estate after paying liabilities and donations, before it is divided into inheritances.

estoppel.   The prevention of a statement or claim contrary to a previous statement or act.

etherialization of money.   The tendency for money to become increasingly intangible. Historically, PURCHASING MEDIA have been evolving from a COMMODITIES to paper notes to electronic accounts.

ethic.   A set of rules which apply to some sets of ACT and which result in MORAL (1) values of GOOD, EVIL, or neutral for each act. The MARKET PROCESS adheres to a UNIVERSAL ETHIC in which VOLUNTARY acts are good or neutral, and invasions are morally wrong (evil). BUSINESS ETHICS deal with the treatment of employees, the collection of debts, contracts, and other such matters.

etiology.   The determination and assignment of causes.

euro. The CURRENCY of the EUROPEAN UNION, scheduled to replace the ECU in 1999 with the creation of the European Monetary Union, with coins and paper notes to be issued in 2002. The currency was established by the Maastricht Treaty of 1992 and the Madrid summit of 1995. According to the plan, European Union national currencies will become denominations of the Euro and will eventually be replaced by it. However, the harmonization of monetary policies remains problematic. The UK obtained the option of not joining the EMU EUROPEAN MONETARY UNION.

European Monetary Union. A common CURRENCY and MONETARY system for the EUROPEAN UNION, now in formation, to replace the European Monetary System of coordinating exchange rates and monetary policy.

European Union. Formerly known as the European Economic Community and the Common Market, it is a CUSTOMS UNION in Europe, established in 1957, that has been moving towards ECONOMIC UNION. This bloc has absorbed members from the European Free Trade Area, with which the EEC now has free trade.

evasion. Escaping a TAX or REGULATION by illegal means.

evenly rotating economy. A model created by LUDWIG VON MISES of an ECONOMY in which the same pattern repeats periodically, there being no entrepreneurship (ENTREPRENEUR). The model is utilized in AUSTRIAN ECONOMICS to examine the introduction of changes. Its EQUILIBRIUM is one of constant MOMENTUM.

evidence. Data derived from observations, which test a HYPOTHESIS, provide facts for premises, and constitute KNOWLEDGE for ECONOMIC HISTORY.

evil. A PERSON's sentiment or the MORAL (1) value assigned by an ETHIC for something coercively harmful or disagreeable.

evolution. See SOCIAL EVOLUTION.

ex ante. *Lat.* Beforehand; intentions before an event. This and the *EX POST* concepts were developed by Gunnar Myrdal.

ex post. *Lat.* Afterwards; actuality after or due to an event.

excess benefit. The BENEFIT of a TAX or charge, besides the expenditure of the funds. A charge for POLLUTION, for example, provides the benefit of reduced pollution, and geo-economists (GEO-ECONOMICS) argue that a charge or tax on site RENTS can provide the benefit of inducing an efficient current use of LAND and dampening BUSINESS CYCLES.

excess burden.   The DEADWEIGHT LOSS or social cost (SOCIAL COSTS AND BEN-EFITS) of a TAX, beyond the PRIVATE (1) costs of paying the tax, which is not an ECONOMY-wide cost but a transfer of funds. A tax on exertion, whether it is based on income, sales, goods, or value-added, shifts the SUPPLY curve to the left, towards lower supplies for each price or higher after-tax prices for each quantity. The DEMAND curve cuts the higher supply curve at a higher price and lower quantity. The reduced quantity, relative to what consumers would have voluntarily (VOLUNTARY) wanted, is the excess burden (graphically, a triangle below the demand curve). This is the social WASTE due to the tax. The excess burden also consists of the time and resources devoted to complying with the tax, the COMPLIANCE COST. When the supply curve is fixed, hence graphically vertical, then the supply does not shift, and there is no excess burden, the full burden borne by the owner in keeping less of the yield.

exchange.   The transfer of a good by one party to another party, and in return, the other party transferring a different good to the first party. Both parties deem themselves to be better off, because each transfers a good with lesser MARGINAL UTILITY for one that has greater marginal utility, utility being SUBJECTIVE. MARKET ECONOMIES are based on the DIVISION OF LABOR, with re-sources devoted to their most productive use, in accord with their COMPARA-TIVE ADVANTAGE, and the exchange of goods. The typical POLITICAL process, in contrast, is based on an imposed extraction of resources (taxes) and the imposed provision of PROGRAMS (1).

exchange control.   Restrictions on importing (IMPORT), exporting (EXPORT), or converting CURRENCY as well as precious metals.

exchange rate.   The ratio at which CURRENCIES are exchanged, that is, the price of a currency relative to another.

exchange value.   The MARKET value of a good, in contrast to its subjective use value.

excise tax.   A tax on a PRIVILEGE or activity, or on sales, rather than directly on wealth or income, though the amount of tax be measured by the amount of activity. A SALES TAX can be considered to be a tax on the activity of the transaction, the tax measured by the amount of the sales, for example a 6 percent sales tax is 6 percent of the sales. The US INCOME TAX is legally an excise tax on the activity of earning income, measured by the amount of income. Some excise taxes have been paid using tax stamps. See also DIRECT TAXES.

excludable. A COLLECTIVE GOOD for which others can be prevented from using and persons using it can be expelled from the set of users. Some economists define collective goods as only non-excludable, but the more comprehensive definition as simultaneous use would include excludable goods. See also CLUB GOODS.

exertion. The application of LABOR to the production of WEALTH.

exhaustion of gains from trade. The reduction in the MARGINAL UTILITY of the next EXCHANGE of the same goods as a result of a voluntary exchange of the goods. Using MENGER's example, if one rancher has cows but no horses, and another rancher has horses but no cows, the first exchange of a cow for a horse provides a great increase in marginal utility, the second exchange less marginal utility, and so on until a further exchange will provide no increase, hence gains from trade have been exhausted.

exhaustive voting. Voters choose their least favored option, which is then removed from the selection pool, and the PROCESS loops until one is left. This process avoids the PARADOX OF VOTING.

existential good. A GOOD that actually exists, rather than a potential or hypothetical one. As an application, collective goods can be defined as existential rather than potential. By that definition, producible collective goods are not excludable through non-production.

exit. Terminating affiliation in an organization, or ending operations in some field such as an INDUSTRY (2), or the option of doing so. The ABILITY to exit a community, jurisdiction, or organization is a vital element of FREEDOM. Internal exit, or SECESSION, is the ability to withdraw from a jurisdiction without leaving its boundaries. As noted by Hirschman (1970), the other option for changing a collective situation is voice (voting and persuading). See also ENTRY.

exogenous. From outside the SYSTEM.

expansion. The phase of a BUSINESS CYCLE in which output is increasing.

expectation. The value that one estimates a future variable will have, or the probability of the occurrence of a future event.

expenditure.   Funds spent for GOODS and SERVICES. GOVERNMENT expenditure can be measured as MONEY spent for inputs for physical services such as hours of streetlights, or for benefits received such as some reduction in crime. Government expenditures are usually measured by the cost of inputs in producing physical services, since the output is difficult to evaluate.

expenditure tax.   A comprehensive TAX on spending, whether it is a SALES TAX or a tax on all income not saved. Usually, only expenditure for CONSUMPTION is intended, which then raises the difficulty of distinguishing between them. An expenditure tax burdens borrowing (BORROW), since an extra amount must be spent to pay the tax and extra INTEREST on borrowings, while an INCOME TAX penalizes SAVINGS. But since overall, borrowings equals savings, an income and an expenditure tax have similar EXCESS BURDENS, although the COMPLIANCE COST might be less for an expenditure tax. Advocates of a changeover to an expenditure tax also need to explain why an expenditure tax is the best of all tax alternatives, not just that it is superior to the income tax, since the alternative of taxing ECONOMIC RENT avoids the excess burdens present in both income and expenditure taxes.

expense.   A payment for a GOOD or SERVICE, or for a loss.

expense ratio.   Operating EXPENSES divided by average net ASSETS. For mutual funds, this ratio indicates the extent of the fees.

experiment.   A test or trial in order to discover the outcome. ENTREPRENEURS engage in experiments when they innovate (INNOVATION), trying out new products and methods in the market. A successful experiment generates an ENTREPRENEURIAL PROFIT.

'experiments never fail.'   While a new ENTERPRISE or INNOVATION can FAIL in the MARKET, the experiment itself does not fail, since failure provides the KNOWLEDGE that the particular product or PROCESS is not profitable.

explain.   To eliminate a puzzle.

explanandum.   That which is to be explained (EXPLAIN), the explanation being the 'explanans.'

explicit.   Having an observable manifestation, such as the exchange of MONEY for GOODS, a written or oral CONTRACT, or TRANSACTIONS that a bookkeeper records. In contrast, IMPLICIT payments or contracts have no visible manifestations, yet are just as REAL (4).

exploitation. 1 Taking advantage of a resource by putting it to use or by obtaining its benefit. 2 Extracting more work or paying the worker less than what would be warranted (WARRANT) in a truly VOLUNTARY exchange. Exploitation is due to legal PRIVILEGES that restrict one party's options, thereby enabling the exploiting party to extract as much gain as possible from the victim.

export. A GOOD that is sold to foreigners, whether they are located outside or inside the exporting country.

expropriation. The CONFISCATION of PROPERTY by a GOVERNMENT, particularly without any compensation.

extended order. The SPONTANEOUS ORDER of a MARKET ECONOMY, thus called by F.A. HAYEK to indicate the society-wide nature of this ORDER, in contrast to organizational order.

extensive margin of production. The area where a new FACTOR such as LAND would be put to PRODUCTION. This area has the least productive land or other factor in use, and the best land or factor not yet under production. For labor, the extensive margin consists of the best workers not yet employed. In the LAW OF WAGES, the WAGE LEVEL is determined at the extensive land margin, where land is still free. Abstracting from capital goods, if rent is zero, then the whole product constitutes wages, and that wage determines the general wage level due to COMPETITION among workers.

extent of the market. The scope of MARKET PROCESSES, and the size of the MARKET. This determines the DIVISION OF RESOURCES.

external economies of scale. ECONOMIES due to the expansion of an INDUSTRY (2).

external effects. Uncompensated effects of ECONOMIC (1) acts on third parties, those who are not party to the ACTIVITY itself. An external effect alters the utility (UTILITY, MARGINAL) of another person, without any compensation for negative effects, and without the party having to pay for received BENEFITS, or positive effects. With COMPENSATION (1), the effects are internalized. Synonyms include external costs, neighborhood effects, externalities, spillovers, and external economies and diseconomies.

A relevant (or Pareto-relevant) external effect is one which would be altered if there were compensation, whereas a non-relevant effect is not altered; for example parents' expenditure for schooling that takes place whether or not they receive funding. In a relevant effect, gains from trade can take place, since compensation can alter the situation to mutual benefit.

In inframarginal external effects, small changes in the situation do not change the effect on others. In marginal external effects, small changes do alter the effects.

The lack of compensation often exists because PROPERTY RIGHTS are not established and enforced for the resources affecting third parties, including the public at large. If, for example, polluters have to compensate the affected parties, the pollution is no longer a negative external effect, and there would be less of it. If TRANSACTION costs are relatively small, then the COASE THEOREM states that the parties will negotiate an EFFICIENT (2) solution.

CONGESTION occurs when an extra user of a route imposes a crowding cost on the others; the users do not have a property right in the unobstructed usage of the route. One remedy there is a CONGESTION FEE that makes the user pay for the congestion cost, reducing congestion, protecting the right to unobstructed usage.

external orientation.   The degree to which foreign markets impact an IN-DUSTRY (2) or ECONOMY, including the share of revenues earned in foreign markets and the cost of imported inputs. The external orientation of INDUSTRY (2) in the USA, UK, and other countries has increased substantially in recent decades. See Campa and Goldberg (1997).

externality.   Synonym for EXTERNAL EFFECT.

extroversive labor.   Labor engaged in for the wages rather than for the satisfaction of the work itself, in contrast to introversive labor.

F

factor. A resource category that is an input for the PRODUCTION of WEALTH. See also FACTORS OF PRODUCTION.

factors of production. The three main classical categories of FACTORS, LAND, LABOR, and CAPITAL GOODS. See also ENTREPRENEUR.

fail. A business fails when it ceases operations after suffering losses. The MARKET PROCESS fails when actors systematically and over the long run do not equilibrate potential gains from trade (real-world failure implies real-world costs, hence when TRANSACTION costs are greater than gains, there is nothing to equilibrate). Real-world failure only exists relative to real-world feasible perfection (PERFECT). See also CONSTITUTIONAL FAILURE, ENTREPRENEURIAL FAILURE, GOVERNMENT FAILURE, MARKET FAILURE.

Federal Reserve Notes. The MONEY in current use in the USA, created by the FEDERAL RESERVE SYSTEM when it expands bank reserves, funds which are then multiplied by bank loans. Federal law makes these notes LEGAL TENDER. Proposals for FREE BANKING would freeze the supply of notes (the monetary base), future notes issued by private banks. See also BANKNOTE, OPEN MARKET OPERATIONS.

Federal Reserve System. The CENTRAL BANK of the USA, referred to as the FED. It regulates the BANKS, controls the MONEY SUPPLY, and provides wholesale banking services to the private banks. In a pure FREE MARKET, the FED would either cease to exist, or else membership would be VOLUNTARY, and future money would be privately issued. See also FEDERAL RESERVE NOTES.

federalism. In economics, federalism can refer either to the division of FISCAL and regulatory (REGULATION) authority between a CENTRAL GOVERNMENT and subordinate administrative units, or it can refer to political federalism, in which the GOVERNANCE of a TERRITORY is split among areas having parallel governing sovereignty.

The USA, for example, has political federalism. The 50 states exert sovereign governing authority parallel to that of the federal government; neither is supreme or subordinate, but they have in some cases distinct roles under the US Constitution. The Indian nations, with governments and territories in reservation lands, are a third parallel series of governments, although their governing powers have been subject to federal authority.

fee. 1 Payment for services. See also DEED FEE, IMPACT FEE, USER FEE. 2 PROPERTY held without ARBITRARY RESTRICTIONS. See FEE SIMPLE.

fee simple. Absolute ownership of LAND and its RENT; ALLODIAL title.

feminist economics. A school of economic thought that asserts that main-stream economic THEORY is male-centered in its premises and applications. Economic development aid, for example, often ignores the PROPERTY RIGHTS and roles of women. HOME PRODUCTION is underrated and not included in GDP. It is not clear, however, how the FOUNDATIONS of economics would differ with a feminist approach. Feminist thought intersects with many other schools, from neoclassical (NEOCLASSICAL ECONOMICS) to POSTMODERN. See Grapard (1996).

feud. LAND held in exchange for service to a feudal lord.

feudalism. A land-tenure system in which one agent ultimately owns the LAND within some jurisdiction, all others having to pay RENT to occupy and use land. In the Middle Ages, rent was paid to a lord, the lord being granted the estate in exchange for military service. Some FREE-MARKET theorists assert that in modern times, the state is the feudal lord. The term 'feudal' often has a pejorative connotation when applied to modern times.

fiat money. Money not backed by or defined as a COMMODITY, hence having no intrinsic VALUE. It exists by *fiat*, the declaration by GOVERNMENT that it is LEGAL TENDER and the official national PURCHASING MEDIUM. As a government MONOPOLY (1) CURRENCY, fiat money can be inflated (INFLATION) without limit.

finance. The handling of FUNDS.

financial. Regarding FUNDS, ACCOUNTS, and INVESTMENTS.

financial assets. FUNDS. These are CLAIMS (1) on WEALTH rather than REAL (2) wealth. Such assets include MONEY, BONDS, shares of STOCK (2), and DERIVATIVES (2).

financial capital. Synonym for FINANCIAL ASSETS.

firm. An organization which transforms inputs into outputs. Internally, a firm reduces TRANSACTION costs, UNCERTAINTY, and OPPORTUNISM by maintaining a hierarchical order. Economic theory typically models the firm as a PROFIT-maximizer. OWNERSHIP types include single proprietor, PARTNERSHIPS, ASSOCIATIONS, and CORPORATIONS. GOVERNMENT agencies and NONPROFIT ORGANIZATIONS also function as firms.

First Amendment.   The first amendment to the US Constitution and first of the 10 Bill of Rights, protecting the free exercise of religion, speech, assembly, and to petition the government for redress of grievances. Speech, religion, and assembly are also ECONOMIC (1) acts and RIGHTS.

first order.   See GOODS OF FIRST ORDER.

fisc.   The treasury of a GOVERNMENT agency.

fiscal.   Regarding the GOVERNMENT treasury, that is, revenues, borrowings (BORROW), INVESTMENTS, and EXPENDITURE.

fiscal drag.   The increase in TAXES with INFLATION when a graduated INCOME TAX is not INDEXED to inflation. It drags economic activity by taxing it at a higher effective rate.

fiscal equivalence.   A situation in which GOVERNMENT services are fully paid for by the recipients of the BENEFITS and no one else, and the payments equal the perceived value of the benefits. Syn. BENEFIT PRINCIPLE.

fiscal federalism.   The division of PUBLIC FINANCES among levels of GOVERNMENT and the relationships among the levels, including transfers between levels. See also INTERGOVERNMENTAL GRANTS.

fiscal gap.   The difference between GOVERNMENT *EXPENDITURES and the smaller TAX revenue available due to political forces.

fiscal illusion.   A lower public perception of TAX *COSTS than is actually the case, because of the multiplicity of taxes, hidden taxes, and IGNORANCE. For politicians who gain from expenditures, fiscal illusion induces greater spending and an illusionary TAX STRUCTURE. Illusion can be minimized with a single, direct, visible tax, constitutionally mandated.

fiscal neutrality.   See NEUTRAL TAX.

fiscal policy.   TAXATION and GOVERNMENT spending, whether for government operations or to influence the ECONOMY. The use of fiscal policy for MACRO-

ECONOMIC effects includes i) geocratic (GEOCRACY) policy which seeks an EFFICIENT use of LAND and the avoidance of disincentives and speculative (SPECULATION) (3) land BOOMS, ii) SUPPLY-SIDE policies that stimulate growth by reducing INTERVENTION, iii) DEMAND-SIDE policies that seek to increase output with greater spending or lower TAXES, or to decrease INFLATION with the opposite. Demand-side policies only treat effects, thus leave the causes to continue, may create long-term instability and WASTE, and may not be effective if anticipated or if offset by CROWDING OUT.

fixed. Unchanging indefinitely, or for a certain period of time such as one year.

fixed capital. CAPITAL GOODS that remain for a long time, such as REAL ESTATE, large machines, and INFRASTRUCTURE. Contrast: CIRCULATING CAPITAL. Too much INVESTMENT (1) in fixed capital can leave a firm short of funds for circulating capital.

flat tax. A tax rate that is the same for all levels of value, income, or sales. The term is usually used in reference to a flat rate INCOME TAX, but such proposals often have several rates, including a zero rate for RENTAL and INTEREST income.

floating exchange rate. EXCHANGE RATES between domestic and foreign CURRENCIES that are set by SUPPLY and DEMAND. Managed or DIRTY FLOATS have INTERVENTIONS to affect the rates.

flow. The movement of a variable such as FUNDS during some time interval, in contrast to a STOCK.

flying geese formation. The observed pattern of EXPORTS from East Asia, in which Japan first produces and exports new goods, PRODUCTION then shifts to the FOUR TIGERS where COSTS are lower, and finally the exports shift to Malaysia, Thailand, Indonesia, and China.

flypaper effect. The effect of GOVERNMENT *GRANTS to lower-level governments to stick, that is, add to EXPENDITURES and not reduce the level of TAXATION.

follow. 1 To go behind a person in the same direction, keeping the other in sight. 2 To result from. 3 Adhere to. 4 Comprehend.

follower. 1 In the sense of FOLLOW (1), a member of the school of thought of a preceding mentor, who looks to the mentor for inspiration, a world view, and some basic theory. 2 In the sense of FOLLOW (3), one who is a follower (1) and also adheres closely to the thought of the mentor.

force.　Physically, a force equals mass times acceleration, which is a change in MOMENTUM, and so, economically, a force is any influence that changes the behavior of an agent, changing the SUPPLY or DEMAND for a good or the quantities supplied or demanded. Legal force is a government mandate, criminal force (as in 'force and fraud') is an invasion, and a market force is a change in VOLUNTARY action. Momentum can consist of a stationary variable or one moving at a constant velocity, hence a change in the former is any movement, while a change in the latter is an acceleration or change in direction.

forced riders.　When GOVERNMENT uses TAXATION to pay for COLLECTIVE GOODS, the taxpayers are forced riders. FREE RIDERS use the good without paying.

forced savings.　An unwanted reduction in CONSUMPTION because of unavailable GOODS or because an expansion of CREDIT (1) beyond the available SAVINGS has channeled more resources into CAPITAL GOODS.

foreign aid.　GIFTS by GOVERNMENTS to other governments. These include GRANTS, low interest loans, loan guarantees, and technical assistance. Much of such aid has been unproductive. Private aid such as the Soros Foundations and the CIVIC EDUCATION PROJECT, as well as funds sent by citizens to other countries, has also been important.

foreign trade.　Trade with agents who are not permanent residents of the country. Besides the IMPORT and EXPORT of goods and services, foreign trade includes tourism and other services exported within the country to foreign visitors.

forfeiture.　The loss of PROPERTY, such as after committing a CRIME or from CONFISCATION.

formal analysis.　The use of mathematics or some other non-verbal language (such as formal logic) as the only language in the construction and ANALYSIS of a MODEL. Verbal text may provide incidental explanations and illustrations, but the actual construct is the logical or mathematical expression. NEOCLASSICAL ECONOMICS is now centered on formalism, and this is criticized by many in the Austrian (AUSTRIAN ECONOMICS), GEO-ECONOMIC, institutional (INSTITUTIONAL ECONOMICS), and some other schools (for example, Boettke (1996)). See also RIGOR.

formal sector.   The sector of an ECONOMY which basically complies with TAXATION, law, and REGULATION, and is counted in the GDP. For some goods and services, restrictions and TAXES make formal production unprofitable, hence these are provided by the INFORMAL SECTOR. In economics, compliance with taxation, laws, and regulations.

foundation.   1 A set of AXIOMATIC *PROPOSITIONS, forming the base for THEORY derived therefrom. 2 A NONPROFIT ORGANIZATION that provides FUNDS for benevolent (BENEVOLENCE) purposes.

Foundation for Economic Education (FEE).   A nonprofit organization, based in New York state, dedicated to the preservation of individual FREEDOM and the private property order. Founded in 1946 by Leonard E. Read and given direction by its adviser, LUDWIG VON MISES, FEE publishes books and *The Freeman* journal, conducts seminars, and has launched the Freeman Society Discussion Clubs.

foundational.   Regarding or based on a FOUNDATION (1).

four tigers.   The rapidly growing East-Asian countries – Hong Kong, South Korea, Singapore, and Taiwan.

fractional reserve banking.   Maintaining a small fraction of BANK deposits (high-powered money) on RESERVE, while lending out the rest. The rationale is that the reserve satisfies normal requirements for cash and liquidity, and a bank can BORROW emergency funds if needed. Fractional reserves enable the banking system to multiply an increase in reserves into new MONEY, since loaned FUNDS are typically redeposited, thus made available for new loans. Some critics accuse fractional reserve banking as fraudulent, since only a fraction of deposits are on hand, but if the practice is known, then the customer has a choice of banking with fractional or full reserves. See also WAREHOUSE BANKING.

Francisco Marroquin.   A private university in Guatemala with a market-oriented economics program.

fraud.   Deliberately making a false description about a product to induce a sale. This is a type of THEFT, since a VOLUNTARY *EXCHANGE is based on a desire for a good based on its known TRUE qualities.

free.   In terms of individual freedom, free means not subject to ARBITRARY legal RESTRICTIONS or IMPOSED costs. A free PERSON is legally able to do anything that does not coercively HARM others. See also FREEDOM.

free banking. A BANKING system FREE from the CENTRAL BANK and other GOVERNMENT controls. With free banking, banks have unrestricted branching, they can issue PRIVATE (1) BANKNOTES, and there are no restrictions on INTEREST RATES or the extension of CREDIT (1). There is also no mandatory DEPOSIT INSURANCE. See Selgin (1988).

With free banking's competitive note issuing, banknotes are MONEY SUBSTI-TUTES convertible into BASE MONEY such as GOLD or a frozen base of government money. The money supply does not expand beyond what the public DEMANDS (1) to hold, since private banknotes can be redeemed for other notes or for the base money. Free banking was practiced in several countries, notably in Scotland (White, 1984).

free capital. CIRCULATING CAPITAL or loanable FUNDS.

free enterprise. ENTERPRISE which is legally FREE. Truly free enterprise is unrestricted and untaxed so long as it is honest and peaceful. The term 'free enterprise' is often applied to private enterprise, even when subject to INTER-VENTION.

free good. A GOOD whose quantity supplied is greater than the quantity demanded at a zero market price. It is not economically free just because an agent is giving it away, but because the market price set by supply and demand is zero, or would be if PROPERTY RIGHTS to it are assigned. A good with a positive price is SCARCE (1), and one with a negative price is a BAD.

free market. A market in which peaceful and honest enterprise and conduct are unrestricted and not arbitrarily (ARBITRARY) taxed (TAX), CONTRACTS are enforced, and PROPERTY RIGHTS specified and protected. The term 'free market' is often applied to mean PRIVATE ENTERPRISE, even when hampered by GOVERNMENT, but a pure free market has no intervention, hence no taxation of profits, wages, sales, produced goods, or value-added, and no restriction on VOLUNTARY action.

free-market economics. THEORIES of the MARKET PROCESS as it would function without INTERVENTION, or the theories of FREE-MARKET-oriented economists and schools of thought. The principle free-market schools are GEO-ECONOMICS, AUSTRIAN ECONOMICS, the CHICAGO SCHOOL, the UCLA school, and the VIRGINIA SCHOOL OF POLITICAL ECONOMY. Law and economics can also be applied to show the inefficiency of much government policy.

free-marketeer. One who views genuinely FREE MARKETS as the BEST ECO-NOMIC SYSTEM and, for some, also the morally proper system of PROPERTY ownership. They are adherents or advocates of genuine free markets. Within this group there is wide variation as to the best particular INSTITUTIONS and the role of GOVERNMENT.

free port. A port into which IMPORTS enter free of TARIFF. They can be taxed (TAX) if the goods are moved from the free port zone into the domestic ECONOMY.

free rider. An agent who uses a SCARCE (1) good without having to pay for it because the provider is not able to charge the user. For alleged free riding, see PUBLIC GOODS.

free trade. Trade free of any tariffs, quotas, and arbitrary regulatory (REGULATION) restrictions or 'non-tariff BARRIERS.' A free-trade policy might include barriers based on considerations of national defense. The policy of trade limitation is called PROTECTIONISM. The BENEFITS of free trade are based on COMPARATIVE ADVANTAGE. HENRY GEORGE stated that 'true free trade' includes the abolition of domestic barriers, including TAXES, as well as barriers to foreign trade.

free-trade area. A trading bloc of countries which eliminates TARIFFS among its members but retains country trade policies. An example is NAFTA. See also CUSTOMS UNION.

free will. The ABILITY of an organism to choose (CHOICE) its ACTION rather than have action compelled by programmed responses to stimuli that effectively leave it without true choice. Determinism seems to be the opposite, stating that actions are inevitably caused by stimuli and programming. Even if determinism is true, the fact that human beings do not know the determination of their acts, and that their own future acts seem uncertain (UNCERTAINTY), is sufficient for them to have free will in effect, that is the feeling that one is in control of one's acts. Human morality and therefore human RIGHTS and LIBERTY are based on such free will.

freedom. An absence of ARBITRARY restrictions. Legal freedom is the absence of legal restrictions on peaceful and honest action. Individual freedom and LIBERTY are synonyms for legal freedom. Physical freedom is an absence of physical restrictions such as prison walls.

The Freeman. A journal devoted to FREE-MARKET ideas, published by the Foundation for Economic Education.

freeze the base. The policy of a transition to FREE BANKING by not issuing any more national CURRENCY. The national currency becomes the MONETARY BASE, to which private BANKNOTES are redeemable.

friction. In physics, resistance to motion, hence in economics, cost-resistance to TRANSACTIONS in the form of opportunity costs beyond the price of the goods, such as travel and search time.

frictional unemployment. Workers not employed (EMPLOYMENT) because they have left one job and are searching for another one. Such unemployment is disregarded for FULL EMPLOYMENT.

Friedman, Milton (1912–). The most famous economist worldwide, he won the Nobel economics prize in 1976 and was influential in shaping the theories of the CHICAGO SCHOOL, having been appointed Professor of Economics there in 1948. His academic contributions include monetarist theory, MONEY AND BANKING theory and history, the methodology of positive economics, HUMAN CAPITAL, and the CONSUMPTION FUNCTION. His books and television shows on economic FREEDOM have had a large audience. Friedman also wrote a textbook, *Price Theory* (1962). Besides his major status as a monetarist (MONETARISM), Friedman originated the PERMANENT INCOME hypothesis, demonstrating the limitations if not ineffectiveness of Keynesian DEMAND-SIDE policy. He co-authored *A Monetary History of the United States 1867–1960* with Anna Schwartz, complementing his theoretical work on the quantity theory of money. Friedman has remained a leading advocate of economic freedom, having played a major role in the research on the ongoing book and project, *Economic Freedom of the World* (Gwartney *et al.*, 1996).

friendly society. A mutual INSURANCE association. These provided healthcare services prior to the socialization of medicine.

fringe benefits. WAGES aside from the NOMINAL money wage, usually paid in kind, such as with insurance and pensions. These benefits are generally tax-deductible to employers, but not taxable income to employees, hence the INCENTIVE is not to pay money wages but to pay them in kind. In a pure FREE MARKET, without any income tax, the tendency would likely be to pay the entire wage in money and then have the employee choose his mix of insurance and savings plans, which would provide portability, CHOICE, and accountability.

fringe doctrine. DOCTRINES beyond the fringes of academic respectability, such as in the newsletters of ideological (IDEOLOGY) interests.

'From each... .'   See ABILITY.

full employment.   An ECONOMY in which the only UNEMPLOYMENT is frictional (FRICTIONAL UNEMPLOYMENT).

full faith and credit.   The pledge by GOVERNMENT to pay the DEPOSIT INSURANCE liabilities even if the insurance fund runs out.

full-spectrum economics.   Economic theory and teaching that encompasses and integrates warranted (WARRANT) theory from all schools of thought, rather than only using the approach and theory of one or two schools.

functional distribution.   DISTRIBUTION (1).

fund turnover.   The amount of buying and selling of securities in a MUTUAL FUND per year. A high turnover generates more fees and CAPITAL GAINS taxes.

funds.   See FINANCIAL ASSETS.

futures contract.   A contract to buy or sell a certain quantity of a COMMODITY by a certain date, typically purchased with a deposit of a small fraction of the value of the contract. The contracts are used for HEDGING and for SPECULATION (3), and there is a buy contract for each sell contract.

G

Gaffney effect. The effect of the public collection of RENT on equalizing the DISCOUNT RATE (1) for LAND usage. People have differing CREDIT (1) costs and availability when buying land. If the LAND RENT is publicly collected, purchasers pay rent in lieu of a mortgage and hence in effect obtain land with universally available credit and a common rate of discount. Coined by NICOLAUS TIDEMAN, based on the work of MASON GAFFNEY.

Gaffney, Mason (1923–). Professor of Economics at the University of California, Riverside. He founded the Institute for Economic Policy Analysis in Victoria, Canada, the Committee on Taxation, Resources and Economic Development (TRED), and was a co-founder of the Geo-economics Society, and has been a consultant on natural resources and LAND RENT. Gaffney's work on BUSINESS CYCLES has integrated Austrian capital theory (AUSTRIAN THEORY OF BUSINESS CYCLES) with GEO-ECONOMIC land theory.

Gaffney's book *The Corruption of Economics* (1994) (with Fred Harrison) reveals how neoclassical (NEOCLASSICAL ECONOMICS) theory has been altered to obscure the role of land rent. His other books include *Land as an Element of Housing Costs* (1968), and *Containment Policies for Urban Sprawl* (1964). Among his many significant papers are 'Adequacy of Land as a Tax Base' in *The Assessment of Land Value* (1970), 'Toward Full Employment with Limited Land and Capital' in *Property Taxation, Land Use, and Public Policy* (1976), 'The Role of Ground Rent in Urban Decay and Revival,' St. Johns University (1989), and 'Land as a Distinctive Factor of Production' in *Land and Taxation* (1994). Gaffney also wrote an unpublished translation of *Studies in Social Economics* by LÉON WALRAS (1896).

gains from trade. The increase in MARGINAL UTILITY for each party in a VOLUNTARY *EXCHANGE. The goods of the other party have more marginal utility (are preferred) to the goods of similar market value that one has. Trading in a particular good will thus take place until the gains are exhausted, that is, the marginal utility of the good relative to its price will be no more than that of other goods. See also EQUILIBRATION.

Galt's Gulch. The place in AYN RAND'S *ATLAS SHRUGGED* where the people of ideas have retreated to while 'on strike' from society. They create their own VOLUNTARY *COMMUNITY, where all is obtained by voluntary exchange, neither sacrificing nor requiring sacrifice. This term has remained as a metaphor for such communities.

game.   Interaction among persons, following specific rules, with specific payoffs for winners and possible penalties for losers. A game can be non-cooperative, with rivalry among the players, or cooperative, in which there is a positive-sum outcome. In a zero-sum game, what one player gains, the other loses. A famous game much used in PUBLIC-CHOICE theory is the PRISONER'S DILEMMA.

game theory.   A theory of decision making with incomplete information, using GAMES, usually with a mathematical METHODOLOGY.

GATT.   GENERAL AGREEMENT ON TARIFFS AND TRADE.

GDP.   GROSS DOMESTIC PRODUCT.

GDP deflator.   A PRICE INDEX used to deflate inflated measures of GDP, to compare REAL (3) GDP among years.

gender.   Grammatically and now with regard also to human beings, sexual identity as either male or female.

General Agreement on Tariffs and Trade.   An international trade agreement adopted in 1947, now called the World Trade Organization (WTO). Through various agreements or 'rounds,' the organization has lowered trade barriers, stimulating international trade and the global ECONOMY. While providing a forum for the settlement of trade disputes, the WTO also poses the possibility of global REGULATIONS that would hamper MARKETS and favor SPECIAL INTERESTS.

general equilibrium.   'General' here means ECONOMY-wide, and the term means the existence of EQUILIBRIUM in the entire economy, the simultaneous determination of all prices and quantities for all GOODS at some moment in time. The economist who formulated this mathematically is LÉON WALRAS, while DEBREU and ARROW confirmed its mathematical existence.

The concept of all markets being interrelated is broader than the general equilibrium mathematical model. General disequilibrium and general economic process theory could be developed for a theory that is theoretically general as well as economy-general.

generalized system of preferences. Policy by which a country permits certain goods to be imported (IMPORT) from developing countries without TARIFFS or with preferential treatment.

geo. A prefix used by GEORGISTS or geoists (GEOISM) for their philosophy and economic theory of self-ownership for LABOR and COMMON ownership for natural land rent (NATURAL RENT). The POSSESSION of land is individualist, conditional on the payment of rent to a relevant COMMUNITY (see COMMUNITY COLLECTION OF RENT). 'Geo' means earth or land, and is also the beginning of 'George.' While 'Georgist' remains the common label for the paradigm, geo is preferred by many adherents to avoid a too tight connection to the thought of HENRY GEORGE. Geoist thought preceded George, was developed further after George, and not all of George's writings are accepted by most of his FOLLOWERS (2).

geo-anarchism. ANARCHISM that proposes a COMMON ownership of natural land rent (NATURAL RENT) but individualist POSSESSION of LAND, and individualist OWNERSHIP of LABOR and GOODS. CIVIC GOODS are provided by VOLUNTARY *ASSOCIATIONS funded by the RENT in the COMMUNITY. Some of the rent is passed on to higher-level associations that lower-level associations voluntarily belong to.

geo-Austrian synthesis. A merging of complementary Austrian (AUSTRIAN ECONOMICS) and GEO-ECONOMIC theory, particularly Austrian CAPITAL THEORY and geo-economic LAND theory. The geo-Austrian BUSINESS CYCLE combines the Austrian INTEREST-RATE and CAPITAL-GOODS elements with the REAL-ESTATE CYCLE. Much of the Austrian-theory malinvested (MALINVESTMENTS) capital goods consist of real-estate construction, creating too much FIXED CAPITAL, leading to a deficiency of CIRCULATING CAPITAL. Geo-economics adds LAND SPECULATION, which adds to the cost of present INVESTMENT, land being priced for future uses, many of which do not become realized. Rising interest rates and land costs reduce investments, leading to the downturn. When real-estate prices collapse, borrowers default, contributing to BANK failures (FAIL). The remedy proposed by the synthesis is FREE BANKING plus the COMMUNITY COLLECTION OF RENT.

geo-economics. A school of economic thought based on the CLASSICAL three FACTORS OF PRODUCTION and the GEOIST ETHIC of SELF-OWNERSHIP of LABOR and COMMON ownership of LAND RENT. The school was founded by HENRY GEORGE and follows much of his thinking, though it has also adopted Austrian (AUSTRIAN ECONOMICS) and neoclassical (NEOCLASSICAL ECONOMICS) concepts. Academic members of the school founded the Geo-Economics Society in 1994. The school has traditionally been known as the Georgist school, but now prefers a more generic label to focus on the social philosophy and theory rather than the historical person. Geo-economic policy consists of FREE TRADE, the abolition of ARBITRARY restrictions and regulations, and the abolition of all TAXATION falling on LABOR, CAPITAL GOODS, INTEREST, and entrepreneurship (ENTREPRENEUR). Geo-economic public finance is based on collecting the rents from land, with all NATURAL RESOURCES included, and rents generated by PUBLIC GOODS remaining with the agency generating them. Geo-economic thought regards this system as the ultimate in SUPPLY-SIDE economics, maximizing EFFICIENCY, stability, and EQUITY. See also COMMUNITY COLLECTION OF RENT. Feder (1996) presents a summary of geo-economic thought.

geo-libertarian.   A libertarian (LIBERTARIANISM) who holds that LAND RENT is the appropriate funding source for GOVERNMENT and COMMUNITY expenditures, or more strongly, adheres to the GEOIST ETHIC. The alternative is ALLODIAL libertarianism. The term was coined by Fred Foldvary in 1983 in an article by that title in *Land and Liberty* magazine, and has been adopted by geoist (GEOISM) libertarians.

geoclassical.   The GEORGIST variant of CLASSICAL ECONOMICS. To the classical theory of LAND and RENT, geoclassical economics adds a theory of the BUSINESS CYCLE, a theory of the effect of LAND SPECULATION on production, the LAW OF WAGES, and an analysis of the taxation of LAND RENT that goes beyond RICARDIAN theory.

geocracy.   The implementation of GEOISM. A GOVERNMENT or ASSOCIATION that practices geoism.

geoism.   The social philosophy and economic THEORY based on SELF-OWNERSHIP of PERSONS and COMMON ownership of LAND RENT. The label is used by followers of HENRY GEORGE, referring both to George and to LAND or the earth. See also GEO-ECONOMICS, GEOIST ETHIC.

geoist ethic.   The view that human beings properly own themselves, and thus own their LABOR and the products of labor, and that SELF-OWNERSHIP does not extend to LAND RENT, hence that land rent is properly COMMON property. The common ownership of the rent can be manifested in its collection by GOVERNMENTS and COMMUNITIES for public expenditures, or to distribute as an equal per-capita CITIZEN DIVIDEND. The ethic originated in the writings of HENRY GEORGE. See also GEOISM.

geonomics.   An alternative name for GEO-ECONOMICS used by some geoists (GEOISM), coined by Jeff Smith.

George, Henry (1839–97).   American economist known for his defense of
FREE TRADE and his proposal to ABOLISH all TAXATION except on LAND RENT. His
books include *PROGRESS AND POVERTY* (1879), *Social Problems* (1883), *Protection or Free Trade* (1886), and *The Science of Political Economy* (1897,
posthumous). His contributions to economic theory include the LAW OF WAGES;
the LAW OF RENT (extending RICARDIAN *DIFFERENTIAL RENT to the CAPITALIZA-
TION (1) of commerce and public works); the effects of LAND SPECULATION; a
theory of the BUSINESS CYCLE based on the REAL-ESTATE cycle; and the effects of
a shift of TAXATION from taxing production to taxing NATURAL RESOURCES. His
proposal to tax only land rent became known as the 'SINGLE TAX.' The school
based on his thought is now called 'GEO-ECONOMIC.' Several organizations
carry on his work in teaching, research, and publications, including the ROBERT
SCHALKENBACH FOUNDATION, the HENRY GEORGE SCHOOL of Social Science, the
Henry George Foundation, Common Ground, the International Union for
Land-Value Taxation and Free Trade, and the Geo-economics Society.

George Mason University.   The base of several market-oriented organiza-
tions, including the Center for Study of Public Choice, Center for Market
Processes, Institute of Humane Studies, the Locke Institute, and the Atlas
Foundation. The Department of Economics has offered courses in AUSTRIAN
ECONOMICS.

Georgist.   Referring to the thought and writings of HENRY GEORGE, or to his
FOLLOWERS and adherents, who also call themselves geoists (GEOIST ETHIC).

gift.   GOODS transferred to another, with nothing directly expected in return.
An inheritance is thus a category of gifts. Normally, the motive is benevolent
(BENEVOLENCE), although often FIRMS provide gifts for publicity. In many
CULTURES, goods are given with the understanding that there will be reciproc-
ity, or for prestige or from obligation, so that they are not pure gifts but part
of a tacit exchange system. A prime example is the potlatch custom among
the American Indians of the Pacific Northwest. See also GRANT.
   A gift has a zero price to the recipient, but it is a different concept from a
FREE GOOD, which has a zero cost of PRODUCTION. A gift, say to CHILDREN, is
also apart from the goods that are normally provided out of parental obligation or custom. Gifts are VOLUNTARY, hence government grants are not gifts
but forced TRANSFER PAYMENTS from taxpayers to the recipients.

gift tax.   A TAX on GIFTS, paid by the donor, normally for gifts above a
certain tax-free amount. If there is a DEATH TAX, it is consistent to also have a
gift tax so that transfers during the life of the donor do not entirely escape
taxation. However, both gift and death taxes violate PROPERTY RIGHTS, espe-

cially when the owner paid taxes when the PROPERTY was obtained. If the property was properly earned by the giver, then it is earned property after transfer, because the transfer does not alter the nature of the origin of the property.

Gini coefficient.   A method of measuring the INEQUALITY of a DISTRIBUTION (3), it is the ratio of the area between the LORENZ CURVE and the diagonal equality line, and the area of the triangle under the diagonal. It can also be calculated with a formula. The values range from one for complete inequality to zero for complete equality. The coefficient was formulated by the Italian statistician Corrado Gini in 1912.

Since one criterion for evaluating ECONOMIES is the inequality of income and wealth, it is important to have a sound method of measuring it. One problem with the Gini measurement (G) is that, given some CONCENTRATION, as the number of units in the distribution increases, G does not decrease proportionally. Likewise, for a given number of elements, as the concentration increases, G does not decrease in the same proportion. G places more weight to transfers in the middle of a distribution than in the tails. These deficiencies are overcome with the inverse–reverse function $1/(1-G)$. This index is consistent with the Tideman–Hall concentration index (Hall and Tideman, 1967).

The EQUATION OF INEQUALITY, $I = CN$, where C is a measurement of concentration and N the number of items, has inequality proportional to both concentration and numbers. The Tideman–Hall–Foldvary index of inequality is thus the product of N and the Tideman–Hall concentration index (Foldvary, 1995).

giro system.   Payments made by transferring FUNDS directly from one account to another, reducing the amount in one account and increasing the amount in the other. This avoids cash and checks. This system has long been used in Europe, and is used in systems such as LETS, where when X sells goods to Y, X receives a balance increase and Y a decrease, minus any transfer fee.

global.   Encompassing the whole earth, particularly economic activity that spans many ECONOMIES and countries. Global investment funds, for example, invest worldwide.

global economy.   Enterprise, finance, and institutions that are worldwide. Multinational corporations operate in many countries, trade relationships span many economies, and there are international institutions such as GATT/ WTO (WORLD TRADE ORGANIZATION) that affect trade in many countries.

Reduced trade barriers since World War II, the vast increase in communications and the internet, and stock and commodity markets with global access and listings have transformed much enterprise into an ECONOMY that is GLOBAL as well as national and local. The mobility of FINANCIAL CAPITAL has gone so far as to limit the effectiveness of MONETARY and FISCAL policy that formerly could be confined to the national economy. High taxes and unstable MONEY can still be implemented, but the result will be CAPITAL FLIGHT and low INVEST-MENT (1) and growth. The global economy thus has had a liberalizing (LIBER-ALIZATION) effect as formerly restrictive countries in Eastern Europe, South Asia, and Latin America have pursued DEREGULATION, reduced BARRIERS to trade, and lowered MARGINAL tax rates. See Gwartney *et al*. (1996).

glut. See SURPLUS.

gold. A heavy, yellow, stable metal that has been in wide use for ornaments as well as MONEY in the form of COINS. By the latter 19th century, most of the world used gold as money. World War I, the GREAT DEPRESSION, and the ascending IDEOLOGY of central controls led to the replacement of gold with FIAT MONEY issued by CENTRAL BANKS. There are companies now that have gold accounts against which one may make payments. Gold is used as a hedge (HEDGING) against INFLATION, as over the very long run, it has maintained its purchasing value.

gold standard. MONEY that is GOLD, with a UNIT OF ACCOUNT measured as an amount or weight of gold. PURCHASING MEDIA then consist of both gold and money substitutes, that is, BANKNOTES convertible into gold. Private money substitutes (competitive banknotes) make the amount of purchasing media flexible. When the world is on a gold standard, there is in effect an international CURRENCY, with each national currency or unit of account having a fixed relation to gold and thus to one another. Trade surpluses and deficits are balanced via the PRICE-SPECIE MECHANISM. Many FREE-MARKET economists and adherents favor a restoration of the gold standard instead of the inflation-prone FIAT MONEY systems of today. Combined with FREE BANKING, a gold standard would eliminate monetary policy. The gold standard of the USA from the Civil War to the establishment of the Federal Reserve (FEDERAL RESERVE SYSTEM) was not a free-market currency, but a national currency convertible into gold as well as using SILVER for coins. The gold exchange standard exists where countries peg their currencies to a country that is on the gold standard, but again the use of monopoly national currencies is not a pure free market.

good. *Ec.* An item that impacts a PERSON. Narrowly, tangible items of positive value that are taken from nature or produced and then exchanged (EX-

CHANGE) and consumed (CONSUME). More broadly, the items include BADS and FREE GOODS. Even more broadly, SERVICES are included as goods simultaneously produced and consumed. Thus, all items involved in the production and consumption process are goods. See also PRIVATE GOOD, COLLECTIVE GOODS.

good, morally.   *Eth.* Agreeable and/or beneficial.

goods of first order.   CONSUMER GOODS, designated as 'first order' by CARL MENGER.

goods of higher order.   CAPITAL GOODS. Goods of higher order are more roundabout (ROUNDABOUTNESS), in that they are used to produce lower-order goods, with a longer period of payoff than goods of lower order.

goodwill.   The market value of a company minus its BOOK VALUE. Reputation, customer base, and favorable EXPECTATIONS are key elements of goodwill. See also CONSUMER GOODWILL.

governance.   The adoption and enforcement of RULES regarding PROPERTY and conduct. GOVERNMENT generally refers to imposed governance, while ASSOCIATIONS generally refer to voluntary rules' agreements. Human society always has governance, hence the actual dichotomy is not market versus government but VOLUNTARY versus IMPOSED governance (Foldvary, 1997a).

government.   An AGENCY (1, 2) that enacts and enforces RULES within some DOMAIN. Generally, the term refers to IMPOSED *GOVERNANCE. Governments also typically operate ENTERPRISES and provide SERVICES (not necessarily welcomed by all). The rules imposed by government can be market-enhancing or market-hampering, that is, INTERVENTIONS. Economic theory distinguishes between the private sector and the government sector, the latter usually called the 'public' sector. CLASSICAL LIBERALS and FREE-MARKET adherents hold that government is best confined to the role of protection and the provision of a few basic collective goods, while libertarians go further and require PUBLIC FINANCE to be voluntary, and anarchists (ANARCHISM) would have no imposed government.

government failure.   GOVERNMENT *FAILS when the PUBLIC (1) would have preferred to spend the funds privately rather than the way the government did. Examples of failure include EXPENDITURES that benefit SPECIAL INTERESTS, wasteful (WASTE) expenditures, excessive expenditures, and violations of LIBERTY contrary to constitutional guarantees. See also CONSTITUTIONAL FAILURE.

government intervention. See INTERVENTION.

government sector. The part of the ECONOMY consisting of government programs, including the goods, bads, and services it provides. This sector is usually labeled the 'public sector.' The other sector is the private sector, notwithstanding its being regulated and taxed by the government.

Gracchi. Roman statesmen and reformers, after Gaius Sempronius Gracchus (153?–121 BC) and Tiberius Sempronius Gracchus (163?–133 BC), who carried out the 'Gracchic revolution.' The Gracchi passed a law restricting the right of Roman citizens to 500 yokes of the Roman common, but made a concession to landowners, conferring upon them the entire ownership of land which they had held in fee from the state. The restrictions were later repealed, but landowners kept their land rights (Oppenheimer, 1917, 1997). These rights became extended throughout Western Europe, and then, through colonization and influence, throughout the world, thus creating the contemporary LAND TENURE system.

graduated. With increasing TAX rates as INCOME increases.

grant. A transfer of assets, usually FUNDS, usually to those meeting certain requirements, but with no quid pro quo exchange. Grants are typically given from a higher to a lower-level government or from governments and foundations to institutions and individuals who do research. Many university departments place great emphasis on obtaining grants. While many local governments seek and are glad to obtain grants, from a global perspective grants are usually DYSFUNCTIONAL in skewing (SKEW) INCENTIVES and wasting (WASTE) resources in BUREAUCRACY and compliance with requirements. A PUBLIC FINANCE system that sent funds from lower to higher-level governments would most likely eliminate grants from higher to lower-level governments.

Great Depression. Critics of MARKETS point to the DEPRESSION of 1929–41 as a prime example of MARKET FAILURE, while free-market economic thought demonstrates the INTERVENTIONS which caused it. ROTHBARD (1975) deals with the expansion of the MONEY SUPPLY in the 1920s, while Hoyt (1933) depicts the role of the real-estate boom and subsequent crash, synthesized with the Austrian (AUSTRIAN ECONOMIC) theory by Foldvary (1997b). Interventions such as high tariffs and the failure of the FEDERAL RESERVE SYSTEM to counter the DEFLATION, as well as controls on INDUSTRY (2), helped make the depression more severe. See also GEO-AUSTRIAN SYNTHESIS.

greed.   Wanting and obtaining more than one morally deserves. Thieves are greedy, and those who use government power to forcibly transfer resources from others or to prevent others from freely using their property are greedy. Greed is thus a root cause of social problems, along with the complementary APATHY, that prevents action against greed, and IGNORANCE, which helps maintain apathy.

Greed is sometimes used as a synonym for AVARICE. It is useful to draw a clear moral distinction between them, since accusations of 'corporate greed' can confuse COERCIVE *TAKINGS with the mere desire for WEALTH, which as a motivator can have social BENEFIT.

green revolution.   The vast increase in agricultural output due to the development of superior seeds and other technology. To maintain a high productivity, large amounts of fertilizer and water are often needed.

green taxes.   Environmental (ENVIRONMENT) USER FEES, and taxes related to the abatement (ABATE) (1) of POLLUTION and other environmental damage. If they compensate for damage, then they are taxes in form but fees and penalties in substance.

Gresham's law.   The principle that bad MONEY drives out good money when the bad money is LEGAL TENDER. It does not apply when the bad money lacks the force of law. The law, named after Sir Thomas Gresham (1519–79), predicts that when two currencies circulate, and one has a lower intrinsic value (such as debased precious metals) than its legal value, then people will hoard the one with more intrinsic value and spend the one with lower intrinsic value.

Gross Domestic Product.   The total value of GOODS and SERVICES produced during a year by the residents in an ECONOMY. As measured, it omits HOME PRODUCTION and also omits the depletion of NATURAL RESOURCES as well as environmental DEGRADATION.

gross income.   INCOME before paying TAXES.

gross national product.   The total amount of OUTPUT by a country's citizens (rather than residents) during a year.

Grossgrundeigentum.   'Large LAND ownership': the personal ownership of unlimited land holdings.

growth.   See ECONOMIC GROWTH.

Gung Yü (124–44 BC).   Chinese official who suggested a SINGLE TAX on LAND, the first historical figure to do so. This idea was rejected by the emperor. Gung's single-tax idea become known to TURGOT (Chandler, 1983: 1075).

H

Haberler, Gottfried (1900–). Austrian-born and Austrian-school American economist (AUSTRIAN ECONOMICS) who in the *Theory of International Trade* (1936) presented the theory of GAINS FROM TRADE based on the OPPORTUNITY COSTS of producing goods. Besides his work on international economics, he wrote *Prosperity and Depression* (1935).

Haig–Simmons income. See INCOME.

happiness. A feeling of WELL-BEING, ranging from transient pleasure to long-term satisfaction.

hard assets. Tangible assets such as GOLD, gems, and REAL ESTATE, which hold their value during an INFLATION.

hard-core unemployment. See CHRONIC UNEMPLOYMENT.

hard currency. CURRENCY which is convertible and readily accepted worldwide in exchange for currencies or goods.

harm. Morally (MORAL (1)), an injury not solely dependent on the views of the party suffering a loss, but the result of an INVASION into the domain of the injured party.

Hayek, Friedrich A. von (1899–1992). A leading Austrian school economist (AUSTRIAN ECONOMICS), known for his work on the TRADE CYCLE, on the role of decentralized KNOWLEDGE, his arguments against SOCIALISM, and also for his work on political theory and law. Born in Vienna, Hayek was a professor at the London School of Economics and the University of Chicago as well as in Freiburg and Salzburg. He won the Nobel prize in economics in 1974 along with G. Myrdal. The Austrian program at GEORGE MASON UNIVERSITY is strongly influenced by Hayekian thought, emphasizing the role of knowledge and RULES, although all Austrians regard Hayek as one of the two giants of Austrian economics, along with LUDWIG VON MISES.

Hayek's *Prices and Production* (1931) showed how the rate of INTEREST changes the structure of CAPITAL GOODS and thus how MONETARY expansion can instigate a trade cycle. Hayek's work on knowledge focused on how tacit, decentralized knowledge is unavailable to a central authority, hence CENTRAL PLANNING *FAILS on that account, aside from the problems of INCENTIVES. His best known book is *The Road to Serfdom* (1944), warning that INTERVENTION can lead to totalitarian socialism (TOTALITARIANISM). His works on political theory include *The Constitution of Liberty* (1960) and *Law Legislation and Liberty* (1973, three volumes).

Hayekian triangle.   A model of the CAPITAL STRUCTURE (1), with goods of lowest to highest order on one axis (see GOODS OF HIGHER ORDER) and the amount of capital goods on the other. A higher rate of INTEREST flattens the triangle, making PRODUCTION less roundabout (ROUNDABOUTNESS), while a lower rate does the opposite.

Hazlitt, Henry (1894–1993).   FREE-MARKET economist, author of many books including Hazlitt (1959). Among his titles are *Economics in One Lesson* (1946), a classic in free-market texts. He wrote several works on inflation. See also HENRY HAZLITT FOUNDATION.

head tax.   Also called a poll tax, it is a lump-sum DIRECT TAX on a PERSON, rather than based on his PROPERTY or ACTIVITY. It is usually the same tax per capita in a jurisdiction. As VOLUNTARY dues, clubs are typically funded by equal per-capita payments, but when imposed by GOVERNMENT, head taxes are considered regressive (REGRESSIVE TAX) and unjust, because the BENEFITS from expenditures are not equal per capita. The head tax was imposed by colonial governments in Africa to force the inhabitants to work for money wages. It was also used in the US southern states for voting, which prevented poor Blacks from voting. The British introduced a head tax in the 1980s, which was unpopular and repealed.

hedging.   The purchase of a FINANCIAL ASSET that offsets another financial or REAL (2) asset or some rate of change, such as a farmer hedging his crop by selling the same amount of produce in a FUTURES CONTRACT. Thus when the asset changes in price, the hedger is in a neutral position. A hedge against INFLATION consists of the purchase of HARD ASSETS or other assets that rise in value at least at the same rate as inflation, or do not depend on the PRICE LEVEL of the currency; this hedge is in effect a futures instrument to buy the currency at a future rate of exchange with the hard asset rather than the current one.

hedonic price.   A PRICE set on a COMMODITY or AMENITY that has no MARKET PRICE, based on its CHARACTERISTICS and factors affecting its DEMAND. This is used in environmental (ENVIRONMENT) economics.

heir. One who inherits property; strictly, one who inherits when there is no will. See also BENEFICIARY.

Henry George Schools. A family of private schools of social science which teach GEORGIST economics. The main school is in New York City, with branches in major cities in the USA and in some other countries. The schools also conduct research on LAND and RENT, host conferences, and network with other organizations.

Henry Hazlitt Foundation. A foundation based in Chicago and started in 1997 that is helping FREE-MARKET advocates communicate online.

hereditary lease holder. The holder of a lease of property, particularly land, who has perpetual RIGHTS of possession so long as the lease payment is made, and who may bequeath the lease to his heirs. Such tenure is as secure and thus has the same economic effects as outright ownership.

Herfindahl index. (Herfindahl–Hirschman index). An index of CONCENTRATION developed by Herfindahl. Given a DISTRIBUTION (3) with n elements, the share of the total of each element (fraction from zero to one) is squared, and the index H totals the sum of the squares. The values of H range from 1 for MONOPOSSESSION to $1/n$ for equal shares. The index thus takes into account both the number of elements and their relative sizes. The EQUATION OF INEQUALITY $I = CN$ can be rewritten as $C = I/N$, or concentration equals the INEQUALITY of the elements divided by the number of elements. The Herfindahl index can thus be used also for a measurement of inequality, using H for C. An alternative both for concentration and inequality is the Tideman–Hall index (Hall and Tideman, 1967). In addition, since DIVERSIFICATION is the inverse of concentration, 1/H offers a measurement of diversification. See also CONCENTRATION.

heterogeneous capital goods. While capital goods are treated as a homogeneous asset in much of neoclassical theory (NEOCLASSICAL ECONOMICS), Austrian (AUSTRIAN THEORY OF BUSINESS CYCLES) theory emphasizes the heterogeneity of capital goods in a structure of GOODS OF HIGHER ORDER and lower order. Neoclassical economics, however, recognizes also specialized capital goods that cannot be used to make different goods or moved to another location; this ASSET SPECIFICITY leads to such assets being owned within the firm that requires them, or else to complex long-term CONTRACTS.

high-powered money. Circulating CURRENCY and bank RESERVES in excess of required minimums, which can therefore be lent, increasing the MONEY SUPPLY by a multiple of these reserves.

higher order. See GOODS OF HIGHER ORDER.

historic cost. A 'historic cost' is the PRICE paid for an ASSET; this rather than the current market VALUE is usually reported on a balance sheet.

Historical School. A school of economic thought centered in 19th-century Germany which studied ECONOMIC HISTORY and rejected the AXIOMATIC-DEDUCTIVE approach of CLASSICAL and AUSTRIAN ECONOMICS. Their methodology, HISTORICISM, as developed especially by Gustav Schmoller, the leader of the school, sought to derive theory from economic history, emphasizing the ever-changing nature of empirical phenomena. This methodology was criticized by Carl MENGER in a famous debate over METHODOLOGY. The German economists greatly influenced US economists during the late 1800s and early 1900s, especially institutionalists (INSTITUTIONAL ECONOMICS) who studied in Germany.

historicism. An economic METHODOLOGY rejecting the deduction of general economic THEORY from a FOUNDATION (1) of premises, instead attempting to derive explanations from detailed historical studies, emphasizing the changing nature of economic life.

history of economic thought. The reporting and analysis of past writing on economic THEORY, a field of ECONOMICS. A study of past thought helps explain present-day theory and may at times provide theoretical insights that have been forgotten and overlooked. Austrian school economists (AUSTRIAN ECONOMICS) have been much interested in the history of Austrian economic thought as well as similar schools and precursors such as Cantillon, TURGOT, and the early Spanish economists. The Virginian school looks to WICKSELL and the Italian public-finance economists, and geo-economists (GEO-ECONOMICS) invoke HENRY GEORGE and physiocratic (PHYSIOCRACY) thought. CLASSICAL-LIBERAL economists still take inspiration from ADAM SMITH and JOHN LOCKE.

home production. GOODS and SERVICES produced in residences, for example, repairing, cleaning, cooking, child care, and gardening. This PRODUCTION is not exchanged (EXCHANGE) with others outside the household, and does not become part of the official GDP. As women work more outside the home and then increase paid-for child care, the GDP shows the child care as an increase, even though in reality it is a replacement for at-home child care. Thus, GDP is distorted. The measurement of the value of at-home production is quite fuzzy, but perhaps a supplement GDP, a more complete domestic product, could be useful.

home rule. A high degree of authority by a MUNICIPALITY for its internal policies, set forth in its charter. See also DILLON'S RULE.

home schooling. Educating (EDUCATION) a child (CHILDREN) at home rather than in a private or government school.

homesteading. Taking TITLE to virgin or vacated goods or TERRITORY by 'mixing one's LABOR with the LAND.' NATURAL-LAW and NATURAL-RIGHTS theory includes the homesteading principle. While titles to products such as fruit and fish are clearly obtainable by homesteading, the question of title to the land itself is more complex and problematical, that is, the Lockean PROVISO may apply. If one goes to the ocean and catches fish, one clearly has proper title to the fish, but has one also obtained title to the sea?

Land titles can be ALLODIAL (ABSOLUTE), or conditional, for example of payment of rents or taxes to an authority as well as being subject to land-use law and EMINENT DOMAIN. The homesteading of land can confer rights only to POSSESSION, as with GEOISM, or also to the RENTS, as with allodialism. In allodialist (ALLODIAL) libertarian (LIBERTARIANISM) theory, the morally proper creation of land titles is either allodial homesteading or the transfer of allodial rights to the current title holders. However, taking legal title implies a legal authority to grant title, hence having jurisdiction over the territory, and thus being the primary landowner. The question then remains as to whether such authority is proper, and if the state has jurisdiction and thus ownership prior to the homesteader, why allodial homesteading is morally proper; that is why the Lockean proviso should not apply.

homo cupiditus. *Lat.* A narrowly self-seeking, self-centered, but not MORALLY CRIMINAL person, the behavioral premise of most NEOCLASSICAL ECONOMIC theory, an assumption for the sake of theory conditional to it, not a proposition about how human beings always ACT. See also BENEVOLENCE.

homo economicus. *Lat.* Economic man, sometimes referring to ECONOMIZING MAN who maximizes utility (UTILITY, MARGINAL), and other times to *HOMO CUPIDITUS*, who is confined to narrow SELF-INTEREST.

homo sympaticus. *Lat.* Sympathetic (SYMPATHY) man, who is COMMUNITY-conscious and who sympathizes with others, as a counter to self-seeking *HOMO ECONOMICUS*.

horizontal equity. Equal treatment of individuals in similar circumstances. While as such it is compatible with classical liberalism (CLASSICAL LIBERAL), when applied to TAXATION, the proposal that equal incomes pay equal taxes overlooks the fact that different sources of income make the circumstances unequal. A thief's income, for example, should not be treated the same as that of an honest worker. Different sources can have different ethical (ETHIC) values. Proper horizontal equity applies the same standard to the same source of income, hence the marriage penalty, higher taxes for married than single people on the same income, is unjust.

Hospers, John (1918–). Libertarian (LIBERTARIANISM) philosopher emeritus at the University of Southern California and editor of *The Personalist* journal. His book *Libertarianism* (1971) laid out its basic principles and applications. Other books of his include *Human Conduct* (1961) and *Meaning and Truth in the Arts* (1967). He was the presidential candidate of the Libertarian Party in 1972, and the Party also adopted his Statement of Principles that year.

human action.   Purposeful and willful ACTIVITIES performed by persons, consisting of means to achieve ends. ACTION (1) involves gain and cost. The actor imagines options that remove UNEASINESS or improve his condition, and chooses that option that in his judgment has the greatest expected net gain. Human action is the basis of the theory of PRAXEOLOGY by LUDWIG VON MISES.

Human Action.   The title of a large treatise on economics by LUDWIG VON MISES (1949), which lays out the method and content of PRAXEOLOGY. It is a landmark, definitive text of AUSTRIAN ECONOMICS, much referred to by Austrian school economists. Originally published in 1949, revised editions were published in 1963 and 1966.

human capital.   Neither a FINANCIAL ASSET nor a CAPITAL GOOD, 'human capital' is a metaphor for the investment in KNOWLEDGE and skills that makes labor more productive. Like capital goods, human capital can depreciate (DEPRECIATION (1)) over time.

human failure.   The failure (FAIL) of human beings to adhere to their commitments and to successfully complete projects. Reasons for failure include unanticipated incompetence, negligence, GREED, avoidable IGNORANCE and personality defects. Contractual protections are thus needed not just to guard against OPPORTUNISM, but human failure of all sorts. The failure of particular enterprises is thus not a MARKET FAILURE but a human failure, since one function of the market process is to discard from the field those who fail and reward the winners.

human rights.   See NATURAL RIGHTS.

humanism. A philosophy and body of theory centered on human beings, with a consciously normative (NORMATIVE ECONOMICS) element. Humanist thought is based on REASON and seeks to promote human flourishing.

humanist economics. An approach to economic theory critical of self-seeking HOMO ECONOMICUS or HOMO CUPIDITUS, as well as excessive consumption. See Smith (1996). While many of its criticisms of NEOCLASSICAL ECONOMICS have merit, the humanist school may be overlooking the SUBJECTIVE nature of value, as well as GEO-ECONOMIC policies that would lead to the ends sought by members of this school.

Hume, David (1711–76). Scottish philosopher who is also known for explaining the PRICE-SPECIE MECHANISM. His writings on economics are mainly in *Political Discourses* (1752). He also wrote on MONEY, INTEREST, and other topics, influencing ADAM SMITH.

hyperinflation. INFLATION which accelerates until the UNIT OF ACCOUNT has almost no value, and prices rise daily. The most famous example was that of Germany in 1923.

hypothecation. EARMARKING.

hypothesis. A PROPOSITION that is abducted (ABDUCTION (2)) and partially warranted (WARRANT) using THEORY but remains to be fully tested by EVIDENCE. In loose language, a 'theory' often refers to a hypothesis.

hypothetical. Possible but not necessarily actual.

hysteresis. A system with systemic non-linearities (as coined by physicist James Ewing). For example, two shocks equal in magnitude but in opposite directions result in an outcome different from the original state. When a shock moves a variable and has no tendency to move back to the initial value even though all other variables have resumed their initial values, it exhibits hysteresis. Some models of UNEMPLOYMENT attempt to explain it with hysteresis: unemployment depends on past unemployment. Prices may also exhibit hysteresis; if the PRICE LEVEL moves up and then back down, relative prices may no longer be in the previous state.

I

iatrogenic. A disease caused by the doctor, hence an economic woe caused by policy or the bad advice of policy advisors.

ideal type. A CONCEPT with a role and particular CHARACTERISTICS, in contrast to a category of PERSON or INSTITUTION. For example, an ENTREPRENEUR is an ideal type, a typical role rather than a category of persons. Ideal types are an important element of Misesian PRAXEOLOGY.

ideology. The social philosophy, social doctrines, and policy believed to be the best, and promoted by a school of thought, a social movement, or political party.

ignorance. A lack of KNOWLEDGE. Superficial ignorance is a mere absence of knowledge, while a deeper ignorance is the ignoring of the knowledge, disregarding its acquisition because of APATHY or antipathy. Ignorance is one of the ultimate causes of SOCIAL PROBLEMS, as both an ignorance of the problems and an ignorance of the solution.

ignoratio elenchi. *Lat.* Beside the point. In logic, the fallacy of an appeal to emotion.

IMF. INTERNATIONAL MONETARY FUND.

impact fee. A charge paid by property developers to finance public works associated with the project. A sounder approach would be an annual assessment for the public works rather than imposing an upfront cost, since the developer passes the cost to the buyers, who then pay higher mortgage interest. However, the impact fee is closer to the BENEFIT PRINCIPLE than the financing of the works by general TAXATION.

imperfect competition. A market structure in which there is more than one firm in an INDUSTRY (2), and they have some control over price. It is called 'imperfect' in contrast to 'PERFECT' COMPETITION because the market price is above MARGINAL cost, thus hypothetically (HYPOTHETICAL) the seller could sell another unit by offering it at a lower price, but if TRANSACTION costs and other market realities preclude this, then there is no real-world imperfection. See also MONOPOLISTIC COMPETITION, OLIGOPOLY.

imperium.   1 The right to command, including the right to use the FORCE of the STATE, an attribute held by the executive branch of government, but also by private persons given such right. 2 Supreme and absolute POWER, authority, and rule.

implementation lag.   The time between a decision to pursue a policy and when it is actually started.

implicit.   Occurring in reality and in effect, but without any overt exchange, agreement, or sign. For example, a self-employed (SELF-EMPLOYMENT) owner of a firm implicitly pays himself a WAGE from his ACCOUNTING PROFIT; the profit above that wage is an ECONOMIC PROFIT. One who occupies his land implicitly pays himself RENT, since that is the OPPORTUNITY COST of the use of the land by the owner.

implicit contract.   A tacit AGREEMENT, where the terms are understood due to widely known custom or law. 'Implicit contract theory' also refers to incomplete labor CONTRACTS.
   Implicit general agreements save on TRANSACTION costs. Some theorists assert that one implicitly agrees with the rules of a government by living in its jurisdiction, but even if one moves into the area, if the entire country and world are divided into country CARTELS, there is no true VOLUNTARY agreement. Since attempts to establish new countries have not been successful, there is no libertarian (LIBERTARIANISM) option, hence no truly free CHOICE in government.

implicit cost.   The OPPORTUNITY COST of an owner's labor and resources, since these could be sold or rented, or the owner could have invested the funds in alternatives.

import.   A foreign good or service purchased, including tourists purchasing them abroad. If a country has a trade DEFICIT, then imports may be financed by selling assets or exporting currency.

imposed.   ARBITRARY *RULES that are enforced regardless of whether the subjects agree to them or not. The two main agencies which do this are GOVERNMENT and family rules for CHILDREN (or in some cases, an unwilling spouse or other family member). The proper imposition on immature children can become an inappropriate prototype for the morally improper imposition of rules by government on adults.

impossibility theorem.   The theorem by KENNETH ARROW states that it is impossible for a voting system to simultaneously satisfy a certain set of fair criteria, that is, a complete and consistent ranking of alternative options in accord with individual PREFERENCES. The basic concept was discovered much earlier by CONDORCET.

impôt unique.   *Fr.* 'Single tax,' a tax on the 'net product' of land, or its ECONOMIC RENT, proposed by the physiocratic economists (PHYSIOCRATS) as having no negative impact on PRODUCTION, unlike other taxes. The concept is similar to the 'SINGLE TAX' proposed by the followers of Henry George, but without the Georgist moral dimension.

improvements.   CAPITAL GOODS that make LAND more usable and productive. Foundations, buildings, gardens, and fences are improvements. Leveling a site, clearing it of plants, and draining water are also improvements to land.

imputation of value.   The determination of the value of HIGHER-ORDER goods (FACTORS OF PRODUCTION) from the goods they produce, a concept developed by CARL MENGER.

imputed income.   A BENEFIT received from an ASSET that is not an explicit TRANSACTION, such as the rent from owner-occupied land or the wages from the profits of a proprietor.

incentive.   The desire of a person to better his condition. INTERVENTION reduces incentives by cutting or cutting off the gains from an ACTIVITY.

incentive taxation.   TAXATION, such as on RENT, which preserves INCENTIVES, but without any privileged (PRIVILEGE) SUBSIDIES.

incidence.   Bearing the ultimate burden of a cost, such as a tax.

incidence of taxation.   The change in the DISTRIBUTION of income after the imposition of TAXATION. The incidence tells who ultimately bears the burden of a tax. INDIRECT TAXES are to some degree passed on to others, such as customers bearing a SALES TAX. The incidence of a FACTOR with an entirely inelastic SUPPLY, that is with a fixed supply, is that the tax burden falls entirely on the owner of the factor. The incidence of items in current production falls partly on the factor owners and partly on consumers. The ultimate incidence is on the owners of LAND and LABOR, since these are the original factors of production. Hence, taxes borne by consumers are also borne by them as owners of factors from which the income is derived. For example, a person whose only source of income is wages pays a consumption tax out of his wage. See also ABSOLUTE TAX INCIDENCE.

income.   The Haig–Simmons definition of income is CONSUMPTION plus the change in net REAL (3) wealth during some time interval. Income consists of funds and goods and other flows of value received, net of costs. Income taxation (INCOME TAX) as practiced also taxes some of the principal. See also PSYCHIC INCOME.

income statement.   An accounting and reporting of the flow of INCOME and EXPENDITURES.

income tax.   A TAX on 'INCOME' as determined by a tax code, which in reality mainly taps cash receipts and sales of ASSETS, typically leaving some income untaxed while also taxing assets. After a Civil War income tax and an attempt in 1894 that was declared unconstitutional, the US federal personal income tax now has Constitutional authority under the 16th Amendment, although its application is disputed by some. The US personal and also the corporate income tax are legally EXCISE TAXES on the ACTIVITY (1) of obtaining income, measured by the amount of income, rather than DIRECT TAXES on income (as economists would hold), since under the Constitution the latter would have to be apportioned by population. Income taxation is based on ABILITY TO PAY rather than the BENEFIT PRINCIPLE.

To avoid taxing assets, an income tax needs to be entirely indexed for INFLATION, including INTEREST, DIVIDENDS, CAPITAL GAINS, and DEPRECIATION (1). By taxing gains not indexed to inflation, the income tax also taxes some CAPITAL.

Libertarians (LIBERTARIANISM) consider the income tax an INTERVENTION because it takes funds that properly belong to the owners and also because it intrudes into privacy, and enforcement can be harsh. See also FLAT TAX.

incomes policy.   GOVERNMENT control over wages and other income. The UK implemented such a policy during the 1960s and 1970s to reduce inflation. This treats effects rather than the MONETARY cause of the inflation, while creating inflexibility and postponing the effects of monetary inflation.

indexed.   A PRICE, TAX, or other variable that is periodically adjusted to account for price INFLATION, so that the REAL (3) variable is not changed or only a real gain or loss is accounted for. For example, if a minimum amount of a gain or transfer is not taxed, then that minimum would be raised each year to account for the increase in the PRICE LEVEL.

indicative planning. See ECONOMIC PLANNING.

indirect taxes. Taxes which are not DIRECT TAXES. These are usually taxes on sales, value-added, or on an ACTIVITY (1) rather than directly on a person, property, or income. Legally, the US federal INCOME TAX is indirect, being on the PRIVILEGE of operating as a corporation or on the activity of earning income.

individualism. Basing policy on the rights of individuals, rather than placing priority on collectives, since without unanimity, collective superiority implies the rule by those with power. Individualism is distinct from ATOMISM.

induction. Reasoning (REASON) from the specific to the general. This involves some rule for obtaining a conclusion from the specifics, and the data. Hence, the inductive conclusion is actually a DEDUCTION (2) from the rule and the data.

industrial organization. A branch of economics studying MARKET STRUCTURE and the conduct and performance of FIRMS. Anti-trust policy is a major subfield. See also ATOMISTIC COMPETITION, MONOPOLY.

industrialization. The transformation of an ECONOMY from agriculture to manufacturing, and from simpler TECHNOLOGY to more complex, sophisticated, and powerful technology. Traditional culture is also transformed into a more commercial culture, and the society becomes more mobile. The former Soviet Union and its satellites, and many developing countries after World War II, attempted to industrialize via government planning and controls, while East-Asian countries were more market-oriented. More recently, there has been a trend towards LIBERALIZATION. See also ECONOMIC DEVELOPMENT.

industry. 1 PRODUCTION and ENTERPRISE. 2 The enterprises producing a class of PRODUCT.

inelastic. The percentage change of one variable such as quantity being rather unresponsive to a percentage change in the price, the ratio being less than one.

inequality. Having or being greater or less than others. See also EQUATION OF INEQUALITY, GINI COEFFICIENT. An unequal distribution of income can be due to market-compatible differences in the quality of labor and effort, or it can be due to non-market gains due to privileges and coercion, including endowments of natural resources.

infant industry. A new INDUSTRY (2) that requires INVESTMENTS until it matures into profitability by achieving sufficient ECONOMIES OF SCALE. This is often invoked as an argument in favor of PROTECTIONISM, the counterarguments being that it is up to investors to nurture a firm or industry's start-up costs; that once an industry receives protection, it creates a vested interest that continues to seek it; that the power to protect will attract special interests, including aging rather than infant industries; and that if an industry is to be assisted, an outright SUBSIDY is less distorting and the cost is made explicit.

infeudation. Making ALLODIAL *REAL (1) property feudal (FEUDALISM), that is subject to a superior such as the STATE, placing it in possession subject to payment of fees or taxes and regulatory obligations, usually by FORCE but possibly by CONTRACT.

inflation. PRICE INFLATION or MONETARY INFLATION. Usually, the former is meant when the term is not qualified, although price inflation usually follows monetary inflation. Cost-push inflation is price inflation due to rising costs of inputs, such as oil or labor. However, price inflation implies that monetary inflation is accommodating the rising price of the inputs, otherwise the demand for other goods falls, their price drops, and the PRICE LEVEL does not rise. Demand-pull inflation means that an increase in AGGREGATE DEMAND raises the price level; this again implies that there is monetary inflation driving up aggregate demand or else funds flowing in from abroad, which is also an increase in the money supply. It is possible for there to be a temporary increase in some wages that drives up some prices, but on an ECONOMY-wide basis this is unsustainable without monetary inflation.

inflation tax. **1** An implicit TAX on MONEY holdings due to PRICE INFLATION. The purchasing power of money decreases, effectively taxing the financial asset. A non-INDEXED tax on INTEREST is a further inflation tax, since the nominal interest is taxed, even though there is no real gain. **2** An explicit tax on wage increases above some government-set rate.

informal sector. (Also, 'informal ECONOMY.') Economic activity which evades REGULATION and TAXATION, but is otherwise not illegal. It also includes the occupation of government lands without permits. Many less developed economies have large informal sectors. Hernando de Soto (1989) shows how the costs of formality make legal production prohibitively expensive. Syn. 'underground economy.'

infrastructure. CAPITAL GOODS that facilitate trade, including communications, transportation routes, utilities, airports, and harbors. Often they are provided by government, but private enterprise has provided these as well. By extension, there is also the legal infrastructure which also facilitates the operation of a market.

inheritance tax. A TAX on an inheritance, either as an ESTATE TAX or an ACCESSIONS TAX.

injection. Governmental action to increase AGGREGATE DEMAND, especially an increase in the MONEY SUPPLY by a monetary authority. If the injection is greater than the increase in the DEMAND FOR MONEY, then not only is the PRICE LEVEL raised, but there will be CANTILLON EFFECTS.

innovations. New products and marketing methods, changes in TECHNOLOGY, and new ways of organizing enterprise. ENTREPRENEURS introduce innovations, hoping to PROFIT, and these changes result in CREATIVE DESTRUCTION as successful innovations push out the less successful methods and products.

input. A FACTOR OF PRODUCTION, a resource that enters a firm and is transformed into products as the output.

inside lag. The duration of time between desiring a policy and implementing it.

inside money. If GOLD is MONEY, gold is outside money and the MONEY SUBSTITUTES created by banks are inside money, inside the banking system, arising from debt. With FIAT MONEY, bank deposits matched by private lending are inside money, and the government or central bank (for example paper dollars) currency as well as bank deposits based on government debt and foreign exchange reserves are OUTSIDE MONEY.

insider–outsider. A model (used for example by New Keynesians) of UNEMPLOYMENT in which employed insiders, such as unions, maintain above-market-clearing WAGES due to their bargaining power with a firm. Neither the firm nor the insiders are atomistic competitors (ATOMISTIC COMPETITION), hence they have MARKET POWER. Outsiders are unemployed even though they would willingly work at a lower wage. This, however, is not a cause of unemployment, but only of insider privilege.

instability. Having a large continuous variation or being vulnerable to a downfall or termination. Interest rates which continuously rise and fall are unstable, and a job is unstable if the employee continuously fears being laid off.

institution. A shared MENTAL CONSTRUCT. Examples include MONEY, organizations, marriage, income taxation, law, property rights, and customs. An institution can also be considered to include the property owned by an organization.

institutional economics. A school of economic thought that emphasizes the importance of INSTITUTIONS, SOCIAL EVOLUTION, and the structure of economies, as well as also a branch of economics that examines the role of institutions. Major institutionalists include T. Veblen, W. Mitchell, and G. Myrdal, J. Commons, and C. Ayres. See Whalen (1996) and 'Dialogues in economics' in Foldvary (1996).

Institutionalists criticize neoclassical theory (NEOCLASSICAL ECONOMICS) for attempting to explain economic phenomena without regard to institutions. However, Austrian (AUSTRIAN ECONOMICS), GEO-ECONOMIC, Virginian (VIRGINIA SCHOOL OF POLITICAL ECONOMY) and other schools do include institutional structures and analysis. Many in the institutional school do not favor FREE MARKETS, which may be the result of not distinguishing pure free markets from markets hampered by INTERVENTION, but the approach *per se* is neutral with respect to policy, and it is possible to have a free-market institutionalist approach, showing that market-enhancing institutions such as property rights and efficient dispute resolution lead to better outcomes.

institutional failure. An outcome whereby the intention of the founders or directors of an institution is not achieved. The structures of an institution may not be suitable to the achievement of the desired outcomes. MASS DEMOCRACY suffers from institutional failure when SPECIAL INTERESTS exploit the structure and thwart the intentions of the supporters of democracy to have the people rule.

insurance. The substitution of a relatively small known COST for a RISK of a large loss. HEDGING might also be considered insurance.

intended consequences. Outcomes of a policy which were those sought by the initiators, in contrast to the UNINTENDED CONSEQUENCES.

intensive margin. The productivity of the next unit of a variable input in the same DOMAIN of a fixed resource, which in EQUILIBRIUM is equal to the productivity of a unit at the EXTENSIVE MARGIN, where the variable input is extended into a new domain of the other resource. For example, when the MARGIN OF CULTIVATION of land for growing corn is extended to new land, which is less productive than the previous margin, the marginal productivity of labor falls, hence wage falls, and new workers can be added to the more productive lands until the productivities at those intensive margins equal those of the extensive margin.

intentional community.   A COMMUNITY which is deliberately founded to achieve certain goals, such as the implementation of a theory or ideology, the ABILITY to express a CULTURE and pass it to posterity, and/or the provision of specialized services. In contrast, a condominium or typical residential association has no such intentions, but are within the mainstream in ideology and culture, although there can be specialized services which make it intentional.

interest.   A premium paid to obtain goods at the present time rather than in the future. As stated by Austrian (AUSTRIAN ECONOMICS) theory, the positive rate of interest is due to TIME PREFERENCE and to CAPITALIZATION. As the rate of interest approaches zero, the present value of future yields rises and becomes infinite at a zero rate of interest, which is impossible, hence the long-term real rate of interest will not become zero or go negative. Interest is a return on financial assets lent, and it can be a return from any factor of production. The productivity of INVESTMENTS has been alleged to affect interest rates, but a highly productive asset will command a high present-day price rather than increase the rate of interest. If people choose not to invest in such assets, the short time preference will make interest rates high. The supply and demand for loanable funds sets interest rates, but these are in turn determined by time preference. See also COMPOUND INTEREST.

interest rate.   The DISCOUNT RATE (1) of future goods relative to present day goods, the conventional time interval for measuring the rate being one year. See also COMPOUND INTEREST, INTEREST. Short-term rates differ from long-term rates, the long-term rates usually being higher to offset the RISK of INFLATION. Premiums for the risk of loan losses are included in NOMINAL interest rates, but are not part of pure interest. The interest income received by an account holder is the gross interest paid by borrowers less the overheads, taxes, and risk premiums. Interest paid on tax-free bonds such as municipal bonds has a lower rate than taxable interest, since the latter has a tax premium. The REAL (3) interest rate equals the nominal interest rate minus the inflation rate. Interest paid by borrowers on unsecured loans has an extra risk premium due to bankruptcy laws making it easy to void one's debts. Free-market interest rates would be much simpler due to an absence of taxes on interest, tax deductions of interest paid, an absence of inflation, and bankruptcy laws that retain responsibility. See also AGIO THEORY OF INTEREST.

intergenerational equity.   Policy that is just for all age levels, rather than forcing one age bracket to subsidize (SUBSIDY) another, as is now the case with TRANSFER PAYMENTS from taxpayers to recipients of SOCIAL SECURITY and transfers of medical aid. Equity to future generations may also involve conserving NATURAL OPPORTUNITIES rather than excessively mining renewable resources and polluting (POLLUTION) the planet.

intergovernmental grants.   Funds transferred from one level of government to another, usually from higher to lower levels, and often with conditions. Such grants typically have a high compliance cost, reduce the power of local voters, and often skew expenditure into projects which have a high carrying cost.

internalization.   The elimination of EXTERNAL EFFECTS by making PRIVATE COSTS equal social costs (SOCIAL COSTS AND BENEFITS), thus making all costs internal to the purchaser. The delineation and enforcement of PROPERTY RIGHTS achieves this, as does the payment of damage fees, and also the inclusion of activities under one owner.

international economics.   The branch of economics dealing with INTERNATIONAL TRADE or FOREIGN TRADE, EXCHANGE RATES, and international institutions such as trade blocs and the WTO (WORLD TRADE ORGANIZATION). The field or courses in it are also called the GLOBAL ECONOMY. A major principle of international economics is the theory of COMPARATIVE ADVANTAGE.

International Monetary Fund.   An agency which makes short-term loans to governments. It was established as an outcome of the BRETTON WOODS conference of 1944, under which CURRENCIES had fixed exchange rates. DEFICITS in international trade as well as government budgets can be financed by loans from the IMF. In some cases, borrowing has been due to changed circumstances, such as the Baltic countries needing to finance oil previously obtained at low prices. The IMF makes loans dependent on meeting certain conditions. Some of these, such as balancing a budget, are sound, but often the means, such as higher taxes on productive effort, impose austerity and hardship on much of the population, and make a recovery more difficult. The IMF obtains funds from the industrialized member countries and extends much of its lending to less developed countries. The IMF thus internationalizes INTERVENTION, obtaining revenues from taxpayers and imposing austerity and loan repayments from the recipient countries. The alternative of a shift in taxation to RENTS and POLLUTION charges would provide revenues without austerity, but this is not an IMF-favored option, since it would reduce the availability of land value as a loan collateral.

International Society for Individual Liberty.   See ISIL.

international trade. The exchange of goods and financial assets among AGENTS (1) in different countries. This differs from domestic exchanges in usually having different CURRENCIES and in having greater BARRIERS. See INTERNATIONAL ECONOMICS.

International Union for Land Value Taxation and Free Trade. A global GEORGIST or GEO-ECONOMIC society based in London. It hosts international conferences every few years, and publishes *Land and Liberty* magazine.

interpersonal. Regarding relationships and comparisons among persons, such as comparing utilities (UTILITARIANISM), or the impossibility thereof.

interstate commerce. In the USA, goods which are used on one state, but which originate in another state or are transported between states. The USA Constitution provides the federal government with authority over such commerce, but this was intended to promote FREE TRADE among the states. The interstate commerce clause became stretched to encompass all goods that cross state borders, hence INTERVENTION into almost all production and trade.

intersubjective values. A community having the same subjective value regarding some item.

intertemporal. Across TIME (2). Exchanges between one moment in time and another. See also INTEREST RATE.

intervention. GOVERNMENT policy which imposes (IMPOSED) costs and ARBITRARY *RESTRICTIONS on peaceful and honest action. Intervention hampers the MARKET PROCESS by skewing (SKEW) prices and profits, thereby misallocating resources. See also REGULATION.

intrinsic value. See VALUE.

invasion. A penetration into a DOMAIN without the AGREEMENT of the domain's owner (OWNERSHIP).

inventory. GOODS ready to be sold. These are CAPITAL GOODS as well as CIRCULATING CAPITAL. INVESTMENT in inventory has been reduced by 'just in time' processing that tracks the amounts sold and is able to deliver goods for sale as needed.

investment. **1** *Ec.* An increase in the stock of CAPITAL GOODS, or funds spent on enterprises which produce capital goods, or funds spent to increase HUMAN

CAPITAL. If EXPENDITURE is considered to be divided into CONSUMER GOODS and capital goods, and income is either spent for consumer goods or saved, then over the long run, investment equals and comes from savings. **2** *Fin.* Funds used to purchase productive assets that provide a yield or increase in value. See also SPECULATION.

invisible foot.   A term coined by Stephen Magee for the POLITICAL forces that shape outcomes in addition to the INVISIBLE HAND.

INTERVENTION is often a visible fist, but much TRANSFER-SEEKING is opaque to consumers and taxpayers, who indeed foot the bill.

invisible hand.   A famous metaphor used by ADAM SMITH in the *WEALTH OF NATIONS* (1776, 1976) for the COORDINATION of economic activity by the spontaneous MARKET PROCESS as if it were deliberately directed. One who pursues his own interest is led by the invisible hand to provide for the social interest by providing wanted services. The metaphor has spin-offs such as the visible fist (coercion), the INVISIBLE FOOT (political and legal forces) and the INVISIBLE HANDSHAKE (custom and social forces), but these are not nearly as widely used.

invisible handshake.   **1** A term coined by Arthur Okun for historical and social forces that shape outcomes in addition to the INVISIBLE HAND. **2** An implicit contract between a firm and its employees or customers.

iron law of wages.   The proposition that in the long run, the WAGE LEVEL tends to SUBSISTENCE if there is population growth, since if there is no change in TECHNOLOGY, then an increase in the labor supply decreases labor PRODUCTIVITY. In some CLASSICAL or Malthusian presentations, it is asserted that population growth will continue and productivity will not keep pace.

IS–LM.   A Keynesian model which has been widely used, but has now fallen out of favor, with two curves, the IS being investment savings or the goods market, and the LM being the liquidity and money-market curve. The axes are the rate of interest and national output. Both curves indicate equilibria in the respective markets, the intersection being a common EQUILIBRIUM. Keynesians have debated the shapes of the curves with monetarists.

ISIL.   The International Society for Individual Liberty, an organization which publishes literature, hosts conferences, and promotes and coordinates libertarian global activity, especially helping FREE-MARKET proponents in less wealthy countries.

J

Jefferson, Thomas (1743–1826). Third president of the USA and author of the US Declaration of Independence, which, echoing LOCKE, proclaimed the right to life, liberty, and the pursuit of happiness, and the equality of man. Jefferson was responsible for the US decimal coinage (Chandler, 1983). Jefferson stated that 'government should not take from the mouth of labor the bread it has earned' (first inaugural, 1801). That evidently implies that Jefferson opposed taxes on wages. It would also imply no consumer taxes. In a letter to Isaac McPherson on August 13, 1813, Jefferson wrote 'no individual has, of natural right, a separate property in an acre of land,' implying that rights of possession were subject to an equality criterion.

joint. 1 Connected, as in joint production or joint account. 2 A place where two items are connected. A prime example is the financial and real sides of the ECONOMY, joined by money; see also BROKEN JOINT, LOOSE JOINT, TIGHT JOINT.

joint stock company. A CORPORATION.

joint ventures. Cooperation between firms or between a firm and a government, harnessing COMPARATIVE ADVANTAGE. For example, a firm from an industrialized ECONOMY provides funding and technology, while the local firm has a knowledge of the local governance, customs, language, resources, and markets.

jus possessionis. *Lat.* The right to possess (POSSESSION) land.

just price. A morally justified or fair price, usually regarded as the normal market price. During an emergency when there are temporary shortages and a firm can obtain a higher price, there may be no violation of market ethics, but customers may resent it as exploitative, and the firm may suffer a loss of GOODWILL. The concept of a just price was developed during medieval times, and the ethical questions are still relevant for issues such as prison and child labor.

justice. Providing each person with his due. The main premise of justice is moral EQUALITY among PERSONS. Those who violate equality are criminals, and their due is to pay restitution and be penalized. See also ECONOMIC JUSTICE, SOCIAL JUSTICE.

justification.   *Log.* Answering the question, how do you know? Propositions are justified by removing the puzzle. See also WARRANT.

K

kakistocracy. GOVERNMENT by the worst persons.

Kaldor–Hicks test. The proposition that a shift from state A to B is preferred if those who lose by it are compensated (COMPENSATION) by those who gain. The test was proposed by Kaldor and Hicks in 1939. The criterion proposes that A is preferred to B even if the compensation does not take place, whereas by NATURAL MORAL LAW such a change is immoral without the compensation, and thus is not preferred. If the losers do not agree to the compensation, the problem of comparing utility makes the criterion problematic.

Keynes, John Maynard (1883–1946). Author of the *General Theory of Employment, Interest and Money* (1936), which rejected CLASSICAL *SUPPLY-SIDE analysis and policy and was influential in restoring Mercantile DEMAND-SIDE thinking, based on the premise that various prices (especially wages and interest rates) are not downwards-flexible. Among the enormous literature criticizing Keynesian demand-side economics, a notable refutation specifically of the *General Theory* is HAZLITT (1959). Keynes was also a major contributor to the BRETTON WOODS conference.

Keynesian economics. A school of DEMAND-SIDE macroeconomics based on the analysis of KEYNES. Key features include the determination of income from autonomous expenditures and the marginal propensity to save, hence policy which increases output by increasing autonomous government spending. However, if the CONSUMPTION FUNCTION has a zero intercept, this analysis collapses. Inflexibilities in a market ECONOMY may be real, but if they are due to INTERVENTION, then Keynesian policy only treats effects, which may then cause further maladies requiring ever further intervention. In response to classical criticism, especially RATIONAL EXPECTATIONS, the New Keynesian school has arisen which continues with sticky-price explanations that persist despite such expectations.

Khaldun. See ABU SAID IBN KHALDUN.

Kirzner, Israel (1930–). British-born Austrian-school (AUSTRIAN ECONOMICS) Professor of Economics at New York University. He has been a leading theorist of entrepreneurship, institutions, and distributive justice. Among his major books are *The Economic Point of View* (1960), *Competition and Entrepreneurship* (1973), *Discovery, Capitalism and Distributive Justice* (1989), and *The Meaning of Market Process* (1992). He heads the Austrian program at NYU.

kleptocracy.   Government by organised criminals.

Knight, Frank (1895–1973).   Professor of Economics at Chicago, a founder of the CHICAGO SCHOOL, and a major influence on economics and free-market economists (FREE-MARKET ECONOMICS). He wrote on methodology, ethics, social cost, and a landmark work, *Risk, Uncertainty and Profit* (1921), in which he differentiated RISK, which has a known probability, from UNCERTAINTY, which does not. ENTREPRENEURS obtain their ECONOMIC PROFITS from facing uncertain market conditions.

knowledge.   Data and PROPOSITIONS, in minds and in texts, that persons believe and which correspond to reality. Knowledge can be an intangible CAPITAL GOOD, and can also be embodied in tangible goods. As HAYEK pointed out, much of the knowledge about production is tacit and decentralized and dependent on time and place, hence there is a KNOWLEDGE PROBLEM in centralized controls. Wise corporations and governments thus decentralize their operations. See also TRUE.

knowledge problem.   The problem inherent in any large organization or the control by central government over an ECONOMY, that much relevant KNOWLEDGE is decentralized, and therefore, central planning fails to be effective.

Kondratieff, Nikolai (1892–1930?).   Russian economist who in *The Long Waves of Economic Life* (1925) posited the existence of long BUSINESS CYCLES spanning many decades. He died in prison at an unknown date.

kratos.   *Gk.* Governmental rule.

L

labor. The FACTOR OF PRODUCTION consisting of human exertion engaged in the production of WEALTH. Labor includes HUMAN CAPITAL and entrepreneurial exertion (ENTREPRENEUR). The yield of labor is WAGES, which can take the form of OPPORTUNITY-COST and ENTREPRENEURIAL PROFITS. See also WAGES.

labor theory of value. An explanation for the value of goods: the value of the LABOR input determines the value of the product. This doctrine was used by classical economists (CLASSICAL ECONOMICS) and then Marxists (KARL MARX). The contribution of capital goods is accounted for by its labor input. LAND does not co-determine the price of goods, since its rent is derived from the value of the goods in accord with the theory of DIFFERENTIAL RENT. Since the ultimate factors are land and labor, it follows that labor creates the value of goods in current production. (The doctrine does not apply to goods with a fixed supply, such as antiques and natural resources.) The rate of interest also needs to be taken into account for different periods of production and different intensities of capital goods.

The marginalist and subjectivist revolutions overturned the labor theory of value and replaced it with SUBJECTIVE VALUES. As CARL MENGER pointed out, the classicals had it backwards: the value of factors is imputed (IMPUTATION OF VALUE) from the subjective value of goods. However, the classical labor theory of value has some explanatory power for goods in current production. Abstracting from capital goods, given a demand curve, the labor supply curve determines the price. If labor becomes more expensive, the price of the products will rise, given the demand. And if there is only one consumer good, then at the rent-free margin, the wage equals the goods. What subjectivism does is differentiate the demand among various goods. Moreover, the supply of labor itself is also subjective, the worker valuing wages and the psychic satisfaction of labor versus leisure or an investment in human capital.

Karl MARX turned the labor theory of value into a DOCTRINE of EXPLOITATION (2), arguing that all value is created by labor, hence value above wages paid is exploitative profit, or surplus value. The counterargument is that in a competitive INDUSTRY (2), ECONOMIC PROFITS tend to be reduced to zero, hence if there is any surplus, it is what the physiocrats identified as the net product, or RENT. But rent goes to the landlord, not the capitalist or entrepreneur. Marx would have had a sounder case if he had become a GEORGIST rather than a Marxist.

labor unions.   See UNIONS, LABOR.

Laffer Curve.   TAX revenues as a function of tax rates, named by Jude Wanniski (1978) after Laffer (1979), but see also ABU SAID IBN KHALDUN. There is a tax rate that maximizes revenues. For a tax on economic rent, the revenue maximizing rate is 100 percent.

lag.   A time interval between the initiation of an ACTIVITY and its taking effect. An example is the time it takes for an increase in the MONEY SUPPLY to become fully manifested in changes in output and price. See ACTION LAG, ADJUSTMENT LAG, ADMINISTRATIVE LAG, APPLICATION LAG, DECISION LAG, IMPLEMEN- TATION LAG, INSIDE LAG, OUTSIDE LAG, RECOGNITION LAG. All these lags make policy less effective.

laissez-faire.   Fr. The policy of having a FREE MARKET, with no INTERVEN- TIONS. In French, it means 'let it be made.' The theory of *laissez-faire* is that a pure free market provides both liberty and prosperity, efficiently (EFFICIENT) allocating resources to meet effective demand. Government's role is mainly to provide protection and enforce PROPERTY RIGHTS. The term originated in France and was espoused by the PHYSIOCRATS and classical economists (CLAS- SICAL ECONOMICS).

There has been no modern *laissez-faire* ECONOMY, yet critics of markets allege that industrial economies have practiced *laissez-faire*, which is to blame for POVERTY, UNEMPLOYMENT, and POLLUTION. In contrast, free-market analysis has pointed to countless interventions and taxes that have hampered markets and caused the distortions that lead to SOCIAL PROBLEMS. See Gwartney *et al.* (1996).

land.   The FACTOR OF PRODUCTION consisting of NATURAL RESOURCES and OP- PORTUNITIES prior to being altered by HUMAN ACTION. This ECONOMIC (2) mean- ing of land, as economic land, includes all usable three-dimensional space, and thus includes lands with a water as well as solid surface.

Economic land includes surface sites, naturally occurring materials (water, oil, minerals), the atmosphere, the ELECTROMAGNETIC SPECTRUM, airline routes, satellite orbits, wildlife, and the genetic stock of all living beings. The in- come or yield of land is LAND RENT, which is an ECONOMIC RENT. Natural materials are altered by human effort to produce REAL WEALTH, but space is not altered and remains land even when used. The quantity of surface land is fixed, hence its SUPPLY curve is vertical. Land is also immobile and its supply independent of human effort. Therefore, the economic rent of land can be collected without affecting its supply, activity using it, or the prices of goods produced with it.

Neoclassical theory (NEOCLASSICAL ECONOMICS) has merged land into capital goods. Geo-economists (GEO-ECONOMICS) consider this reduction of the three classical FACTORS into two to be a theoretical defect, with major policy implications. See Gaffney (1994).

Land and Liberty.   An international magazine published from London, with news and analysis of economics from a GEORGIST or GEO-ECONOMIC perspective.

land reform.   A change in LAND TENURE towards a more equal (EQUALITY) DISTRIBUTION (3) of the land area or the land value, or to consolidate inefficient smallholdings, or to privatize titles to lands owned by the STATE. Land reform is often sought by farmers where a small proportion of the people own much of the land. Two methods of land reform include a physical redivision of land and titles, or a tax on the land rent, which either compensates society for the use of land or turns over land that was inefficiently used to new owners who can pay the rent tax by putting the land to its most productive use. The rent-tax method is more market-compatibly EFFICIENT. Countries that enacted successful land reforms with a rent tax include Taiwan in 1950 and Japan in the 19th century; both subsequently industrialized rapidly (Harrison, 1983).

land rent.   The RENT (1) of ECONOMIC LAND.

land-rent tax.   See LAND-VALUE TAX.

land speculation.   The purchase and holding of land in the expectation that its value will appreciate, sometimes postponing development until a time when it will be more profitable. A tax on LAND RENT reduces land SPECULATION (3) by taking the future rents. HARRY GUNNISON BROWN pointed out that market agents have different EXPECTATIONS. Because land markets are incomplete, with no futures market, a tax on rent reduces the offer prices of those who have the most extreme beliefs about high future land rent, making the lot more attractive to those who wish to develop it immediately. The charge on rent thus increases efficiency, since those who believe that site rents will be higher are more likely to be incorrect. Land speculation fueled by easy money helps cause the boom and bust cycle. See also BROWN EFFECT, WINNER'S CURSE, GEO-AUSTRIAN SYNTHESIS, LAND-VALUE TAX.

land tenure.   The pattern and CONCENTRATION of LAND ownership and possession. See LAND REFORM.

land trust.   A TRUST (2) which owns land, usually for wildlife or farmland conservation or for leasing. Some land trusts such as Arden, Delaware, have been set up by GEORGISTS to implement and demonstrate the principles of funding COLLECTIVE GOODS from LAND RENT and to eliminate the disincentive of PROPERTY TAXES on real-estate improvements by having the trust rather than the leaseholders pay those taxes (Foldvary, 1994b).

land-value tax.   A TAX proportionate to the market value of LAND, often referred to as LVT. It is equivalent to a tax on RENT: given a tax rate t as a percentage of the land value, the percentage of the rent taxed is $t/(i+t)$, where i is the REAL (3) INTEREST RATE. Land-value taxation or the equivalent in land trusts and other organizations (the COMMUNITY COLLECTION OF RENT) is advocated by GEORGISTS or geoists (GEOISM) as a SINGLE TAX or charge, all other taxes to be abolished (ABOLISH), along with abolishing arbitrary REGULATIONS.

The effect of LVT is to induce an EFFICIENT use of land, since its possession then has a carrying cost. LVT also eliminates market-hampering LAND SPECU-LATION, since future rents are collected. Advocates state that this elimination is beneficial, since such speculation prices land for future uses, sometimes locking out present-day uses, and often speculative booms result in malinvestments and busts. (With LVT, land speculation is market-enhancing.) The taxation of rent enables government to shift taxes away from productive exertion, and is thus a market-enhancing policy. LVT also avoids intruding on private finances and is less costly to implement than taxes on income and sales.

LVT has been estimated to collect about half the revenues that governments currently obtain by taxation. The other half of the revenues could be eliminated by reducing expenditures or be obtained with user fees and POLLU-TION charges.

land-value tax options.   OPTION (2) markets on land value that may arise with land-value taxation (LAND-VALUE TAX). A landholder could purchase an option for all future increases in LVT to be paid by the option seller. This would leave the land-titleholder with only the opportunity-cost of developing the land as rents rose. These are also called rent-collection options.

landholder.   A person who has TITLE to LAND.

landowner.   One who has either the RIGHTS of POSSESSION to LAND or also the rights to obtain the RENT.

larcenous.   Taking the PROPERTY that rightfully belongs to others without their consent. A larcenous MARKET includes legalized larceny. For example, a SLAVE (1) market is not free, but larcenous, because the slaves are human beings who have a right to their own labor and wages, which are instead legally stolen by the slave owner. When a government allows POLLUTION without compensation, or protects some firms from the competition of other firms, these all transfer wealth and constitute a larcenous market.

large cap.   See CAP.

law.   1 *Sci.* A THEOREM about a fundamental PHENOMENON, expressing a major regularity, such as the law of gravity. In economics, the LAW OF DEMAND or the LAW OF DIMINISHING RETURNS are key regularities. A synonym is a 'principle,' although the 'law' label is used for specific laws. 2 *Leg.* A command issued by a GOVERNMENT, or a RULES agreement by an association. 3 *Phil.* A universal ethic, derived from human nature, thus a law of nature or NATURAL MORAL LAW. True legal law is based on such moral law rather than the arbitrary commands of the rulers.

Among the key classical-liberal works on law are works by BASTIAT, Benson (1990), Berman (1983), and SPOONER. Berman's *Law and Revolution* (1983) shows how in the development of Western-European law, competition among jurisdictions and sources of law led to the emergence of greater liberty.

law and economics.   The positive and normative application of economic theory to law, the effects of legal decisions, property rights, contracts, regulation and monopoly, and PUBLIC-CHOICE decisions regarding law. RONALD COASE spurred much of this analysis, and R. Posner is another key theorist.

law, Director's.   See DIRECTOR'S LAW.

'the law is an ass'.   A phrase used colloquially to refer to absurd government law, by Charles Dickens in *Oliver Twist*. Mr. Bumble, manager on site of the orphanage, expresses this when informed that 'The law presumes that a man controls his wife,' to which he replies, 'If the law presumes that, sir, then the law is a ass!' (*sic* 'a ass').

law of demand.   An inverse relationship between the PRICE and the quantity demanded of a GOOD, when all other elements are held constant. The law is based on the substitution effect: as the price of a good drops, consumers buy more because they substitute this good for others they would have bought. The law also depends on the DIMINISHING MARGINAL UTILITY of goods: with more items, the utility of the next one falls, so consumers are willing to obtain more only at a lower price. The law is fundamentally based on the economizing principle (ECONOMIZE). There is also an income effect as lower prices create more purchasing power, but this does not necessarily and universally lead to a greater amount purchased of any particular good, since some goods are inferior. The law of DEMAND is a fundamental principle of economics.

law of diminishing returns.   Given a fixed input and a variable input, eventually the MARGINAL PRODUCT of the variable input declines, extra inputs yielding ever less extra output. This is an AXIOMATIC, foundational (FOUNDATION) proposition of economics. The law was known by TURGOT in the 1700s.

law of reflux.   The proposition in BANKING theory that there cannot be a permanent overissue of competitive private BANKNOTES, since any issued exceeding the demand will be returned for redemption (REDEEM).

law of rent.   'The RENT of LAND is determined by the excess of its produce over that which the same application can secure from the least productive land in use.' Henry George (1879; 1975, p. 168). The 'same application' means the same quality of labor and capital goods, and that quantity at which the INTENSIVE MARGIN produces the same marginal yield as the extensive margin (EXTENSIVE MARGIN OF PRODUCTION).

law of supply.   A direct relationship between PRICE and the quantity supplied of a good in current production, when all other variables are held constant. As the price rises, a greater quantity is produced and offered because of substitution, as production shifts to that good from other goods. With greater quantity, resources that are less suitable are obtained, at a lower productivity and higher price, hence these are only warranted at a greater price of the product. Downward-sloping SUPPLY curves due to ECONOMIES OF SCALE do not violate the law of supply because the production methods are not held constant as the quantity increases.

law of variable proportions.   *Syn.* LAW OF DIMINISHING RETURNS.

law of wages.   A law in GEO-ECONOMIC theory that states that the WAGE LEVEL is determined at the EXTENSIVE MARGIN OF PRODUCTION, where land has a zero RENT. Abstracting from CAPITAL GOODS, the entire product at the rent-free margin constitutes wages, and competition among labor makes the wage level equal in an ECONOMY. The law of wages is related to the LAW OF RENT, since output above the wage level in the more productive lands is distributed as rent. When capital goods are added to the model, productivity increases, but the relationship between wages and rent remains the same. The law of wages was developed by Henry George in *Progress and Poverty* (1879), and was an improvement over RICARDO's subsistence theory of wages. For a recent examination of the law of wages, see Foldvary (1994a). See also WAKEFIELD.

legal tender. MONEY which by law must be accepted for the TENDER or payment of DEBT, although one may refuse small denominations for large debts.

lex non cogit ad impossibilia. *Lat.* Law does not recognize impossibilities: impossible acts should not be legislated.

lex non curat de minimis. *Lat.* Law does not concern trifles. Trivial invasions should not be ACTIONABLE.

liability. A DEBT or other obligation, reducing net worth.

liberal. 1 CLASSICAL LIBERAL. 2 Favoring egalitarian, redistributionist, and welfare-state policies and also some civil liberties, an IDEOLOGY descended from classical liberalism, which opposed PRIVILEGE, but then taking on socialist (SOCIALISM) overtones as the unwarranted conclusion was reached that social problems derived from MARKETS rather than INTERVENTION.

In Europe, 'liberal' still means classical liberal, while in the USA, it has for the most part become liberal (2). US liberals tend to favor greater civil liberties than conservatives (CONSERVATIVISM), though not to a full extent, while favoring more intervention to treat the symptoms of poverty, unemployment, discrimination, and other economic and social maladies, policies which reduce liberty and are classically illiberal.

liberalism. LIBERAL (1, 2) DOCTRINE and philosophy.

liberalization. The reduction of INTERVENTIONS, such as price controls, on ENTERPRISE.

libertarianism. The ethical and political philosophy that VOLUNTARY *ACTS (1, 2) should be free of any legal restrictions or IMPOSED costs. Libertarians oppose INTERVENTIONS, including arbitrary taxation and any restriction on the activities of consenting adults. Libertarians are more radically and consistently pro-liberty than CLASSICAL LIBERALS, who might give way to some taxation and minimal intervention in order to provide security and the rule of law. In foreign policy, libertarians tend to be non-interventionist and do not support paying for the defense of other countries; some favor a strong military for domestic defense.

Libertarians are divided into several factions: i) those who espouse natural rights, versus utilitarians and pragmatists who reject natural law or NATURAL RIGHTS; ii) anarchists (ANARCHISM) versus minarchists (MINARCHISM); iii) GEO-LIBERTARIANS versus ALLODIAL libertarians; iv) supporters of political participation versus those who shun any politics or even voting; of those who favor political participation, there are those who favor libertarian political parties versus those who favor joining the major parties to influence them.

libertopia.   A libertarian (LIBERTARIANISM) version of UTOPIA.

liberty.   Political freedom, the absence of any restrictions or IMPOSED costs on acts which do not coercively HARM others and the presence of restraints and penalties on coercively harmful acts. The delineation of harm is determined by an ethic, and if liberty has a universal meaning, then it derives from a UNIVERSAL ETHIC.

license.   **1** An official document permitting one to do certain activities, such as practice a profession. Such licensing can be a BARRIER to entry, creating a PRIVILEGE. **2** Acts which violate the rights of others.

life.   Beings with internal, autonomous activity that they can change. The right to life is the right not to have life forcibly taken; that is, the right not to be murdered.

life-cycle hypothesis of consumption.   The hypothesis that people tend to plan CONSUMPTION over their expected lifetime, and so consumption is spread over that lifespan. Thus people BORROW when young, save (SAVINGS) in middle age, and then consume savings when old.

lifespan.   The expected length of a human life. This has profound economic applications, unappreciated for its being familiar. For example, TIME PREFERENCE would most likely differ if the human lifespan were multiplied by 10; time would be less valuable.

limited government.   Government confined to a few functions, such as national defense, courts, and foreign affairs, or government effectively constrained by a constitution. Some libertarians (LIBERTARIANISM) and CLASSICAL LIBERALS favor a limited government, while others regard proper governance as based on the consent of all the governed, thus whatever is voluntarily (VOLUNTARY) agreed to is consistent with LIBERTY.

limited liability.   Limiting the loss of a shareholder to his investment in the shares. The board of directors of a corporation of the general partners of a limited partnership do not have limited liability. Some FREE-MARKETEERS question the concept, alleging that it is a PRIVILEGE granted by the state. However, it can also be regarded as an extension of limited partnerships.

limited partnership. See PARTNERSHIP.

line item reduction. The ability of a government executive to reduce the expenditure of a BUDGET item. This greater authority than a veto can reduce government EXPENDITURES.

local government finance. A synonym of LOCAL PUBLIC FINANCE.

local public finance. The PUBLIC FINANCES of local governing agencies.

local public good. A good which is collective within some territorial (TER-RITORY) neighborhood, which can be as large as a metropolis. From the perspective of the greater ECONOMY, such as a country, the total amount of local COLLECTIVE GOODS is the sum of the COMMUNITY goods, hence they function as private goods, that is they are summable and separately consumable, with consumers revealing their preference by choosing a community. There is a MARKET among the goods, as the communities compete for residents and enterprise, as in the TIEBOUT MODEL. The theory of CLUBS applies to such local collective goods.

location. The geographical coordinates of a TERRITORY, often described in relationship to its neighbors. Location is said to be the key to REAL-ESTATE values, but it is actually location and timing.

location theory. The determination of geographic positioning or placing of economic ACTIVITY (1). Location theory intersects with the theory of RENT. The field was pioneered by von Thünnen in 1826.

Locke Institute. An educational and research organization based in Virginia, founded in 1989. Named after JOHN LOCKE, the Institute seeks to engender a greater understanding of natural rights and their implication for democracy and the ECONOMY. Its research includes rights theory, PUBLIC CHOICE, law and economics, and the new institutional economics.

Locke, John (1632–1705). A foremost CLASSICAL-LIBERAL *NATURAL-LAW philosopher, Locke highly influenced the American Revolution and the US Constitution. His *Two Treatises on Government* (1690, 1947), especially his 'Second Treatise of Civil Government,' had a major impact on the subsequent philosophy and theory of PROPERTY RIGHTS, GOVERNMENT, and NATURAL RIGHTS. Locke's political philosophy has been regarded also as a defense of the British 'Glorious Revolution' of 1688, which shifted power from the monarchy to parliament. Locke also wrote on economics (Vaughn, 1980). For a dictionary explaining Locke's terms, see Yolton (1993). See also PROVISO.

locked-in effect.   The effect of inhibiting sales of property or other economic activity because of having to pay TAXES. The taxation of realized gains locks in property ownership, while the taxation of gains even if unrealized does not lock in. Some investors may feel locked in also when the price of the asset falls, even though the unrealized loss is actual.

logic.   A relationship between two propositions A and B such that if A is true, then B must be true. The truth is intuitive. For example, if A is a subset of B, then if A exists, B must exist. Propositions A and B may each consist of sets of propositions; for example A might be a set of premises and B a set of conclusions. THEOREMS are warranted by logic and EVIDENCE.

logrolling.   Vote trading. Representative A offers to vote for B's program if B votes for A's. This is how SPECIAL INTERESTS are able to get a majority vote for their SUBSIDY. The term derives from logging, where logs are rolled down a mountain, one log bumping another and making it roll down too.

long cycle.   A BUSINESS CYCLE spanning several decades, such as the KONDRATIEFF, overlapping shorter trade cycles. The evidence for long cycles is considered to be inconclusive. See also REAL-ESTATE CYCLE.

long purchase.   The purchase of an ASSET prior to its sale, the usual practice, in contrast to the opposite, SHORT SALES.

long run.   The length of TIME (2) in which all resources are variable, or the time in which fundamentals take effect.

long run labor supply.   The labor SUPPLY curve is horizontal until all households seeking employment are employed, and then it becomes upward-sloping, and possibly vertical or backward-sloping at higher wages. At the horizontal level, it is possible to have UNEMPLOYMENT at market wages, since some of the labor force is unemployed at the same market wage that workers earn.

loose joint.   HAYEK'S term for the role of money, loosely tied to the real ECONOMY, rather than tightly as in CLASSICAL models or in a broken way as with DEMAND-SIDE theory.

Lorenz curve. A graph, devised by the US statistician Max Otto Lorenz in 1905, that measures INEQUALITY, with the vertical axis measuring cumulative income or wealth, and the horizontal axis measuring cumulative population, both starting at the lower left corner. Complete equality is a 45° degree line, and progressively more unequal distributions get ever closer to the axes. The GINI COEFFICIENT provides a numerical summary measure of the curve.

Lucas critique. A criticism made by LUCAS about the application of econometrics for policy. POLICY changes the parameters of the model, thus placing the previous results in question.

Lucas, Robert E. (1937–). American economist at Chicago University, he is a major NEW-CLASSICAL theorist. The Lucas supply function puts output as a function of errors in the EXPECTATION of the price level, based on RATIONAL EXPECTATIONS. See also the LUCAS CRITIQUE.

Ludwig von Mises Institute. A charitable and educational organization dedicated to scholarship and teaching in the Austrian school of economics (AUSTRIAN ECONOMICS). It is based in Auburn University, Alabama. In the tradition of LUDWIG VON MISES and MURRAY N. ROTHBARD, the institute opposes statism, welfarism, and central banking, and defends the FREE MARKET, private property, and sound money. The Institute hosts conferences and publishes books and periodicals, including *The Review of Austrian Economics*.

lump-sum tax. A fixed tax regardless of overall activity or ABILITY. As a one-time charge, the marginal tax rate is zero and the lump-sum tax preserves INCENTIVES or even stimulates them. This amounts to forced labor for those with only wage income. A LAND-VALUE TAX or COMMUNITY COLLECTION OF RENT is lump-sum for the period of the tax. If a periodic lump sum exceeds the market land rent paid by an enterprise, it taxes its returns to capital goods and labors, which has a disincentive effect.

luxury tax. Economically, a luxury is a good with an income ELASTICITY greater than one, hence when income rises, proportionally more is consumed. Politically, luxuries are goods bought only by the rich, such as yachts and expensive cars. Attempts to tax luxuries are often futile, since consumption is often shifted to other goods (including travel and purchase abroad) or the tax is evaded. Usually, poorer countries attempt to tax luxuries, especially as imports, but the USA also has attempted it, with poor results.

LVT. LAND-VALUE TAX.

LVTO. LAND-VALUE TAX OPTIONS.

Lycurgus.   Spartan lawgiver, perhaps legendary, of the 9th century BC. Some of the alleged SOCIALISM of the Lycurgian system may be a wishful reading by socialists into the Spartan past.

Lydia.   An ancient country in Asia Minor, now Turkey. Around 600 BC it originated COINS as money. Lydia was later conquered by Persia.

M

M.   Commonly an abbreviation for the MONEY SUPPLY or demand.

macroeconomics.   The branch of ECONOMICS that deals with theory and policy applying to an entire ECONOMY. Because of COMPETITION, rates of INTEREST are economy-wide. POLICY provides an economy with one currency, hence the money supply is macroeconomic. Aggregates such as national output or income and their fluctuations in BUSINESS CYCLES are key variables in macroeconomic analysis, and a key concept is the PRODUCTION FUNCTION for the entire economy, with output as a function of economy-wide inputs (usually labor, with other factors constant). Some concepts such as labor have both microeconomic and macroeconomic applications. Economy-wide UNEMPLOYMENT, for example, is a major macroeconomic topic. Some economists question some aspects of conventional macroeconomic theory, such as a macroeconomic production function.

Mercantilist (MERCANTILISM) and CLASSICAL theory were concerned with macroeconomic issues, such as the wealth of a nation and its growth. The PHYSIOCRATS originated a model of a national economy, and there were theories of cycles and other macroeconomic phenomena by KARL MARX, HENRY GEORGE, and others. JOHN MAYNARD KEYNES overturned classical SUPPLY-SIDE theory and established DEMAND-SIDE theory as the new orthodoxy. The tide turned again during the 1970s as concurrent inflation and high unemployment, along with rational-expectations theory and criticism by monetarists (MONETARISM), Austrians (AUSTRIAN ECONOMICS), and others, restored supply-side theory to the mainstream.

Macroeconomics for the past half century has been a tug-of-war between the 'classical' and the Keynesian, that is supply- versus demand-side theory, and textbooks typically present both sides of the argument. Austrian, GEO-ECONOMIC, and other approaches to macroeconomics provide alternatives to this debate, such as FREE BANKING as an alternative to both fixed-rule and discretionary monetary policy, and the public collection of rent (COMMUNITY COLLECTION OF RENT) as a remedy to the usual trade-off between efficiency and equity. For a view of Austrian macroeconomics, see Garrison (1978, 1984, 1997). See also GEO-ECONOMICS.

majority rule.   The most common voting system in which the candidate or proposal getting more than half the votes wins. The method is subject to the PARADOX OF VOTING and inconsistent results.

malinvestments.   A term used in AUSTRIAN ECONOMICS for INVESTMENTS that turn out to be unprofitable. In the Austrian BUSINESS CYCLE theory, this is due to artificially low INTEREST RATES in a policy of credit expansion, which induces too much investment in HIGHER-ORDER goods, distorting the structure of CAPITAL GOODS. GEO-ECONOMIC theory also posits locational malinvestments, as LAND SPECULATION holds land closer to city centers out of current use, making development move to lands further from the city as urban sprawl. The public collection of rent (COMMUNITY COLLECTION OF RENT) would reverse this by inducing infilling.

management.   The administration and control of an ENTERPRISE. A principal–agent problem arises when the managers are hired by the owners. One remedy for large CORPORATIONS is to make the top executives owners with stocks and options, but this then leads to enormous compensation. Managers have to possess people skills as well as competency over the operations of the enterprise.

managerial socialism.   The type of SOCIALISM in which the government plans and controls the ECONOMY, that is *DIRIGISME*, as distinct from socialist redistribution and the socialist concept of workers owning their CAPITAL GOODS.

Manchester School.   A 19th-century British group of manufacturers and politicians favoring *LAISSEZ-FAIRE* and FREE TRADE, so named by Disraeli.

manipulative policy.   Policy by the monetary authority which seeks to manipulate the MONEY SUPPLY to exploit (EXPLOITATION (1)) wage rigidities and lower real wages, to increase employment. See (Foldvary and Selgin, 1995).

margin.   **1** *ec.* The next unit of input used in production or a good in consumption. The marginal cost, for example, is the cost of one more unit. In the case of land, see MARGIN OF CULTIVATION. See also EXTENSIVE MARGIN OF PRODUCTION, INTENSIVE MARGIN, MARGIN OF PRODUCTION. 'At the margin' means the boundary between the last unit used and the next one to be used. **2** *Fin.* Revenue minus cost, as in a profit margin.

margin of cultivation.   The borderline where the least productive land is being cultivated. Worse lands are submarginal. In a model with just one crop, land at the margin is free and has no RENT, and so the whole produce goes to labor, either directly or as payments for CAPITAL GOODS. With many products, land at the margin of cultivation for a particular product is not free, but is priced according to the next best use, with a cascade of margins reaching to the one that is rent free. Land more productive than at the margin commands a rent. See DIFFERENTIAL RENT, LAW OF RENT, LAW OF WAGES.

margin of production. By extension from the MARGIN OF CULTIVATION, the EXTENSIVE MARGIN OF PRODUCTION is the least productive land in use for a particular product, worse lands being submarginal. The wage level is determined by the extensive margin of production.

marginal. 1 Extra, of one more unit. 2 Small and slight.

marginal analysis. Economic analysis using MARGINAL (1) rather than total quantities, since the MARGIN (1) determines the price. Profits or benefits are maximized at quantities where marginal cost equals marginal revenue. The price a consumer is willing to pay for a good depends on its marginal utility. A wage is equal to the marginal product of labor, and rent equals the marginal product of land. In economics, the tail wags the dog.

marginal-cost pricing. Setting the price of a good at its MARGINAL (1) cost, done by markets in ATOMISTIC COMPETITION, and advocated for regulated utilities and transportation by economists as EFFICIENT. For territorial services, the remaining expenses can be covered from the collection of the RENT generated by the services. However, as a price fixing for monopolist or oligopolist firms, the policy faces the problems of subjective costs, the issue of short and long-term marginal costs, problems in measuring marginal cost, and the question of intervention in general. William Vickers was a key analyst of marginal-cost pricing.

marginal product. The additional output obtained by using one more unit of an input or factor.

marginal propensity to consume. The percentage of extra income a typical person consumes. In KEYNESIAN ECONOMICS, the premise is that this percentage decreases with increasing income, resulting in crossed expenditure and income curves, upon which investment and government spending piggyback to determine output. However, studies show that in the long run, the percentage is constant, thus the curves do not cross and national income is not economically determined by the marginal propensity to save.

marginal propensity to save. One minus the MARGINAL PROPENSITY TO CONSUME.

marginal rate of tax. The tax rate on one more unit of the item taxed, such as income or wealth. For income taxes, it is also called the tax bracket.

marginal utility.   In NEOCLASSICAL ECONOMICS, the utility (UTILITY, MARGINAL) generated by obtaining one more unit of a good. In AUSTRIAN ECONOMICS, a good serves various ends, and marginal utility diminishes as a good is used for ever less important ends, such as water used for bathing after there is enough for drinking.

market.   EXCHANGE which is VOLUNTARY among the parties, within a certain context. A market is a PROCESS encompassing the totality of voluntary economic ACTS (2) within some context. Regarding third parties and EXTERNAL EFFECTS, markets can be free, skewed, or larcenous. See also FREE MARKET, LARCENOUS *SKEWED MARKET.

market clearing.   A PRICE of a good, determined by the market PROCESS, where there is neither a GLUT nor a SHORTAGE. Therefore, the market CLEARS (1) the good from inventory.

market distortion.   A skewed (SKEW) market, with WASTE and inefficiency, resources not being allocated to where people most want them.

market economy.   An ECONOMY in which most goods are produced via the MARKET PROCESS. Contemporary economies are market economies with INTERVENTION superimposed.

market enhancing.   Law and policy which make MARKETS work better, by delineating and protecting PROPERTY RIGHTS. The enforcement of laws prohibiting and punishing force and fraud are market-enhancing.

market ethics.   The ETHIC on which a MARKET is based, as it determines which ACTS (1) are market-compatible. Theft, for example, violates market ethics.

market failure.   The inability of the MARKET PROCESS to provide an OPTIMAL amount of goods. The proposition that the market for COLLECTIVE GOODS systematically fails due to FREE RIDERS is unwarranted, since in practice most civic goods are territorial, generating an economic rent that is always paid. For non-excludable goods, sympathy does in fact generate a benevolent (BENEVOLENCE) provision of goods, so the presumption of market failure begs the question of why sympathy would be lacking. See Foldvary (1994b). Many alleged market failures such as POLLUTION are actually due to interventions or the absence of enforced property rights.

market for legislation.   The POLITICAL process of seekers of PRIVILEGES, protections, and transfers (TRANSFER PAYMENTS) contributing funds to politicians and campaigns in an attempt to buy such favors. This is a political market for legislation, a PUBLIC-CHOICE concept.

market forces. Voluntary FORCES such as a change in tastes, plans, or ends, which shift SUPPLY and DEMAND, or else the reaction of market agents to data, such as a SURPLUS or SHORTAGE, altering their plans. For example, a surplus of a good at some price indicates to the seller that the price is higher than MARKET clearing (CLEAR). He lowers the price to move the inventory. Such changes in prices and quantities are changes in the MOMENTUM of these variables, hence forces of the MARKET PROCESS.

market hampering. Legislation and policy which intervenes (INTERVENTION) in the MARKET PROCESS, stopping activity or making it more costly. Income and sales taxes are market-hampering, for example.

market mechanism. The operation of MARKET FORCES. 'Mechanism' is a term Austrian economists (AUSTRIAN ECONOMICS) do not care for, since it implies that the MARKET is mechanical rather than being a human, all too human, PROCESS.

market power. The ABILITY of a firm to set a price for a PRODUCT (1), or to influence the DEMAND for the product.

market price. The PRICE of a good or factor as determined by SUPPLY and DEMAND. Given INTERVENTION, this is a skewed (SKEWED MARKET) or LARCENOUS market price rather than a FREE-MARKET price.

market process. Ideally, production, distribution, exchange, and consumption by VOLUNTARY means. CONSUMPTION is freely CHOSEN by individuals and families. ENTREPRENEURS are unhampered in deciding which PRODUCTS (1) and methods to engage in. Producers are free to supply goods of their choice, without any imposed costs. CONTRACTS govern the relationships between workers, tenants, owners, and customers. The governing agency pursues, tries, and penalizes those who transgress on the property of others, as well as providing services as determined by mutual agreement. Market processes occur over time; its study emphasizes change, uncertainty and knowledge.

market process analysis. An analytical framework used by the CENTER FOR MARKET PROCESSES emphasizing three aspects: INCENTIVES as affected by rules, KNOWLEDGE as it is discovered and affects markets, and VALUES as reflected in the market process and are affected by it.

market socialism.   **1** An economic SYSTEM in which enterprises are owned by the GOVERNMENT, but operate in a decentralized, competitive fashion. The separation of ownership and control, and the lack of capital and land markets still precludes efficient ECONOMIC CALCULATION. **2** A GEOCRACY if the COMMON ownership of RENT is considered socialist; here, rents are determined by the market process, since the possession of land is still individual. Geocratic market socialism, if so labeled, is EFFICIENT. **3** A market made up of worker-owned, worker-managed firms.

market structure.   The CONCENTRATION of firms in an INDUSTRY (2).

marketable discharge permits.   Permits to pollute, which have a fixed supply and are traded in exchanges. In some applications, firms are grandfathered, so they may continue to pollute without penalty. While the permits make new polluters pay a cost, the gains from increasing permit prices go to the seller rather than the victims of the pollution.

marketing.   Activities that promote the sale of goods, such as advertising (ADVERTISE) and packaging. ENTREPRENEURS innovate with better marketing as well as with new PRODUCTS (1).

marketing boards.   Government bureaus that purchase goods from producers, usually farmers, and sell them in international markets. In some less-developed countries, farmers are paid less than the MARKET PRICE, a TAX that creates a disincentive to produce. In other cases, the boards subsidize (SUBSIDY) farming, imposing costs on the taxpayers while skewing (SKEW) the market.

marketization.   The creation and enforcement of the legal preconditions of RULES and RIGHTS of the MARKET, and the transfer of enterprise from government controls to the market process.

Markowitz, Harry (1927–).   American economist, sharing the 1990 Nobel prize with M. Miller and W.F. Sharpe. He helped develop modern portfolio theory, showing how the optimal investment choice balances the expected return with the variance of a portfolio. See also EFFICIENT PORTFOLIO.

marriage penalty.   A tax rate on the income of married people which is higher than the tax rate on single people for the same income. In the USA, the penalty can be substantial if both spouses have a significant income. The opposite is a 'marriage allowance.'

Marx, Karl (1818–83). One of the foremost anti-market theorists, he was a German philosopher and economist who settled in Great Britain. Though he derived his basic ideas from CLASSICAL ECONOMICS, Marx conflated LAND with CAPITAL GOODS, and thus misidentified capital as producing a SURPLUS VALUE. Marx's triumph was in propaganda, including the adoption of the term 'CAPITALISM' by both his followers and his critics.

Marxism, nondeterminist. Also called 'postmodern Marxism,' this branch of Marxism does not reduce prices to labor inputs, but sees them as simultaneously causing one another, which the adherents claim is not vulnerable to BÖHM-BAWERK's critique of Marx. See Amariglio *et al.* (1996).

Marxist economics. A now diverse school of economic thought based on the thought of MARX, retaining key concepts such as CLASS (2) struggle and the EXPLOITATION (2) of labor.

mass democracy. Voting by groups so large that the typical voter has no personal knowledge of the candidate and little personal ACCESS to his representative. To win elections, candidates need publicity in the media, and to pay for it, they receive funds from SPECIAL INTERESTS, who then expect favors in return. TRANSFER-SEEKING is thus an endemic disease of mass democracy no matter what the voting method. See also COMMUNITARIAN DEMOCRACY.

matter. One of the rudiments of the universe, along with TIME and SPACE, matter consisting of mass and energy. In economics, matter manifests itself as LABOR, tangible CAPITAL GOODS, and material types of LAND. Some capital goods such as KNOWLEDGE are intangible and not strictly matter, but consist of MENTAL CONSTRUCTS, or SOCIAL programming (PROGRAM (2)).

means of production. The FACTORS OF PRODUCTION.

measurement. The determination of the extent of an item, which with a complex item such as an index also involves making distinctions regarding inclusion and weighing among the subcategories.

median voter. A voter at the center of a political spectrum for a particular issue. The concept originated with Duncan Black, Scottish economist, in 1942.

median voter theorem. In an election, candidates seeking to win will tend to claim to represent the views of the MEDIAN VOTER. There are exceptions where IDEOLOGY is important to a candidate. Where there are two dominant political parties, as in the USA, the parties' positions on issues will often tend to converge to the median.

mediation.   A resolution of a dispute by a neutral third party, which the parties may accept or reject.

medium of exchange.   A COMMODITY or MENTAL CONSTRUCT with standard units, which is readily accepted in exchange for goods, and is therefore MONEY.

meme.   An idea, which like biological genes, propagates across the generations.

Menger, Carl (1840–1921).   Founder of the Austrian school of economics (AUSTRIAN ECONOMICS) and one of the pioneers of MARGINAL-UTILITY and SUBJECTIVE-VALUE theory. He became a professor at the University of Vienna in 1879. His landmark book *Principles of Economics* (1871, 1976) established the main themes of Austrian theory, including deductive-theory methodology (DEDUCTIVE METHOD). Menger originated the theory of price imputation (IMPUTATION OF VALUE), that FACTORS derive their value from the value of CONSUMER GOODS, rather than the classical doctrine that goods derive value from the costs of production. His theory of EXCHANGE is based on GAINS FROM TRADE due to the greater marginal utility of the goods of others. Menger engaged in a famous methodological debate with the German historicists (HISTORICISM), initiating the tradition of Austrian economists debating with other schools such as Marxists (MARXIST ECONOMICS), Keynesians (KEYNESIAN ECONOMICS), and determinist neoclassicals (NEOCLASSICAL ECONOMICS).

mental construct.   A concept created by one's mind, in contrast to a CONCRETE EXISTENT. INSTITUTIONS and CULTURE are shared mental constructs. For example, GOVERNMENT, the DOLLAR, and a police officer are mental constructs.

menu costs.   The COST of changing prices, as with a restaurant menu. It is one of the costs of an inflationary policy (INFLATION).

mercantilism.   The economic system as well as thought from the 1500s through the 1700s, the most famous doctrine being that of having a trade SURPLUS in order to import precious metals. Mercantilism is a DEMAND-SIDE policy, with government control over the ECONOMY, on the premise that economic interests diverge from those of the country's leaders. The colonial policy associated with mercantilism restricted the economies of the colonies, which were to provide raw materials. The mercantilist doctrine was undermined by HUME, who showed that bullion imports raised the PRICE LEVEL and restored a BALANCE OF TRADE, by the PHYSIOCRATS who opposed intervention, and by ADAM SMITH's *WEALTH OF NATIONS* (1776, 1976). The American Revolution was to a large degree a rebellion against mercantilist policy. Mercantilism lives on in demand-side policy as well as the terminology and viewpoint of a 'favorable' balance of trade consisting of an export surplus.

merit goods and bads. The notion that certain GOODS are intrinsically socially desirable or, for bads, undesirable. Unless the criterion is an objective universal ethic, the criterion for merit goods is ARBITRARY and implies that individuals cannot best judge their own welfare, or that the culture of the majority is to dominate by sheer force. Such notions are contrary to the principle of SUBJECTIVE VALUES and to CONSUMER SOVEREIGNTY.

Merton, Robert. See MYRON SCHOLES.

methodological individualism. Placing the individual PERSON at the FOUNDATION of economic theory. The rationale is that all action is individual. A person is influenced by and socially dependent on others, but people's minds are distinct and independent. A person's SUBJECTIVE VALUES are the basis for all HUMAN ACTION and thus of economics. In contrast, holism posits an independent status for society or culture. Culture does have its own existence, but it is a result of an evolutionary process in which each contribution was individual. See METHODOLOGY.

methodology. An approach and method of deriving THEORY. Methods include i) axiomatic deduction (AXIOMATIC DEDUCTIVE), using deduction to derive propositions, ii) INDUCTION, iii) HYPOTHESIS testing. Axiomatic deduction is used to derive pure theory, universal to the field. Specific theory, regarding particular phenomena dependent on time, place, circumstance, and culture, are observed and examined with hypothesis testing. Various methodological alternatives include METHODOLOGICAL INDIVIDUALISM versus holism, ENVALUED versus non-valued, FOUNDATIONAL versus anti-foundational, and mathematical versus verbal. FREE-MARKET thought usually rejects holism and uses METHODOLOGICAL INDIVIDUALISM. Austrian (AUSTRIAN ECONOMICS) and GEO-ECONOMICS are both FOUNDATIONAL, the former being non-valued and the latter envalued. See Boettke (1996) for a critique of neoclassical methodology (NEOCLASSICAL ECONOMICS).

MFN. MOST FAVORED NATION.

microeconomics. The branch of economics dealing with the units of an ECONOMY, such as consumers, workers, firms, and government, rather than aggregates. The field also deals with the interaction of the units, as with market structures with various types of competition and GENERAL EQUILIBRIUM. INTERNATIONAL TRADE is often included in a microeconomics course, the units in this case being countries in a global economy. Much of the field consists of price theory, using partial EQUILIBRIUM analysis. AUSTRIAN ECONOMICS has an alternative microeconomic theory, such as a different theory of utility (UTILITY, MARGINAL) and an emphasis on PROCESS and DISEQUILIBRIUM, as well as a different approach to WELFARE ECONOMICS. Some economic concepts such as the FACTORS OF PRODUCTION are neither exclusively microeconomic nor macroeconomic, but what could be called 'mezoeconomic,' having aspects of both.

microfoundations.   The proposition that MACROECONOMICS has a FOUNDATION in MICROECONOMICS, that is in the ACTIONS of individuals and FIRMS.

militarization ratio.   The number of full-time military per 1000 population.

milker bills.   New or increased TAXES or REGULATIONS introduced in a legislature to 'milk' the potential tax victims. The subjects are expected to contribute funds in order to prevent the milking, at which point the legislation is withdrawn.

Mill, John Stuart (1806–73).   British philosopher and CLASSICAL economist. Mill expanded the theory of INTERNATIONAL TRADE with the concept of RECIPROCAL DEMAND, which determined the terms of trade. His treatise, *Principles of Political Economy* (1848), was the standard economics text until the end of the 19th century. In his essay 'On Liberty', a classic of LIBERAL (1) ethical philosophy, Mill expressed the free-society prescription that law should only prohibit HARM to others, and leave all other action unrestricted. Yet in economic policy, Mill thought that there was a role for government in providing EDUCATION and programs to further social welfare, which from a FREE-MARKET viewpoint is a result of not delving deeply enough into the root causes of the problems for which J.S. Mill sought the treatment of the effects.

minarchism.   The political philosophy and theory of MINARCHY.

minarchy.   A GOVERNMENT limited to the defense of the country and of the persons and property within the country against invasions (for example force, theft, and fraud) and the provision of a court system for the ultimate resolution of disputes. Some minarchists would add a few COLLECTIVE GOODS. The government is still IMPOSED, disallowing at-will SECESSION. *Syn.* minimal government, limited government, nightwatchman state. (See Burris, 1983, pp. 394–5.) If at-will secession is permitted, then the system is anarchist (ANARCHISM).

mind. That which consciously thinks, feels, wills, and perceives, and causes the body to act as a result. A brain is the biological tissue whose functioning produces a mind. METHODOLOGICAL INDIVIDUALISM presumes that minds are independent.

minimal government. MINARCHY.

minimum wage. A legislated WAGE, below which employers may not pay. While some workers receive a higher wage due to this floor, others become unemployed because the cost of labor becomes too high. If policy makers truly wish to increase the income and employment of the poor and least skilled, the effective remedy is to deregulate and untax labor and enterprise, increasing the DEMAND for all labor. The minimum wage is thus a prime example of an INTERVENTION to treat the problems caused by other interventions.

Mises, Ludwig von (1881–1973). A great economist of the Austrian school (AUSTRIAN ECONOMICS) as well as a major contributor to economic THEORY and METHODOLOGY. He taught in Vienna, Geneva, and New York University, his seminars having influenced key economists such as HAYEK and ROTHBARD. His *Theory of Money and Credit* (1924, 1980) is a major work in theory of money, interest, and banking. In *Socialism* (1922, 1937), he showed how efficient economic calculation was not possible under a command socialist ECONOMY. *HUMAN ACTION* (1949, 1966) was his grand treatise of economics, based on PRAXEOLOGY, using the Austrian subjectivist, deductive, marginalist methodology. He wrote many other works on methodology, theory, and applications to policy. The LUDWIG VON MISES INSTITUTE provides a base for Misesian thought.

Misesian. Regarding the work and thought of LUDWIG VON MISES.

mixed economy. A SKEWED MARKET *ECONOMY with government controls as well as government enterprises. All contemporary economies are a mixture of markets, INTERVENTION, and government production. A key work is Littlechild (1978).

mixed goods. CLUB GOODS, also called 'impure public goods,' so designated because they are EXCLUDABLE, according to a definition of COLLECTIVE GOODS by which they are non-excludable, though this does not follow the landmark Samuelson (1954) definition. The term is also applied to collective goods which become crowded, so that another user reduces the benefits enjoyed by others. If collective goods are defined as CHARACTERISTICS of physical goods, then the 'mixed' nature disappears, since some characteristics remain collective and others do not. If 'mixed goods' refers to the characteristics of physical goods, then almost all goods are mixed, that is they have severable (SEVERABLE GOODS) and COLLECTIVE characteristics.

model. A scientific model is a set of concepts and propositions which demonstrate the main features of the PHENOMENON or THEORY being analyzed.

modern portfolio theory. See EFFICIENT PORTFOLIO.

Molinari, Gustave de (1819–1912). A Belgian, editor of *Journal des Economistes*, and perhaps the first anarcho-capitalist. His book *The Society of Tomorrow* (1904, 1972) is a visionary program for peace, liberty, and prosperity. He advocated a non-monopolistic legal system.

momentum. Physically, mass times velocity, thus economically, the movement of a price or quantity or other variable. With zero velocity, a price does not move, while with a constant velocity, a price is moving at a constant rate either up or down. The EVENLY ROTATING ECONOMY, an Austrian (AUSTRIAN ECONOMICS) model developed by LUDWIG VON MISES, economic activity repeats at a constant rate, and thus has an EQUILIBRIUM of constant momentum. Equilibrium exists when a set of variables are in constant momentum, even when the velocity is non-zero.

moneta abatuda. *Lat.* MONEY diminished in value.

monetarism. A school of economic thought that espouses the QUANTITY THEORY OF MONEY, the term 'monetarist' introduced by Karl Brunner in 1968. The school argues that instability in the money supply is the main cause of instability of output. MILTON FRIEDMAN has been central in the rise of the monetarist school.

Monetarism has challenged Keynesian (KEYNES) doctrines, but in many respects it differs more in degree than in substance from it. Monetarists advocate a fixed monetary rule (increase in the MONEY SUPPLY) and Keynesians advocate a flexible DISCRETIONARY POLICY, while many Austrians (AUSTRIAN ECONOMICS) argue that the paradigm of central banking (CENTRAL BANK) is DYSFUNCTIONAL altogether.

monetary. In connection with MONEY SUPPLY and the BANKING system. The 'monetary authority' is usually the CENTRAL BANK.

monetary base. See BASE MONEY.

monetary inflation. An increase in the MONEY SUPPLY greater than warranted by the DEMAND FOR MONEY. This normally results in PRICE INFLATION.

monetary policy. Control over the rate of expansion of the MONETARY BASE, INTEREST RATES for FUNDS lent to BANKS, required bank RESERVES, and other variables that determine the MONEY SUPPLY, and thus, at least in the short run, interest rates. These variables, especially the money supply, are manipulated to achieve ends such as stability, growth, the exchange rate, and inflation, not always all compatible. With a completely FREE MARKET in money and banking, there is no monetary policy other than letting the MARKET PROCESS operate.

monetization of debt. The purchase of DEBT by the CENTRAL BANK, increasing the MONEY SUPPLY.

money. A MEDIUM OF EXCHANGE and the final means of payment. It can be a COMMODITY, such as gold, or a MENTAL CONSTRUCT, such as FIAT MONEY. A desirable quality of money is that it should be a store of value, maintaining its purchasing power, but, contrary to some textbooks, this is not part of the definition of money. Money has a UNIT OF ACCOUNT, the unit in which it is counted, such as the dollar, but this is not part of its definition, but an implication of its being a medium of exchange. PURCHASING MEDIA include both money and MONEY SUBSTITUTES; true money includes only the final means of payment. The dynamic money supply includes both the quantity of money and its VELOCITY, that is the money supply times the velocity. (See the EQUATION OF EXCHANGE.) The DEMAND FOR MONEY is the quantity that people wish to hold at some price level, usually for TRANSACTIONS.

The purchasing power of money is based on its historical value, in accord with the regression theorem of LUDWIG VON MISES. As in the scenario by CARL MENGER (1871, 1976), money evolved from readily exchangeable commodities, and then became usurped by governments as a MONOPOLY, and now is fiat. The tendency has been for money to become increasingly etherialized (ETHERIALIZATION OF MONEY), going from a physical commodity to a paper symbol to electronic accounts and transactions. See also INSIDE MONEY, MONEY SUPPLY, OUTSIDE MONEY.

money and banking. The branch of macroeconomics dealing with an ECONOMY-wide MONEY SUPPLY and BANKING system, both in monetary theory and in the actual INSTITUTIONS and economic history (HISTORY OF ECONOMIC THOUGHT).

money market.   The market for short-term, liquid loans. Money-market accounts usually provide checks, but with restrictions.

money substitute.   An item, usually a BANKNOTE, which is used as a SUBSTITUTE for true MONEY, for convenience, such as the use of banknotes convertible into gold COINS. It is readily accepted as money, thus travellers' checks are quasi-money substitutes.

money supply.   The quantity of MONEY and MONEY SUBSTITUTES in an ECONOMY. With FREE BANKING, the supply consists of the monetary base (OUTSIDE MONEY or true money) plus BANKNOTES and deposits (inside money, or money substitutes.) With the current FIAT MONEY, there are various measurements of the money supply, with labels such as M1, M2, M3, MZM, and so on, for ever broader measurements. The broader the money supply, the slower the VELOCITY, hence MV is not affected by the measurement. See also DIVISIA MONEY INDEX.

monopolistic.   Regarding a FIRM's *ABILITY to set the PRICE of its PRODUCT (1).

monopolistic competition.   The MARKET STRUCTURE in which there are many firms in an INDUSTRY (2) with differentiated PRODUCTS (1), such as having different brand names or minor variations in ingredients and quality. This is monopolistic in that a firm has some control over the price – a price maker rather than price taker. Firms compete with advertising (ADVERTISE) as well as with quality and price. Critics argue that this market structure is wasteful, but advertising conveys information and reputation, and many consumers value the variety.

monopoly.   1 ABSOLUTE MONOPOLY. 2 ENTRY MONOPOLY.

monopoly capitalism.   A derogatory term for contemporary economic systems, the monopoly being an ENTRY MONOPOLY for land or a high CONCENTRATION of industry or wealth in a few firms or owners.

monopoly profit.   The ECONOMIC PROFIT obtained by a MONOPOLY of either type. The profit is due to barriers to entry, and can be taxed without affecting the quantity of the output if it is a LUMP-SUM TAX rather than based on output.

monopossession.   A distribution in which one unit owns the entire amount, the others owning nothing. See INEQUALITY.

monopsony.   A market in which there is one buyer, whether of goods or of a resource such as labor.

Mont Pelerin Society.   One of the foremost group of CLASSICAL-LIBERAL scholars and leaders in business and government, with about 500 members, founded in 1947 by LIBERALS (1) who met at Mont Pelerin in Switzerland. They sought to reassert the ideas of PRIVATE ENTERPRISE and CIVIL LIBERTIES. The original members included HAYEK, Popper, Polanyi, Robbins, and VON MISES. FRIEDMAN and STIGLER joined later.

moral.   1 Referring to an ACT done by a PERSON, that is the rightness (good), wrongness (evil), or neutrality of an act done by a person. 2 Morally GOOD.

moral hazard.   The tendency of insured persons to take more RISKS or use more the service, raising the cost for others, an example of INSTITUTIONAL FAILURE. Increasing the user's co-payments reduces this hazard, as does obtaining more information on the user.

morality.   The assignment of MORAL (1) values to ACTS (1) by an ETHIC.

morally criminal.   Committing MORAL (1) EVIL. Using the moral standard of NATURAL LAW, a morally criminal ACT is one that coercively HARMS others. Morally criminal acts thus violate the ethical basis of a FREE MARKET.

morally good.   See GOOD, MORALLY.

Moses.   The leader of the Israelites who took them on an Exodus from slavery in Egypt. He also is said to have brought the TEN COMMANDMENTS to the Israelites. According to Chandler (1986), Moses's influence ranged far beyond the Middle East, Moses being instrumental in spreading the concept of democracy and the ideal of peace to the world. Religious conservatives who seek to implement restrictive laws based on Mosaic Biblical prescriptions miss the point that these rules were a Covenant voluntarily adopted by the Israelites; those not party to the covenant are not bound by them.

most favored nation.   Countries whose imports have the lowest TARIFFS, aside from trading blocs and special cases. A most favored nation clause in trade agreements requires each party to extend tariff reductions to all countries having MFN status.

multilateral governance.   GOVERNANCE that is a mutual agreement among the parties, rather than unilaterally IMPOSED.

multinational corporation.   A CORPORATION with operations and subsidiaries in several countries.

multiplier.   The effect of increasing the final amount of a good or of output by a multiple of the initial input. For example, a money or credit multiplier expands an increase in BASE MONEY into a much larger money supply. A new factory employing 100 workers will induce enterprises to serve them. However, the Keynesian income multiplier based on the MARGINAL PROPENSITY TO CONSUME is a mathematical manipulation that only applies economically when idle resources are stuck, if at all, since if all income not consumed is invested, the marginal propensity to save is irrelevant.

municipality.   An incorporated town or city.

mutual fund.   A COMPANY which owns shares of other companies and does not directly engage in PRODUCTION. Owners of shares of the mutual fund are thus able to diversify (DIVERSIFICATION) their INVESTMENTS and ASSETS.

MZM.   A measure of the MONEY SUPPLY, equal to M2 plus institutional money-market funds minus small time deposits.

N

NAFTA. North American Free Trade Agreement.

national debt. The DEBT of the central government, such as the US federal government. Besides the official debt, manifested in government BONDS, there are unfunded LIABILITIES not usually included in the government budget. Both are liabilities of the taxpayers. See also BUDGET. National debts are built up especially during war, and more recently, because of a lack of constitutional and cultural/ethical restraints on spending, since spending generates votes and taxing is unpopular.

national income. An official measure of the income (or output) of a country, such as GROSS DOMESTIC PRODUCT. Critics say that much economic activity, such as HOME PRODUCTION, is not included, and that the consumption of environmental capital is also not accounted for.

nationalization. The EXPROPRIATION of the firms in an INDUSTRY (2) by a government, making government the owner. Recently the tendency is the reverse, to privatize (PRIVATIZATION). Nevertheless, in many countries, CONFISCATION remains a risk.

natural. 1 Referring to everything that is prior to HUMAN ACTION. 2 Society and an ECONOMY without government INTERVENTION. 3 PRODUCTS (1) produced without chemical treatments. See also NATURAL LAW, NATURAL MORAL LAW, NATURAL OPPORTUNITY, NATURAL RIGHT.

natural law. Propositions UNIVERSAL to a subject matter. In science, natural law consists of theory describing and explaining REGULARITIES. In ETHICS, NATURAL MORAL LAW consists of propositions applying universally to all humanity, thus independent of cultural or personal views.

natural law rent. See NATURAL RENT.

natural monopoly. A PRODUCT (1) whose production involves a large fixed cost and a small MARGINAL (1) cost, with no close SUBSTITUTES, for which a duplication of the fixed cost would not be profitable. Technology has reduced the scope of territorial monopolies, such as telephone service, if it ever was

NATURAL (2). COMPETITION can be achieved in many cases by having competitors supply the service over the same INFRASTRUCTURE. Other market remedies include bidding for the franchise and the horizontal integration of utilities into privately organized COMMUNITIES, providing competition among communities.

natural moral law.   PROPOSITIONS about ETHICS which have UNIVERSAL application and are logically derived from EMPIRICAL premises about human NATURE, hence NATURAL (1). Their formulation into moral rules is the UNIVERSAL ETHIC. It is often referred to more briefly as 'natural law' or, as JOHN LOCKE called it, the 'law of nature.'

natural opportunity.   An unhampered OPPORTUNITY provided by NATURE or NATURAL RESOURCES. Geo-economists (GEO-ECONOMICS) include equal access to LAND, made possible by the equalization of the BENEFITS as manifested by RENT.

natural rate of interest.   A concept used by KNUT WICKSELL, essentially the rate of INTEREST that would exist if there were a pure FREE MARKET, due to TIME PREFERENCE. The actual MARKET rate of interest may be a skewed (SKEW) rate affected by the rate of money issuing by a CENTRAL BANK, along with other INTERVENTIONS. More narrowly, the market rate can be compared to the quasi-natural rate that would exist if the MONEY SUPPLY matched the money DEMAND.

natural rate of unemployment.   1 The level of UNEMPLOYMENT consistent with a lack of price inflation or with an absence of wage increases, as related to the PHILLIPS CURVE. This rate cannot be increased in the long run just by increasing AGGREGATE DEMAND. 2 The amount of unemployment that would occur in a pure market ECONOMY, that is only FRICTIONAL UNEMPLOYMENT. 3 The level of unemployment that would be the hypothetical outcome of Walrasian GENERAL EQUILIBRIUM (MILTON FRIEDMAN).

natural rent.   The RENT of ECONOMIC LAND due to value provided by NATURE rather than human-made IMPROVEMENTS.

natural resources.   LAND.

natural right.   A MORAL (1) RIGHT, the correlative of a moral wrong. Given a UNIVERSAL ETHIC as the formulation of NATURAL MORAL LAW, since the one moral wrong is COERCIVE *HARM to others, there is one basic natural right, the right to be free of coercive harm, which also endows a person with the right to do whatever is not coercively harmful. The right is NATURAL (1) because the moral law derives from human nature. A society which has LIBERTY is one in which people may legally freely exercise their natural rights.

nature. Everything that is NATURAL (1); that is, everything prior to being altered by HUMAN ACTION.

naturism. The philosophy of living in harmony with NATURE, which in its widest sense includes living in accord with NATURAL MORAL LAW, avoiding harming one's body with toxic substances, accepting the natural body's appearance as wholesome, and having respect and appreciation of the natural ENVIRONMENT.

needs. Goods considered a necessity, with an income ELASTICITY of demand of less than unity, so that as income rises, its consumption does not rise proportionately. The term also refers to merit goods (MERIT GOODS AND BADS).

negative rights. See PROTECTIVE RIGHTS.

neighborhood effects. See EXTERNAL EFFECTS.

neo-Austrian. As indicated by ISRAEL KIRZNER (1987), the post-1970 revival of the ideas of the early Austrian school (AUSTRIAN ECONOMICS), especially the work of MISES and HAYEK, emphasizing MARKET PROCESS rather than EQUILIBRIUM analysis. The 'neo' indicates the modern time frame rather than any substantial difference in theory from the early Austrians.

neoclassical economics. Also spelt neo-classical. The contemporary mainstream of economic theory, probably coined by Veblen. The school has several aspects. First, the neoclassical revolution of the latter 1800s replaced cost of production and LABOR THEORIES OF VALUE with SUBJECTIVE VALUES and MARGINAL analysis, MENGER, WALRAS, and Jevons being the main pioneers. Second, neoclassical theory merged LAND with CAPITAL GOODS, making it a two-factor school, in contrast to the classical three-factor analysis. Third, the formalist revolution (FORMAL ANALYSIS) of the mid 1900s brought determinist partial and GENERAL EQUILIBRIUM mathematical modeling into the mainstream. See Boettke (1996) and Gaffney (1994) for critical views of the development of neoclassical theory.

The Austrian school (AUSTRIAN ECONOMICS) is neoclassical in the first sense, is split in the second, but is not neoclassical in the third. For the most part, 'neoclassical' theory includes all three aspects. Some schools of thought with a more focused domain of study use neoclassical analysis or combine it with other methods (for example the Virginia School, which uses neoclassical as well as Austrian theory), while others, such as the Marxists (KARL MARX), institutionalists (INSTITUTIONAL ECONOMICS), and post-Keynesians, fundamentally reject the theory and approach. Keynes's macroeconomics did not at first have neoclassical microeconomic foundations, but the NEOCLASSICAL SYNTHESIS integrated it into the neoclassical paradigm.

neoclassical synthesis.   The merging of Keynesian DEMAND-SIDE macroeconomics with neoclassical (NEOCLASSICAL ECONOMICS) utility-maximizing theory. Don Patinkin in the 1940s was instrumental in this synthesis, saying that UNEMPLOYMENT is a DISEQUILIBRIUM phenomenon. Unlike Keynes's assertion of presenting a general theory with CLASSICAL theory a special case, the synthesis reverses the relationship.

net domestic product.   GROSS DOMESTIC PRODUCT minus DEPRECIATION (1).

net investment.   INVESTMENT (1) net of DEPRECIATION (1).

net profits.   PROFITS less DEPRECIATION (1) and TAXES.

neutral tax.   No TAX is completely neutral in having no effect on the behavior of persons. However, taxes on fixed NATURAL RESOURCES have the least EXCESS BURDEN. The more ELASTIC the supply of a resource, the less neutral the tax. A tax can also be neutral among different classes of the targeted source, such as an income tax treating all income alike, rather than, say, having a MARRIAGE PENALTY.

new classical.   A school of MACROECONOMICS, not really CLASSICAL in the 'classical–classical' sense, but SUPPLY-SIDE neoclassical (NEOCLASSICAL ECONOMICS). It uses RATIONAL EXPECTATIONS theory and the premise of flexible prices to demonstrate the futility of expected DEMAND-SIDE policy, especially an attempt to reduce UNEMPLOYMENT with monetary expansion. The school argues that the AGGREGATE SUPPLY curve is always vertical, so that changes in aggregate demand only change the PRICE LEVEL even in the short run. In contrast, monetarists (MONETARISM) and Austrians (AUSTRIAN ECONOMICS) believe that demand policy can have effects in the short run, often with adverse long-term CONSEQUENCES.

new Keynesian.   A branch of the Keynesian school of macroeconomics (KEYNESIAN ECONOMICS) which embraces RATIONAL EXPECTATIONS theory and argues that macroeconomic variables such as wages can nevertheless be stuck, because of long-term fixed-wage labor contracts. However, if expectations are rational, then long-term fixed-wage contracts would only exist if the monetary authority did not pursue a demand-side manipulative monetary policy (Foldvary and Selgin, 1995).

New Right. Advocates of PRIVATIZATION and less INTERVENTION, who became influential during the 1980s in the USA and Western Europe.

Ninth Amendment. This amendment in the US Constitution recognizes RIGHTS even if not enumerated in the Constitution. These would be NATURAL or COMMON-LAW rights, which would protect liberties and lead to a FREE MARKET if recognized as such by the legal community and the courts. The constitution of the Commonwealth of Virginia has a similar clause.

Nock, Albert Jay (1870–1945). GEO-LIBERTARIAN author of *Our Enemy the State* (1935), influenced by Franz OPPENHEIMER's *The State* (1914, 1975). Both distinguished between the ECONOMIC MEANS and the POLITICAL MEANS.

nominal. In name, or as set in the numbers rather than in economic reality. Nominal income over the years is income in current prices, rather than purchasing power adjusted for inflation, and nominal interest rates are the quoted rates rather than the REAL (3) returns after subtracting inflation.

non-excludable. Of a COLLECTIVE GOOD, the inability to exclude persons from using it or being impacted by it once provided. See also COLLECTIVE GOODS, EXCLUDABLE.

non-rival consumption. A feature of COLLECTIVE GOODS, where each person uses the entire good, and so there is no RIVALRY among the users. Some CHARACTERISTICS of a collective good can be non-rival while others of the same physical good are rival, so no conclusion can be drawn regarding the pricing or provision of a good just from non-rivalness. Also, the use of a TERRITORIAL GOOD can be non-rival while the occupation of space to access the good is rival. See also CONGESTION.

non-tariff barriers. Trade BARRIERS such as quality regulations, inspections, and quotas.

non-valued science. Science whose METHODOLOGY excludes ethical values. Whether social science, such as economics, can be 'value-free' is debated. The interests of the scholar influence his choice of topics, at the least. Some economic topics are non-valued, but others, such as policy, may be unavoidably ENVALUED.

non-wage labor costs.   The overheads associated with hiring employees, fringe benefits, plus costs imposed by government such as social security, unemployment, and disability taxes as well as the costs induced by government policy such as litigation.

nondeterminist.   Theory not having any determined result, unlike neoclassical (NEOCLASSICAL ECONOMICS) or orthodox Marxist theory.

nonmoral.   Lacking morality. Physical and biological science are nonmoral, but economics is MORAL (1), since its behavioral concepts implicitly recognize moral rules, for example consumer BEHAVIOR rather than misbehavior, the choice being between paying for A or B, rather than stealing both.

nonprofit organizations.   Organizations whose intention is to serve their members, the public, or charitable purposes. If not subsidized, these are part of the MARKET PROCESS. See CHARITY.

normal.   **1** Typical, hence not extraordinary. **2** A type of bell-shaped frequency distribution commonly used in regressions. **3** A good whose DEMAND is positively related to income, for example rising with increasing income.

normal profits.   Revenues that just cover all costs, including implicit costs, hence ACCOUNTING PROFITS but not ECONOMIC PROFITS.

normative economics.   Theory passing moral judgment on phenomena (PHENOMENON), or proposing ideal situations, or evaluating how an ECONOMY or POLICY should be.

North American Free Trade Agreement.   An agreement between several countries of the Americas (currently Canada, the USA, and Mexico) to eliminate TARIFFS on most trade as well as liberalize capital transactions. The agreement contains many complexities, hence it is a movement towards more FREE TRADE rather than establishing true free trade. Some free-marketeers think the net result is less freedom of trade or loss of US sovereignty.

notional demand.   The desire for a GOOD, whether or not one has the resources with which to obtain them.

Nozick, Robert (1938–).   American philosopher known for his *Anarchy, State and Utopia* (1974) in which he presented a scenario of the development of a minimal state (MINARCHY) arising from anarchist (ANARCHISM) protection agencies.

NSPIC.   Neuro-Semantic Political Illusion Complex. These are words, meta-phors, and expressions which help maintain COERCIVE institutions by setting a linguistic AGENDA.

nudity.   Being without any significant clothing. Nude or naturist (NATURISM) clubs and resorts are an example of an activity which is in most places legally not permitted, yet can be practiced in a PRIVATE COMMUNITY.

nulle terre sans seigneur.   *Fr.* No LAND without a lord. If land is within human control, someone effectively owns it.

O

objective. Independent of persons' values, beliefs, and CULTURE.

Objectivism. The philosophy and movement founded by AYN RAND, which regards life as the standard of value, and derives an OBJECTIVE ethic. Its key prescription is that it is wrong to initiate force. While FREE-MARKET oriented, many Objectivists do not favor LIBERTARIANISM.

obligation. A debt, duty, promise, it being morally or legally wrong if one does not do it.

obligational rights. MORAL (1) RIGHTS to goods which others are morally obligated (OBLIGATION) to provide to the recipient. Parents, for example, have obligational rights to care for their CHILDREN. In contrast, TAKINGS RIGHTS are legal rights to takings not morally warranted (WARRANT).

occupational licensing. A restriction on practicing a craft or profession unless one obtains a certificate, usually after passing some requirement. Once government has the power to license, it can be used by the INDUSTRY (2) to limit entry, and licensing also violates consumer sovereignty. Private certificates can assure quality without restricting consumer CHOICE.

ochlocracy. Government of mobs, or mob rule.

oligopoly. An INDUSTRY (2) with only a few FIRMS. The firms are affected by the actions of others. There is no one type of behavior in this case, since the outcomes can range from CARTELS to price wars and strategic GAMES. Except for cartels, which generally do not last long, there is still COMPETITION, since there is RIVALRY among the firms. If the firms are cooperatives, however, they may try to coexist in harmonious competition.

one hundred percent reserve banking. See WAREHOUSE BANKING.

opacity. The CHARACTERISTIC of not letting light pass through, hence by extension, not visible to the PUBLIC (1). When one buys an appliance, the BENEFITS are visible but the faults may be opaque. The public BADS in an area may also be opaque to a prospective resident. TRANSFER-SEEKING and corruption can also be opaque unless there is a systematic method of making government processes and acts transparent.

open access. Of a resource that is owned by government or in COMMON, without any entry restriction or payment requirement. This unmanaged common tends to be overly exploited. With assigned property rights, the owner will charge admission.

open economy. An ECONOMY engaged in INTERNATIONAL TRADE.

open market operations. In the USA, the purchase or sale of government securities (bonds) by the Federal Open Market Committee of the FEDERAL RESERVE SYSTEM, or in other countries, the equivalent action by the CENTRAL BANK. The FED increases the MONEY SUPPLY by purchasing government bonds and paying for them by increasing bank RESERVES, thus creating money by fiat (FIAT MONEY).

open society. A society which permits immigration and respects basic CIVIL LIBERTIES, particularly freedom of speech and association. The term was coined by Henri Bergson in *The Two Sources of Morality and Religion* (1932), and was used by Karl Popper in his book *The Open Society and Its Enemies* (1945). Totalitarian (TOTALITARIANISM) countries are closed societies. Financier and philanthropist George Soros adopted the term for his Open Society foundations.

Oppenheimer, Franz (1864–1943). German historian and sociologist; as author of *The State* (1914, 1975), he held that STATES originate in conquest and involve domination. He originated the concept of distinguishing the ECONOMIC MEANS (VOLUNTARY production and exchange) and the POLITICAL MEANS (using force), a theme elaborated upon later by ALBERT JAY NOCK. A 'liberal socialist,' Oppenheimer also held that LAND was originally owned collectively by nations, tribes or villages, and that the exploitation of workers is made possible by the usurpation of the land by government-enforced titles to landowners who are not user/occupants. See Foldvary (1997c).

opportunism. Originally a French political term, economic opportunistic behavior is the EXPLOITATION (1) of an informational or physical advantage (such as due to ASSET SPECIFICTY), thus taking all or most of the GAINS FROM TRADE. Communists used the term for those willing to compromise with bourgeois parties.

opportunity.   A chance to achieve some outcome. The chance consists of the possible availability of the means and an absence of BARRIERS, such as legal or physical barriers. See also NATURAL OPPORTUNITY.

opportunity cost.   The true economic cost of something, consisting of the best foregone OPPORTUNITY. When one buys an item, the true cost is not the cash, since one is exchanging it for something one prefers. The true cost is what one could have otherwise obtained, but did not. For example, the opportunity cost of self-employment is the best employment one could have working for another. The concept was developed by Friedrich von Wieser, but also recognized earlier, for example by Henry George (1871).

oppress.   To severely control another in a harsh or painful way, as some GOVERNMENTS do to their subjects, especially dissidents and minorities.

optimal.   The best possible, given the constraints and criteria. Opposite term: PESSIMAL. In mathematical economics, the optimal is usually a maximum or minimum of some function. In FREE-MARKET economics, what is optimal is regarded as what is voluntarily chosen, given the constraints of morality. Optimizing is equivalent to economizing, and the general rule is that one optimizes when MARGINAL (1) benefits equal marginal costs, and when the marginal benefits of items compared to (divided by) costs are equal. For example, the socially optimal level of POLLUTION is the level where the marginal costs of additional pollution equal the marginal costs of reducing pollution.

option.   1 OPPORTUNITY or alternative. 2 A CONTRACT to buy or sell an asset at a certain price within some time interval, a call (CALL OPTION) being the buy and a put (PUT OPTION) the sell option. One can hedge (HEDGING) the ownership of stocks with a put option if one fears a decline.

order.   An environment in which a person can learn to form reliable EXPECTATIONS as to the elements of the system and their rates of change. As HAYEK noted, the two types of order are organizational orders and SPONTANEOUS ORDERS, the latter being the order of the MARKET PROCESS, which Hayek also called the extended order.

ordinal utility.   Utility (MARGINAL UTILITY) defined as a ranking from most to least important, so that one can only have PREFERENCES rather than utility directly from a single item, and it is not possible to evaluate the degree of ranking, that is by how much A and B differ compared to B and C. AUSTRIAN ECONOMICS uses ordinal marginal utility. Some theorists argue that a quantified though not measurable utility is also meaningful and real world, as when one says that one likes mangoes a great deal more than papayas, and papayas just a bit more than oranges.

orthogonal.   At right angles, with zero correlation. Two variables are orthogonal if they have nothing to do with one another, or one does not affect the other.

output.   The goods and services that firms produce, including bads as by-products.

outside lag.   The time interval between the implementation of a policy and the completion of its effect.

outside money.   Under a GOLD STANDARD, outside money is GOLD (its quantity determined outside the banks) and the INSIDE MONEY is substitutes for gold, that is BANKNOTES and deposits. With fiat government money (FIAT MONEY), outside money consists of coins and paper currency as well as bank reserves and foreign exchange reserves.

overdetermined.   Psychologically, it means having several factors affecting some condition. Economically, it means that all aspects of a system mutually cause and affect one another. See, for example, Amariglio *et al*. (1996).

ownership.   A bundle of RIGHTS.

P

P. A symbol for PRICE or the PRICE LEVEL.

Paine, Thomas (1737–1809). British CLASSICAL-LIBERAL political philosopher, Thomas Paine emigrated to America and advocated independence in *Common Sense* (1776). Back in Europe, he wrote the *Rights of Man* (1791). After publishing *The Age of Reason* (1794, 1796) on his desist belief, he returned to America. His more economic work is *Agrarian Justice Opposed to Agrarian Law, and to Agrarian Monopoly; Being a Plan for Meliorating the Condition of Man* (1797), where he argued for equality in the right to the benefits of land.

panarchy. A system with multiple and overlapping jurisdictions of VOLUNTARY, contractual ASSOCIATIONS. It is a type of ANARCHISM, but with local governing agencies that provide a variety of economic and social systems, hence 'pan' meaning embracing all. The term has been propagated by JOHN ZUBE.

panic. A widespread sudden fear of the collapse of the ECONOMY, especially the BANKING system, leading depositors to withdraw their deposits, which leads to delays and bank failures, furthering the panic. With DEPOSIT INSURANCE and FIAT MONEY, panics no longer occur. They would also not normally occur with FREE BANKING, since the banks would have agreements to provide one another with BASE MONEY, and there could also be private insurance as well as super-safe banks.

paradox of voting. Simple majority-rule voting may give inconsistent results, giving power to those who set the AGENDA of the sequence of the voting. See IMPOSSIBILITY THEOREM.

paratransit. Small private transportation services such as jitneys (vans and small busses), shared-ride cabs, and car pooling. These are often restricted by municipalities such as New York City to limit COMPETITION with the city transit system.

Paretian liberal. The label by A.K. Sen in a theorem that states that no social decision RULE can be PARETO OPTIMAL yet allow individual LIBERTY without regard to the effects on others. Sen's example is A reading a book to which B objects, when both would prefer that B read it and A not read it (B would rather suffer the book in order to prevent A from reading it). If they are not able to meet to agree on the latter outcome, the PARETO IMPROVEMENT and Paretian liberal is impossible. Sen prefers liberty to the Pareto rule. The example seems bizarre, since most persons who enjoy some activity derive more utility (MARGINAL UTILITY) from doing it than from having others who don't like it do it, and those who dislike something would rather not experience it themselves.

Pareto improvement. UNANIMOUS IMPROVEMENT.

Pareto optimal. The situation where it is impossible to make a UNANIMOUS IMPROVEMENT in the allocation of resources, since any change would make someone worse off.

Pareto relevant. See EXTERNAL EFFECTS.

partnership. A firm which is owned and controlled by several people, and which itself is not a legal person. In a limited partnership, the limited partners are not liable for more than their investment, and control is held by the general partners. Partners may have differing shares of the firm. In the US, profits and expenses flow through to the partners for INCOME TAXES, while CORPORATIONS as legal persons have their own income.

patent. A PROPERTY RIGHT to the design of an invention, prohibiting others from copying it for a number of years. It can be considered an extension of contracting, where purchase is conditional on not copying. The utilitarian argument is that without patents, many inventions would not be developed. A moral argument is that the creator has a right to his invented design as well as physical implementations. Those opposing patent rights argue that these are a PRIVILEGE granted by the state, and that there are other ways of protecting inventions.

path. The historical sequence of events. An outcome is path dependent if it depended on a particular sequence which was arbitrary in the sense that some other sequence could have occurred; the path is an accident of history, that is, of the persons and natural events (earthquakes, and so on). An outcome is path independent if the outcome is independent of other alternatives. If voting on A, B, and then C leads to a different outcome than voting on C, B, and then A, the result is path dependent. Pure economic theory is path independent, but as practiced, it is path dependent because it develops within schools of thought that resist challenges from other schools, and the thought of key individuals can alter the path.

payroll tax. A TAX on money WAGES, such as for social security or, in the UK, national insurance. The tax induces a SKEW to non-taxed FRINGE BENEFITS, as well as imposing a burden on both labor and employment, inducing a preference for non-labor substitutes.

peak-load pricing. Pricing a FLOW according to its CONGESTION, thus charging users for inflicting a social cost (SOCIAL COSTS AND BENEFITS). Examples of such congestion fees include bridge tolls and rapid transit during rush hours, electricity during peak use, and discounts by movie theaters for non-peak hours.

pensience. The capability of a VOLITIONAL purposive being to direct its actions using REASON; it includes awareness and implies the ABILITY to choose actions and know the effects of acts on others. Related but not identical terms include intelligence, sentience, and volitional consciousness.

pensient. Having PENSIENCE.

perestroika. *Russ.* The economic reforms initiated in the former Soviet Union by Mikhail Gorbachev. Initial attempts to decentralize operations and allow some private MARKET initiatives such as COOPERATIVES and land leasing were often reversed and restricted, and had little overall effect, because the basic structure was unchanged. After 1988, central commands were loosened, but the preconditions (PRECONDITIONS FOR MARKET) for COORDINATION by a MARKET PROCESS were not in place, and prices remained fixed, and the ECONOMY began to disintegrate. After the breakup of the Soviet Union in 1991, more fundamental reforms transformed Russia and other former Soviet republics into MIXED ECONOMIES. See Boetkke (1993) on why perestroika failed.

perfect. Complete and pure. See also FAIL.

perfect competition. An absence of long-run MARKET POWER by firms in an INDUSTRY (2), an outcome of ATOMISTIC COMPETITION. It is more accurate to call the market structure ATOMISTIC COMPETITION, and to use the term 'perfect non-monopoly' for that outcome. The term 'perfect competition' conflates rivalry and non-monopoly, and misleadingly implies that there is something imperfect about market structures that are not atomistic, when real-world realities necessitate such structures.

perfect complement. A GOOD without which another good will not be used, such as left shoes and right shoes, completely complementing (COMPLEMENT) one another. The goods are always bought in the same ratio.

perfect information.   Complete relevant information, known to all relevant parties. This is typically a premise of MODELS, such as for PERFECT COMPETITION, and then critics of markets cite informational imperfection as a flaw of real-world markets because they don't conform to the model. Since government officials also lack perfect information, there is no policy implication in not being omniscient. See *LEX NON COGIT AD IMPOSSIBILIA*, FAIL.

perfect substitute.   A GOOD which can completely SUBSTITUTE for another, such as blue and red pencils if one does not care about the color. If a good is priced higher than its perfect substitute, it will not be bought.

period of production.   The payback time, or duration between an INVESTMENT and the time that the cost plus PROFIT are recovered. This is an important element of the Austrian theory (AUSTRIAN ECONOMICS) of CAPITAL GOODS.

permanent income.   Average lifetime INCOME that does not reduce one's WEALTH.

permanent income hypothesis of consumption.   The HYPOTHESIS by MILTON FRIEDMAN that one's CONSUMPTION depends on one's PERMANENT INCOME, in contrast to the life-cycle hypothesis of planning to consume all lifetime income and wealth. This contradicts the Keynesian CONSUMPTION FUNCTION that posits more SAVINGS with more income.

perpetuity bond.   A CONSOL.

person.   A living being which exists on the PENSIENT level. A person has a functioning mind and the actual or potential ABILITY to make CHOICES based on reason and awareness. Such choices rather than reflexes (genetically programmed (PROGRAM (2)) responses) dominate the BEHAVIOR of a person. NATURAL MORAL LAW applies to persons. Persons are the subjects of social science, including economics.

personal evil.   A PERSON's sentiment that something is harmful or disagreeable to him.

personal good.   A PERSON's sentiment that something is beneficial or agreeable to him.

personal neutral.   A PERSON's sentiment which is neither PERSONAL GOOD nor PERSONAL EVIL.

personification.   The depictions of a non-human or collective entity as though it were a human being, such as saying 'France favors European integration' or 'the market does not like uncertainty,' when in fact it is real human beings who do such things.

pessimal.   The worst possible, given constraints and criteria. Opposite of OPTIMAL.

phenomenon.   An object or event.

Phillips curve.   Originally, as presented by A.W. Phillips in 1958, a relationship between WAGE increases and UNEMPLOYMENT. This became extended to a relationship between price INFLATION and unemployment, with the implication that policy could reduce unemployment at the expense of higher inflation. However, the Phillips curve is not stable, and in the long run it is considered by SUPPLY-SIDE economists to be vertical, as expected inflationary policy will only raise prices.

physiocracy.   The rule of NATURAL LAW, thus named by the PHYSIOCRATS for a *LAISSEZ-FAIRE* economic system with policy in accord with NATURAL MORAL LAW.

physiocrats.   A French school of political economy during the 1700s whose policy was *LAISSEZ-FAIRE*, with FREE TRADE and an *IMPÔT UNIQUE*, a SINGLE TAX on the net product, or LAND RENT. They also developed the first DYNAMIC *MACRO-ECONOMIC model, the *tableau économique*. The physiocrats had the first theory of ECONOMIC DEVELOPMENT, based on a tax only on land rent, which would be used for 'advances' or investments in CAPITAL GOODS, especially to create INFRA-STRUCTURE, which would generate more rent, leading to an upward spiral of development, with private enterprise unshackled by regulation and taxation. This model was applied successfully by 19th-century Japan and post-1950 Taiwan (Harrison, 1983), and no better model has been developed by development theory. ADAM SMITH wrote that it could do no harm. HENRY GEORGE one century later expanded on these themes, with an added moral dimension, and some Spanish-speaking Georgists refer to themselves as neo-physiocrats. The physiocratic emphasis on agriculture has been misunderstood, since by 'productive' the physiocrats meant productive of rent. Their error was to not recognize the rental productivity of urban commerce, an error rectified in GEORGIST or GEOCLASSICAL thought. Key physiocrats were QUESNAY and TURGOT. Adam Smith visited them in France and was influenced by their thought.

Pigovian tax.   Named after Arthur Pigou, a tax on a negative EXTERNAL EFFECT equal to the cost it imposes on others, making the PRIVATE COST equal the social cost (SOCIAL COSTS AND BENEFITS). The COASE THEOREM shows that if the TRANSACTION costs are low enough, the parties can negotiate a settlement that is the smaller of the cost of avoiding the effect or of paying for the damage. If transaction costs are too high for direct negotiations, then an institutional method (INSTITUTIONAL ECONOMICS) can be sought to achieve such a result.

planned economy.   See CENTRAL PLANNING.

plunder.   To take by FORCE, and the goods so taken. OPPENHEIMER and NOCK identified the two means of obtaining goods as the political way, through plunder, and the economic means, through VOLUNTARY exchange. Given the premise of SELF-OWNERSHIP, the taxation of WAGES and the PRODUCTS (2) of labor is a wrongful taking.

Governmental means of raising revenue does not need to be plunderous, since voluntary USER FEES are consistent with the economic means, as is the community collection of rent, which NOCK (1935) himself regarded as properly economic.

Pöhlmann, Robert von.   In his *Geschichte des antiken kommunismus und Sozialismus im klassischen Altertum* (1893), he discredited the view that communism arose with the agricultural stage of development. Communism instead arose when war compelled COMMON ownership in military camps and fortresses. See also OPPENHEIMER, Foldvary (1997c).

point of inflection (*Br.* inflexion).   The point on a curve, such as the representation of a BUSINESS CYCLE, where the rate of change of the slope changes sign, thus the rate of expansion or decline slows, foreshadowing the change in the slope, that is the peak or bottom.

policy.   See ECONOMIC POLICY.

political.   Relating to POWER and AGREEMENTS concerning RULES, especially regarding GOVERNMENT.

political business cycle.   Macroeconomic CYCLES caused by increased government expenditures prior to elections.

political economy.   The classical name for ECONOMICS, the term now meaning the theory of governmental ECONOMIC POLICY, including PUBLIC CHOICE and CONSTITUTIONAL ECONOMICS.

political means.   See PLUNDER.

politicization.   The process by which PRIVATE (1) CHOICE is altered by the political process and overridden by SOCIAL CHOICE.

politics.   The pursuit of POWER, and also of RULES *AGREEMENTS.

poll tax.   A HEAD TAX.

polluter pays.   The policy of POLLUTION charges to compensate for damages. See also EFFLUENT FEE, LARCENOUS, OPTIMAL, POLLUTION CHARGE.

pollution.   A substance that reduces the utility (MARGINAL UTILITY) of an ENVIRONMENT.

pollution charge.   An EFFLUENT FEE. See POLLUTER PAYS.

pollution rights.   Legal permits to pollute (POLLUTER PAYS), which trade in a MARKET. With the supply fixed, the price of a permit has some of the effect of an EFFLUENT FEE, inducing a reduction of pollution. If some firms are grandfathered, granted original rights to pollute, it is in effect a subsidy to those firms. Pollution rights avoid the problem of estimating the pollution damage, but they do not generate continuous revenues, and they do not necessarily compensate the victims for the damages.

polycentric law.   Bell (1991) defines it as overlapping private jurisdictions in free and open COMPETITION.

polycentricity.   The degree of polycentric or decentralized GOVERNANCE, measurable by the DIVERSIFICATION index.

portfolio.   A collection of ASSETS held for gain. In MODERN PORTFOLIO THEORY, the assets are grouped into relatively uncorrelated categories. See DIVERSIFICATION.

positive economics.   The analysis of economic phenomena (PHENOMENON), in contrast to NORMATIVE ECONOMICS that evaluates systems and policy.

positive rights.   TAKINGS RIGHTS or OBLIGATIONAL RIGHTS.

positivism.   The philosophy and METHODOLOGY originating in the work of Saint-Simone and Compte, dealing with what are considered to be objective facts, observed and measured, and purports to be non-valued (NON-VALUED

SCIENCE). It has been adopted by NEOCLASSICAL ECONOMICS in HYPOTHESIS testing, where the assumptions need not be realistic, so long as they are falsifiable and the results are sufficiently predictive. Critics say that the allegedly objective facts are actually theory-laden, so the factual objectivity is problematic. Austrian (AUSTRIAN ECONOMICS) and GEO-ECONOMICS use AXIOMATIC-DEDUCTIVE methodology, where the assumptions are intended to be realistic, which does not preclude testing specific propositions.

possession. 1 TITLE to PROPERTY giving the owner RIGHTS of control and transfer so long as usage is peaceful and honest. 2 The physical holding of property.

Rights of possession can be separated from the rights to the yield (return or income) from property.

'possession is nine points of the law.' Thomas Fuller in *The Historie of the Holy Warre* (1639).

post-Keynesian. A DEMAND-SIDE school of economics drawing from KEYNES, MARX, and RICARDO. Some elements in common with AUSTRIAN ECONOMICS include an emphasis on the DYNAMIC nature of the ECONOMY, UNCERTAINTY, and the importance of INSTITUTIONS. However, as an outgrowth of Keynesianism, post-Keynesians believe that MARKETS do not function well, and they favor indicative planning (PLANNED ECONOMY).

postage money. Postage stamps used as MONEY, as during the US Civil War, or the possibility of a money unit based on postage, such as first class mail, which would be COMMODITY MONEY based on a service rather than a stock of physical commodity.

postmodern. A paradigm that rejects universal (UNIVERSE) and OBJECTIVE *TRUTH and determinism (DETERMINIST).

poverty. Absolute poverty is a family income too low to obtain sufficient food, shelter, and medical services to maintain normal health. Relative poverty is some bottom percentage of a distribution of income or wealth. One also needs to distinguish pre-assistance and post-assistance poverty. A society with poverty means that it has a non-trivial number of persons who are in absolute pre-assistance poverty.

Pre-assistance absolute poverty is due to a low marginal PRODUCT (2) of LABOR in a local ECONOMY, which persists due to several factors: the taxation and restriction of labor and enterprise that reduce opportunity and wages, poor government schooling, a WELFARE (2) trap that penalizes those who attempt to escape with high marginal tax rates, and a culture of poverty with poor work attitudes.

power.   Kinetic power is the exertion of one's own or others' energy over time; potential power is the ABILITY to act and make things happen. A powerful theory has great explanatory effect. POLITICAL power commands the energy and resources of others.

praxeology.   The general theory of HUMAN ACTION, derived deductively (DEDUCTIVE METHOD) from the concept of HUMAN ACTION. Praxeology is closely associated with LUDWIG VON MISES, who developed the concept in works such as *Human Action* (1949, 1966). Mises states in that work that the term was first used in 1890 by Espinas. ECONOMICS is a subset of praxeology.

precious metals.   Metals of very high value per ounce, mainly GOLD, SILVER, and platinum, the first two commonly used for coins until the establishment of FIAT MONEY. These metals, commonly as COINS, appreciate (APPRECIATION) in nominal value during periods of high inflation, and are therefore held as inflation hedges (HEDGING). Gold is an especially good store of value because it does not corrode and is easily molded.

preconditions for markets.   A FREE MARKET presumes an ETHIC that determines which acts are market-compatible and which ones are outside the market, for example theft. Moral PROPERTY RIGHTS are a function of the ethic. The ethic is implemented in LAW, which delineates and protects property rights, including the enforcement of contracts and the resolution of disputes. A cadastre (CADASTRAL SURVEY) of land titles is useful for the registration of titles as well as the assessment of value and charges on the rent.

preference.   A foundational premise of economics is the ABILITY of a person to rank ends. Goods then have preferences, or a ranking relative to price, as instrumental in achieving the ends. If A is preferred to B, it means the ACTOR chooses A, given some budget constraint that does not enable him to have both A and B.

preference demonstration.   See DEMONSTRATED PREFERENCE.

preference revelation.   The determination of PREFERENCES before a choice is actually made. This is alleged to be a problem for PUBLIC GOODS, since one may use the good as a free rider, once provided, and if asked, people may not reveal their true preference in order to avoid paying. However, the demand-revealing tax (DEMAND REVELATION) method has been developed to accomplish this (Tideman and Tullock, 1976). Also, most CIVIC GOODS are territorial (TERRITORIAL GOODS), and the RENT paid reveals the preference for the public goods located in that territory (Foldvary, 1994b).

present value. The VALUE at present of future yields during some time interval (or infinite time). The stream of yields is discounted (divided) by the INTEREST RATE. The net present value uses gross yields minus costs.

price. The amount of MONEY a good EXCHANGES for. Price theory is about the determination of prices and quantities of goods by markets, and the resultant allocation of resources, that is MICROECONOMICS. Prices convey signals regarding profits, gluts, and shortages; prices distorted by intervention provide skewed signals.

price ceiling. A PRICE CONTROL setting a maximum PRICE, as with RENT CONTROL. This results in a SHORTAGE and a BLACK MARKET.

price control. The fixing of PRICES or PRICE CEILINGS or PRICE FLOORS by government.

price discrimination. Charging different prices for different customers purchasing the same good or for different quantities of the good. This enables a monopolist to sell more PRODUCT (1) without diminishing PROFITS, reducing the DEADWEIGHT LOSS of monopoly, but in practice, such discrimination is limited to youth and the aged, and special situations.

price-earnings ratio. The price of a stock divided by the earnings per share, an indication of the profitability of a company and the prospects for a rising price of the stock. The P/E of a stock-market index is used to evaluate the market as a whole.

price elasticity of demand. The responsiveness of the quantity purchased to a change in PRICE, calculated as the percentage change in quantity divided by the percentage change in price.

price fixing. Collusion among firms to sell at a certain price or to limit output rather than compete. This is illegal under US ANTI-TRUST law. Some view price fixing as market-compatible and others view it as market-violating.

price floor. A PRICE CONTROL setting a minimum PRICE, such as a MINIMUM WAGE. The result is a SURPLUS (such as UNEMPLOYMENT), and a BLACK MARKET for the good or resource.

price index. The sum of the prices times quantities of a list of goods sold. Various years are compared using past prices and/or quantities.

price inflation. A continuing increase in the PRICE LEVEL. See also MONETARY INFLATION.

price level. The general purchasing power of a unit of CURRENCY, usually measured by a PRICE INDEX. Real prices are indicated by dividing the nominal price by the price level, hence w/p is the real wage when w is the nominal wage and p the price level.

price-specie mechanism. The automatic long-term BALANCE OF TRADE under a GOLD STANDARD. When there is a trade SURPLUS, trade is balanced with IMPORTS of GOLD that raise prices, reducing EXPORTS and increasing imports until trade balances. Trade deficits become balanced with the opposite movement, gold being exported. This process, described by DAVID HUME, occurs with any global currency.

price support. A SUBSIDY to agriculture by government purchasing the crop to prop up the price and warehousing the SURPLUS.

price taker. A firm that has to take the prevailing market price, being unable to set its own price, due to ATOMISTIC COMPETITION.

price theory. See PRICE.

primacy of the abstract. A term used by HAYEK to indicate that in observing phenomena (PHENOMENON), one already has an ABSTRACT theory about it with which to make sense of it, human beings being genetically programmed to create abstract generalizations.

primal economy. The ECONOMY of primal or 'primitive' people who derive much of their materials directly from hunting and gathering. Many such societies do not have an IMPOSED *GOVERNMENT. The few remaining primal groups are threatened with extinction, since governments usually do not recognize their PROPERTY RIGHTS.

primary products. Raw materials such as minerals, oil, water, crops, fish, and lumber.

primitive accumulation. An original store of WEALTH, provided by NATURAL RESOURCES.

primogeniture.   The exclusive right of a first-born son to inherit his father's estate.

principal and agent.   A principal hires an agent to do something, but the agent has his own AGENDA. Examples include shareholders and the management of a CORPORATION and elected representatives. Methods of dealing with the principal–agent problem include monitoring, providing incentives, and shaping the culture.

principle.   A scientific law. 'Principle' also means the basic subject matter.

prior right.   The right to possess some land, a right inherent in being a member of a COMMUNITY or nation, and with the community or nation having the right to exclude outsiders. From Oppenheimer (1917, 1997).

prisoner's dilemma.   A zero-sum GAME in which two prisoners have the CHOICE of informing on the other or not. Each gains most if he informs but the other does not, and they lose more by informing on each other than if they both do not inform. The 'dilemma' is that the player's rational self-interest is to inform, but then they are both worse off than if neither informed.

But it is not really a dilemma, since the payoffs are pre-assigned by the designer of the game. There is, in fact, no choice to be made, but only the inevitable conclusion inherent in the assignment of the payoffs. In reality, true dilemmas are caused by SUBJECTIVE utilities which are not known beforehand, often to the player, and where genuine choices are difficult to make.

If the model shows how rational individual decisions lead to irrational social outcomes, it is only under the restrictions of the model where there is no communication.

private.   **1** Not part of GOVERNMENT. **2** Of a PERSON and his PROPERTY when not part of a collective. **3** A firm that is not a corporation.

private community.   See CONTRACTUAL COMMUNITY.

private cost.   A cost which is PRIVATE (2). SOCIAL COSTS equal private costs plus EXTERNAL EFFECTS.

private enterprise.   Enterprise which is PRIVATE (1).

private good.   A GOOD which is not COLLECTIVE. This meaning of PRIVATE (2) is ORTHOGONAL to private (1). Private goods are rival (RIVALRY) in that given a pie, a slice that one consumes is not consumable by another. See SEVERABLE GOOD.

private sector. The section of an ECONOMY not owned or operated by GOVERNMENT, hence PRIVATE (1), and unrelated to private (2). This is also the VOLUNTARY, contractual sector (CONTRACTUAL COMMUNITY).

privatization. The transfer of property or operations from GOVERNMENT to PRIVATE (1) owners.

privilege. Legislation providing special subsidies protection, or exemptions to a group or persons rather than benefitting (BENEFIT) the public as a whole.

process. A pattern of ACTIVITY (1) over time.

product. **1** A particular GOOD, being the output of a FIRM. **2** Output in general, such as the produced goods of a firm, or the totality of goods produced in an ECONOMY during some time interval, as in GROSS DOMESTIC PRODUCT.

product differentiation. Minor but subjectively significant variations in the characteristics of PRODUCTS that are very close substitutes, such as different brands of laundry detergent. MONOPOLISTIC COMPETITION is characterized by brand names that carry such differences. In some cases, the brand reputation may be the main differentiation. Much of the competition is then carried out by advertising (ADVERTISE). This has been accused of being wasteful, but variety is a good that many people like, and the advertisements pay for media that people want to consume.

production. The transformation of inputs into PRODUCTS.

production function. A relationship between inputs and outputs of PRODUCTION, the function encompassing technology, organization, and INTERVENTION. Microeconomic production functions are of FIRMS, while a macroeconomic production function is of the whole ECONOMY, where, for example, output is a function of labor. Some economists question whether a macroeconomic production function is meaningful. It is used in macroeconomic models to generate an AGGREGATE SUPPLY curve, which is vertical in SUPPLY-SIDE models. See also COBB–DOUGLAS PRODUCTION FUNCTION.

production possibility frontier. A model with two goods, showing the transformation of one to another as resources are so shifted, the curve indicating maximum production. The curve is concave to the origin, since as resources are shifted, they become less productive, as the most productive inputs are used first.

productivity.   Output per designated set of inputs, a function of efficiency, natural resources, technology, and labor skills.

profit.   Revenue minus costs. See ACCOUNTING PROFIT, ECONOMIC PROFIT. See also NORMAL PROFIT.

profit maximization.   In microeconomics, firms are usually assumed to attempt to maximize PROFITS, which are maximized at the quantity where MARGINAL revenue equals marginal cost.

profit motive.   The typical motivation for firms is to make PROFITS, but some owners and ENTREPRENEURS may have other goals.

program.   **1** A service or policy such as one IMPOSED on society by GOVERN-MENT. **2** A sequence of instructions.

progress.   An improvement in the WELL-BEING of a group of PERSONS as judged by their own evaluations. Also, advancement towards some goal.

Progress and Poverty.   Book published in 1879 by Henry GEORGE which inquired into why POVERTY persists in the midst of PROGRESS. Based on classical economics while criticizing and extending it, George traced poverty to LAND TENURE and TAXATION. WAGES could be increased and BARRIERS to EMPLOY-MENT eliminated by eliminating taxes and ARBITRARY restrictions on labor and ENTERPRISE, and placing all taxation on land value or LAND RENT, which has no EXCESS BURDEN.

progressive.   **1** Favoring PROGRESS and change, hence in opposition to CONSERVATIVISM. **2** Favoring WELFARE STATE and redistributionist (REDISTRIBU-TION) LIBERALISM (2), or SOCIALISM. **3** One measure increasing as another does, such as with a PROGRESSIVE TAX.

progressive tax.   A tax that is PROGRESSIVE (3), the proportion of income or wealth taxed increasing with increasing INCOME or WEALTH. This is often accomplished with GRADUATED tax rates, but it can also be done simply by exempting income under a certain amount and then taxing the rest at a flat rate. A completely flat tax is not progressive, but has one rate for all amounts of the item taxed. FREE-MARKET public revenues are based on the benefit principle, normally at flat rates.

proletariat.   An IDEAL TYPE of person who owns no CAPITAL GOODS or LAND and only gets INCOME from WAGES. SISMONDI originated the term, from the

Roman lowest class, and also the concept of a SURPLUS VALUE and CLASS warfare, which Karl MARX would later amplify on. Had Sismondi been careful to distinguish land from CAPITAL GOODS, he may have identified the surplus with land, sparing the world the specter of Marxist *digirisme*.

property.   Anything subject to human control. See also OWNERSHIP.

property rights.   RIGHTS. All rights are PROPERTY rights, since one's body and life are also one's property. The three aspects of property rights are rights of transfer, rights of use, and rights to the yield. Rights of transfer and use are rights of possession, which can be separated from the right to the yield. See *DROIT–DROIT*, NATURAL RIGHTS.

property tax.   A TAX on PROPERTY, the term often applying to the taxation of REAL ESTATE. The tax is typically *AD VALOREM*. A tax on produced property is an INTERVENTION into production.

proportional tax.   A flat tax, the MARGINAL and average tax rates being equal for all amounts of the item taxed.

proposition.   A statement asserting some general TRUTH.

proprietary.   Having a PRIVATE (1) owner.

proprietary community.   1 A COMMUNITY with unitary ownership by one FIRM, including multiple-tenant income property, leaseholds, COOPERATIVES, and LAND TRUSTS. The term was coined by Spencer Heath. 2 A privately owned subdivision community (CIVIC ASSOCIATION), with democratic governance by the proprietors or co-owners. See also CONTRACTUAL COMMUNITY.

prosperity.   Widely shared WEALTH and EMPLOYMENT, flourishing with little or no POVERTY and unemployment. Good times.

protection agency.   A private firm that provides police and security services, protecting its customers from theft and violence. Some libertarians (LIBERTARIANISM) and anarcho-capitalists (ANARCHO-CAPITALISM) envision such services as a VOLUNTARY substitute for that governmental role. It is also likely that PRIVATE COMMUNITIES would provide such services for their members.

protectionism.   Trade limitation. The use of trade BARRIERS to protect a domestic industry from foreign COMPETITION. This raises prices for consumers and reduces the efficiency of the ECONOMY, since it cannot take advantage of global COMPARATIVE ADVANTAGES.

protective rights.   So-called 'negative rights,' RIGHTS to be free from coercive HARM. Rights to life, liberty, and property are not claims on others' property but the right to not have one's life, liberty, and property taken or restricted. They thus morally protect the right to do whatever does not harm others.

provision.   The selection of goods, funding, and arrangement for production. When government provides a SERVICE, it is responsible for making it available to the public.

proviso.   A condition that has to be satisfied, the famous one in economic philosophy being JOHN LOCKE's (1690, 1947) proviso for claiming LAND in the *Second Treatise*. One may homestead (HOMESTEADING) unclaimed land so long as enough of that quality is left for others. This implies that if land of the quality is all appropriated, then one should compensate the others with a payment of RENT.

psychic income.   The joy and satisfaction from working, beyond the WAGE income.

public.   1 Any group of more than one PERSON. 2 The GOVERNMENT sector of the ECONOMY.
   In the term PUBLIC GOODS, 'public' refers to the first meaning, although in many texts the two meanings become merged.

public choice.   A branch of economics consisting of theory applied to COLLECTIVE decisions and their processes and outcomes. It is also called the 'economic theory of politics.' In its typical models, all agents, including government officials, are motivated by their narrow SELF-INTEREST. Voters maximize utility, and POLICY makers seek to satisfy the MEDIAN VOTER, but this raises the question of why *HOMO CUPIDITUS* bothers to vote. Other players include politicians who seek election, political parties, BUREAUCRACIES, and SPECIAL INTERESTS which finance campaigns and politicians in order to obtain transfers of wealth and privilege. A key principle in TRANSFER SEEKING is concentrated interests and spread-out costs, making it feasible for special interests to organize, while the public at large has little incentive to resist imposed cost. See also CONSTITUTIONAL ECONOMICS.

public economics.   The economics of the GOVERNMENT or PUBLIC SECTOR. Fields include PUBLIC CHOICE (collective decisions), SOCIAL CHOICE (the decisions of voters), PUBLIC FINANCE and PUBLIC GOODS. In a free-market world of PRIVATE COMMUNITIES, the same theory would apply to the economics of contractual communities.

public finance.   The branch of PUBLIC ECONOMICS dealing with the revenue, budgeting, and expenditures of governing agencies.

public goods.   COLLECTIVE GOODS. The term PUBLIC (1) in 'public goods' has a different meaning than PUBLIC (2) in 'public sector.'

public sector.   The government sector, that is PUBLIC (2).

purchasing media.   MONEY and MONEY SUBSTITUTES.

pure.   Not mixed with anything else.

pure free market.   A market with no INTERVENTION at all. The qualifier 'pure' would be redundant, except that in some literature, 'free market' is used to refer to MIXED ECONOMIES. See also PURE MARKET ECONOMY.

pure interest.   INTEREST as such, excluding RISK and INFLATION.

pure market economy.   A market ECONOMY with no INTERVENTION. It could take various forms, but there would be no TAXATION or restriction of productive exertion. Theory indicates that such an economy would have FULL EMPLOYMENT, since there would be no BARRIERS between labor and non-labor resources, and there would be no POVERTY, since PROSPERITY would induce a high DEMAND for labor, and without any TAX WEDGE.

pure theory.   THEORY not mixed with any particulars of time, place, or culture, thus UNIVERSAL to the subject matter.

purposeful.   Using REASON to choose (CHOICE) an ACTION aimed at achieving some END. A premise of ECONOMICS is purposeful behavior.

put option.   The right to sell an asset at a certain price within some time interval. The opposite is a CALL OPTION.

Q

Q. A symbol for the quantity of output.

qua. *Lat.* In the capacity as, or to the extent that one is. A homeowner qua homeowner is one strictly in that capacity, and not also as a worker, citizen, or consumer; he is a homeowner as an IDEAL TYPE.

quango. *Br.* A quasi-nongovernmental organization, such as an independent central bank linked to a government.

quantity theory of money. A theory based on the EQUATION OF EXCHANGE, $MV = PT$. The price level P is determined by MV/T. The modern version by MILTON FRIEDMAN, the DEMAND FOR MONEY is a function of several variables, including INTEREST rates. The point remains that if VELOCITY is stable, then nominal output (PT) is a function of the supply of MONEY, M.

quasi-rent. The ECONOMIC RENT of a good in temporary fixed supply.

Quesnay, François (1694–1774). Founder and key economist of the PHYSIOCRATS. His writings include the *Tableau Economique* (1758), a circular flow of an ECONOMY. He espoused FREE TRADE, in opposition to Mercantilist trade barriers, and the *IMPÔT UNIQUE*, a single tax on the *produit net* or RENT of land. He believed that there was a NATURAL LAW that would let the economy run itself with *LAISSEZ-FAIRE* policy.

quiritarian. Having RIGHTS to the RENT as well as rights of POSSESSION of LAND. From Latin 'quiris,' citizen, originally a spear carrier, hence the right of conquest with the spear (Oppenheimer, 1917, 1997).

R

rack-rent. A rental payment higher than the FREE-MARKET rate because the landlord exploits (EXPLOITATION (2)) the lack of mobility of the tenant.

radical. Going to the roots of a subject matter. By association, the term also means extreme relative to the mainstream, since radical thought can challenge a system down to its FOUNDATIONS (1).

radical economics. A school of thought based on Marxism and other socialist sources, critical of both mainstream economics and market economies. Main themes include inequality, labor conditions, and the problems of market economies and less-developed countries.

Raffles, Sir Thomas Stamford (1781–1826). British governor of Java 1811–16 and founder of Singapore in 1819. In Java he made CHATTEL SLAVERY a felony, abolished (ABOLISH) torture, and instituted trial by jury. Favoring FREE TRADE, he abolished transit duties and other taxes except on LAND RENT. He based Singapore's public finance on land rent and made the city a free port, with no taxes on trade or industries. Although taxes were introduced after Raffles left, Singapore has retained much of Raffles's policy and has had one of the world's most successful economies (Hodgkiss, 1942).

Ramsey taxes. TAXES on INELASTIC *SUPPLY or DEMAND.

Rand, Ayn (1905–1982). Russian-born American novelist, philosopher, and founder of the philosophy and movement, OBJECTIVISM. Her novels, influential among libertarians, include ATLAS SHRUGGED (1957), *We the Living* (1936), and *The Fountainhead* (1943). Her key philosophical works include *For the New Intellectual, The Virtue of Selfishness*, and *Capitalism: The Unknown Ideal.*

rate of interest. See INTEREST RATE.

rate of return. The yield of an asset divided by the principal.

rates. In the UK, a TAX on non-agricultural REAL ESTATE.

rational. See RATIONALITY.

rational expectations. Unbiased logical EXPECTATIONS based on all available data, including a model of the behavior of the expected phenomenon. This implies that actors do not make systematic errors. It does not imply that the expectations are correct. In contrast, ADAPTIVE EXPECTATIONS are based on projections from the recent past, not taking into account a model of the phenomenon. However, if the model is foggy, then rational expectations become adaptive: given no knowledge about the behavior of a monetary authority or the economic environment, the best estimate of the future is the present, since for example, it would be equally likely for interest rates to rise as to fall.

Rational expectations are applied by NEW-CLASSICAL and NEW-KEYNESIAN economists to government policy, new-classical theory arguing that expected DE-MAND-SIDE policy is ineffective, if market prices are flexible, a premise denied by the new Keynesians. The expression 'rational expectations' goes back at least to Nassau SENIOR, the modern concept developed by Muth in 1961.

rational ignorance. The proposition that it is RATIONAL (1) for voters not to bother to invest resources in information and voting, since one vote is quite unlikely to change an outcome. This is so for instrumental motives, but most voters cast ballots out of SYMPATHY for issues, candidates, political parties, and the democratic system.

rationality. 1 The use of LOGIC in making decisions. This includes being consistent and making use of available information, so long as the MARGINAL cost of gathering it does not exceed the marginal benefit. Consistency includes harmony between long and short-term goals. In applying rationality to decision making, it is assumed that a person is able to rank his ends, and thus his goods relative to the ends, but the ends themselves are non-rational. TRANSITIVITY is also assumed as an element of consistency. Economic theory presumes rationality (1). 2 Social efficiency in achieving social ends. Hence, policy can be socially irrational, although it is rational for the policy-maker's ends. 3 Cultural conformity; having ends which conform to cultural norms, and time preferences near the cultural norm. Those with different desires are considered irrational, if not insane or wicked. Those with very short time preferences who do things for short-run gains at the expense of long-term utility are considered irrational.

rationing. A method of allocating SCARCE (1) resources, the one common to market economies being price. Within families, rationing is usually by equity and BENEVOLENCE. Governmental rationing is based on POLITICAL *POWER as well as rules agreement.

Reaganomics. The economic policies of the administration of Ronald Reagan, the US president from 1981 to 1989, which included tax reforms, an increase in military spending, and some relative reduction in non-military spending, but not enough to prevent a great increase in the national debt. Reaganomics did accomplish a turn from increasingly greater government and INTERVENTION to at least the rhetoric of decreasing government and recognizing the limitations of government policy.

real. 1 Referring to REAL ESTATE. 2 Physical rather than financial. 3 Based on purchasing power rather than NOMINAL numbers. 4 Genuine, actual, and TRUE, rather than a mere label or appearance.

real assets. Physical assets rather than FUNDS.

real business cycle. Theories of business cycles based on REAL (2) causes, such as clusters of inventions, or the REAL-ESTATE cycle.

real capital. CAPITAL GOODS.

real estate. LAND and improvements tied to land.

real-estate cycle. A CYCLE of a period of about 15–20 years (18 years in the USA) in which real-estate prices and construction rise and fall. The troughs have coincided with major depressions. The GEO-ECONOMIC theory of BUSINESS CYCLES is based on the real-estate cycle, which was first analyzed by Henry George.

real GDP. GDP adjusted for INFLATION by a PRICE INDEX, when comparing different years.

real interest. The NOMINAL *INTEREST rate less the INFLATION rate.

real wage. The nominal WAGE divided by the PRICE LEVEL.

real wealth. WEALTH other than financial assets. Some geo-economists (GEO-ECONOMICS) exclude LAND, including only produced wealth.

realism of assumptions. Having premises which are in accord with reality rather than simply assumed for the sake of argument. Conclusions derived are true if the premises are.

reason. Basing beliefs on LOGIC and EVIDENCE, and basing decisions on rational (RATIONALITY (1)) methods. Vertical reasoning deduces conclusions from premises, while lateral reasoning evaluates the premises and investigates alternative or additional premises. ABDUCTION (2) creatively synthesizes HYPOTHESES from facts and logic.

recession. Falling national OUTPUT. Officially, in the USA, national output falling in two consecutive quarters. Colloquially, a recession is often used to mean a minor depression.

reciprocal demand. The DEMAND by a country for the goods of another country, offering its own goods in exchange. The concept originates with J.S. MILL in determining the terms of trade.

recognition lag. The time between the occurrence of some event and the recognition by policy makers that they should react to it.

recursive auction market. An AUCTION in which a buyer may resell the item at the same auction market.

redeem. Exchange a MONEY SUBSTITUTE (banknote) for money (for example gold coins) at a fixed rate, or turn in a security for money at its face value.

redemption. The act of redeeming (REDEEM).

redistribution. The taxation of market-determined income and the reallocation of these revenues according to some normative goal such as equalization or aid to the poor. Redistribution can occur across income classes and across geographic regions.

If certain sources of revenue are considered to already belong equally to the members of a community, then when a higher-level agency collects them and distributes them to a lower-level agency or provides SERVICES that benefit the residents, this would be egalitarian without being redistributive. POLLUTION charges, for example, can be interpreted as compensation to a community for damages, hence the use of such charges for egalitarian purposes would not really be redistributive. Rental income from NATURAL RESOURCES could also be in this class. Therefore, anti-poverty or egalitarian goals do not necessarily require redistribution.

reductio ad absurdum. *Lat.* A type of argument in which a concept is taken to an absurd extreme, whereby the conclusion is obviously false, in contradiction with the premises, implying that at least one of the premises is false.

reflexivity.   A feedback mechanism between thinking and events; coined by financier George Soros.

reflux, law of.   The proposition put forth by the BANKING SCHOOL that holders of private convertible banknotes will redeem those notes that are in excess of market demand as determined by the needs of trade.

regression theorem.   A theorem by LUDWIG VON MISES (1924) that the current purchasing power of MONEY derives from that of the recent past. It is thus difficult to introduce an entirely new currency.

regressive tax.   A TAX which takes an increasingly smaller proportion of income or wealth with increasing amounts of either. SALES TAXES on goods are considered to be regressive, because the rich spend a greater proportion of their income on non-taxed services. HEAD TAXES are also regressive.

regularity.   A pattern that typically responds in the same way to the same changes in variables, making it predictable. The laws of science, such as the law of gravity, describe these regularities. Examples of economic regularities include the law of demand and the law of diminishing returns.

regulation.   Laws and administrative RULES that persons and enterprises are legally obliged to follow. These can be market-enhancing or market-hampering, but when economists and business persons speak of regulations, they typically mean excessive, market-hampering ones. Regulation is a SUBSTITUTE for TAXATION, since government can mandate an activity rather than taxing and providing the activity.

There is no official measurement of the costs of regulation in the USA Regulatory costs are estimated to be more than $500,000,000,000 (half a US trillion), or $6830 (19 percent) per average household. Costs imposed on small firms are proportionally greater than on large ones. See Crews (1996).

regulatory capture.   The control of a government regulatory agency by the INDUSTRY (2) it is supposed to regulate.

relatively absolute absolutes.   A term coined by JAMES BUCHANAN to indicate rules and concepts that are fixed relative to some cultural standard.

renewable resource.   A resource whose yield can be harvested while maintaining its principal and source. Examples include wildlife, soil, timber, fish, and water.

rent.   1 LAND RENT. 2 ECONOMIC RENT. 3 RENTAL. To rent property other than land means to obtain a rental. Land rent is also an economic rent. See also RACK-RENT.

rent control.   A PRICE CEILING on the RENTAL of housing. This creates a shortage of housing for prospective tenants, and can also lead to a deterioration of the housing stock as owners cease making sufficient investments.

rent seeking.   See TRANSFER SEEKING.

rental.   The payment to the owner for hiring or renting property. In terms of factors, a rental paid for housing includes RENT (1) for the LAND, a yield on the capital goods (buildings and other improvements), and a wage to the owner for his services.

rentiers.   Those who obtain income from LAND RENT and returns from investments, without exerting any labor.

representative democracy.   Delegating decision making to elected representatives. With MASS DEMOCRACY, this becomes DYSFUNCTIONAL, since it induces TRANSFER-SEEKING. In a VOLUNTARY club or with COMMUNITARIAN DEMOCRACY, the members retain more control, but there is always a principal–agent problem when one delegates.

reputation capital.   The value of a FIRM due to its reputation and goodwill. This value is an intangible CAPITAL GOOD. For example, firms invest in advertising brand names as a signal of quality. One benefit of PRODUCT DIFFERENTIATION is having such brand capital.

reserves.   BANK reserves, MONEY held by banks which may not be lent, held as a reserve for depositor withdrawals as well as to regulate the supply of credit expansion.

residential association.   A CIVIC ASSOCIATION whose members are owners of residences. Such associations own and provide CIVIC GOODS, COLLECTIVE GOODS similar to those provided by local governments, but based on contract and funded from assessments usually based on property value, rather than an arbitrary multitude of taxes. Such associations typically also have architectural covenants.

resource.   A source of supply.

restriction.   A RULE that keeps an activity within specified limits. At the extreme, the limit is the null set, a prohibition. An ARBITRARY restriction is based on whim, culture, or special interests and gains. An arbitrary legal restriction is an INTERVENTION, a violation of liberty. Generally, the use of the term 'restriction' implies arbitrary restriction.

return.   Income from an asset.

return, total.   See TOTAL RETURN.

revealed preference.   Observations of how CONSUMERS react to changes in price and income. As theorized by Paul Samuelson, given certain premises, one can derive a DEMAND curve from this. See also DEMONSTRATED PREFERENCE.

revenue neutral.   A shift in the items taxed (TAX), which does not alter total government revenue.

revenue sharing.   True revenue sharing is the generation of revenue by some agency, and then allocating the revenue to two or more receiving agencies, such as GOVERNMENTS. As practiced by central governments, 'revenue sharing' is TAXATION by the central government, which then transfers some of the funds to lower-level governments conditional on fulfilling certain policies.

rhetoric.   The study of the conversations (arguments and metaphors) as well as the actual methods of economists in contrast to their claimed methods, pioneered by A. Klamer and D. McCloskey.

Ricardian.   Relating to or derived from the theories of DAVID RICARDO, a central figure in CLASSICAL ECONOMICS. Among the major themes are differential rent, comparative advantage, deductive methodology, and the value of goods deriving mostly from labor. Several theorems have been labeled 'Ricardian,' since they draw from Ricardo even if the modern version differs from his.

Ricardian equivalence theorem.   The proposition by ROBERT BARRO that government DEBT is equivalent to TAXATION in economic effect, since the debt is eventually financed with taxes. The theorem depends on premises contrary to actuality, such as that taxes are lump sum. However, with land-value taxation (LAND-VALUE TAX), the theorem becomes realistic, since the debt is a liability against future LAND RENT, and is capitalized into lower land values.

Ricardo, David (1772–1823).   British CLASSICAL economist whose contributions to the theory of DIFFERENTIAL RENT, COMPARATIVE ADVANTAGE, and the distribution of income among the FACTORS OF PRODUCTION were highly influential. Ricardo theorized that rent is a surplus to the owner of land superior to that at the MARGIN OF PRODUCTION, hence that price determines rent rather than rent determining price. His major work is *Principles of Political Economy and Taxation* (1817). Ricardo's AXIOMATIC-DEDUCTIVE methodology, using abstract models, and his analysis of factors, and focus on the long run, became the heart of classical economic theory. His theory of wages was deficient, since he posited a long-run subsistence wage rather than, as later corrected by HENRY GEORGE, whatever the productivity was at the margin of production.

right to work.   Law in some US states prohibiting a UNION SHOP. This 'right to work' is the right not to have to join a union (UNIONS, LABOR) as a condition of employment.

rights.   A right is the correlative of a wrong. The right to have X or to do X means that it is wrong or evil to negate (take away) X. The right to own property, for example, means that it is wrong to steal another's property. Rights can be moral, legal, or contractual.

NATURAL RIGHTS are those determined by NATURAL MORAL LAW (some theorists consider natural rights to be distinct from or prior to natural law). See OBLIGATIONAL RIGHTS, PROTECTIVE RIGHTS, TAKINGS RIGHTS.

rightsizing.   Reducing assets and operations to an efficient size relative to output, rather than reduction for the sake of cutting expenses.

rigor.   In ANALYSIS, precision, accuracy, and thoroughness. Rigorous analysis is considered by some to be necessarily mathematical, but this is only one language, and one with limits. Verbal logic can be precise, accurate, and thorough. Both Austrian (AUSTRIAN ECONOMICS) and geo-economists (GEO-ECONOMICS) use verbal rigor in their analysis.

risk.   **1** A possible loss. When the probability is known, the risk can be insured or hedged against. **2** The volatility of a stock or mutual fund, that is the short-run risk (1). Investments with greater volatility warrant a higher return. See also UNCERTAINTY.

rivalry.   Gain at the expense of another; the attempt by more than one party to obtain the same gain, such as sales. With quantity rivalry, the quantity consumed by one person cannot be consumed by another. With quality rivalry, the utility obtained from a good decreases when others use it. With marginal rivalry, the utility from a physical good diminishes with the addition of another user, even when there is no existing quality rivalry; marginal rivalry is potential rather than actual.

Robert Schalkenbach Foundation.   Based in New York City, an educational organization incorporated in 1925 under the will of Robert Schalkenbach, a printer. The foundation publishes and provides books and other literature based on the thought of HENRY GEORGE. It makes grants and sponsors studies on FREE TRADE, LAND economics, PROPERTY TAX reform, and economic justice. The foundation also sponsors the *American Journal of Economics and Sociology*.

Robinson Crusoe.   A novel by Daniel Defoe written in 1719, based on a true story about Alexander Selkirk, a Scottish sailor. In the novel, Robinson Crusoe spends 26 years on an isolated tropical island and learns how to live from the resources of the island, but also takes goods from the shipwreck. He rescues a man from a tribe on the island, whom he names Friday, and the man becomes Crusoe's slave. Economists have adopted Crusoe as a metaphor in models with one person, which can then become extended to a second person.

Rothbard, Murray (1926–95).   Austrian school economist (AUSTRIAN ECONOMICS), historian, philosopher, and founder of the modern libertarian movement (LIBERTARIANISM). An adherent of natural rights, his expositions on libertarian thought include *For a New Liberty* (1973) and *Ethics of Liberty* (1982). He was a professor of economics at the University of Nevada at Las Vegas after teaching at the New York Polytechnic Institute in Brooklyn. He was also vice-president for academic affairs of the LUDWIG VON MISES INSTITUTE and editor of the *Review of Austrian Economics*, and frequent contributor to *The Free Market*. Rothbard's *Man, Economy, and State* (1962) remains a key Austrian treatise on economics. His *Power and Market* (1970) presented the case for a FREE MARKET and the ill effects of INTERVENTION. In *America's Great Depression* (1963, 1975), Rothbard focused on the role of the FED and the money supply growth. Rothbard favored a GOLD STANDARD and ONE HUNDRED PERCENT RESERVE BANKING; among his theoretical monetary works is *Method, Money, and the Austrian School* (1997). His historical works include *Conceived in Liberty* (1974–79), a four-volume history of colonial America. He also wrote *An Austrian Perspective on the History of Economic Thought* (1995–96). In his academic writing, Rothbard upheld Misesian PRAXEOLOGY, and he wrote a multitude of articles on policy and economic issues for many publications.

roundaboutness.   Indirect production, which rather than directly producing a CONSUMER GOOD, first produces CAPITAL GOODS that then increase the productivity of making the consumer goods. The concept was developed by the Austrian school (AUSTRIAN ECONOMICS), especially by BÖHM-BAWERK. See CAPITAL STRUCTURE.

royalty.   A dividend paid to the owner or tax paid to government by mining and oil extraction operations, based on output. It is one way of obtaining some of the ECONOMIC RENT of a NATURAL RESOURCE, but to better obtain the RENT (1), it should be flexibly combined with fees paid to obtain the franchise and a charge on the net profits. For high-cost operations, there may be no ECONOMIC RENT, and the royalty as a tax would make the operation uneconomical. See also SEVERANCE TAX.

Rückenrecht.   *Ger.* In Germanic law, the right of USUFRUCT, occupation and active use, of LAND. One who possesses land may not be evicted so long as he has his *Rücken* (back) on it.

rule.   A statement specifying certain ACTIONS (1) or inactions which are to be penalized. Rules prohibiting action penalize their performance, and rules commanding an action penalize those who do not so act. Rules can be AGREEMENTS, or they can be commands by an authority. Government rules are called laws, statutes, or ordinances; non-profit organizational rules are often called bylaws; and business rules are often called policies and procedures. Often, rules are just called 'rules.'

rule of law.   Government policy which follows known, usually written, RULES, ultimately based on its CONSTITUTION, including specified ways of seeking remedies for incorrectly applied rules. The opposite is the rule of man, where rules are applied according to the whim of the authority, and there is no effective remedy.

rules agreement.   A CONTRACT among the members of an organization specifying the RULES of the organization. Consensual community rules are based on VOLUNTARY membership, while governmental rules are usually IMPOSED on the residents of some territory.

ruling class.   The set of persons who wield ruling (RULE) authority, in some cases a distinct group, such as a monarch, dictator, oligarchy, or aristocracy. In modern MASS DEMOCRACIES, the ruling class depends on the particular policy, so that there can be one ruling class for economic policy and another for civil liberties, the rulers being a combination of voters, political parties, pressure groups, and government officials.

S

sacrifice. Giving up something of significant value without receiving any tangible good or service in return, but rather for the sake of others or for some perceived moral, spiritual, religious, or legal value or duty.

sacrifice argument for taxation. The notion that those with ABILITY TO PAY should be forced to SACRIFICE their income and wealth allegedly for the public welfare, but actually to maintain PRIVILEGES, since the BENEFIT PRINCIPLE makes sacrifice redundant.

sales tax. A tax imposed on the transfer of property at the point of sale, usually an *AD VALOREM* tax. Usually, each transfer of an item is taxed, so that the sale of a second-hand item becomes taxed again, unlike a VALUE ADDED tax which does not tax transfers as such but only gains in value. The sales TAX is called a TRANSFER TAX in the case of real estate, for which general sales taxes usually do not apply. See also AMUSEMENT TAX, CONSUMPTION TAX, EXPENDITURE TAX, TURNOVER TAX.

satisficing. Achieving some goal, which then satisfies one's ends, even if profits are not being maximized. But if this approach saves on TRANSACTION costs to achieve some goal rather than the brute attempt to maximize profits, then that is in practice also maximizing, that is economizing (ECONOMIZE).

savings. INCOME not used for CONSUMPTION. Savings are the source of INVESTMENT (1), and tend to equal investment as the INTEREST RATE equilibrates (EQUILIBRATION) the supply and demand for loanable funds. But see also FORCED SAVINGS.

Say, Jean Baptiste (1767–1832). French CLASSICAL economist famous for his theory of MARKETS, especially SAY'S LAW OF MARKETS. Unlike other classicals, Say theorized SUBJECTIVE VALUES. One of Say's key contributions to classical thought was to delineate the three factors of production (THREE-FACTOR ECONOMICS) and their shares of produced wealth. His key work is *Trait d'Économie Politique* (1803).

Say's law of markets. The proposition first proposed by SAY that in the production of wealth, the payment to FACTORS equals the value of the products, so the aggregate quantities of SUPPLY and DEMAND (2) are equal. This normally precludes any general glut or excess of goods. Say's law is often incorrectly defined as 'supply creates its own demand.' Rather, the resources with which demand is effective are created by the quantity supplied. The law has been challenged by assertions such as that price changes can leave a surplus of goods even when factors have spent their resources, but then one may inquire as to why the price level is not equilibrating the market for goods. Say's law does not preclude depressions, when there are both gluts of goods and idle workers, but this implies that market coordination has broken down, usually due to INTERVENTIONS which preclude coordination or that precipitate the breakdown (see BUSINESS CYCLE).

scarce. 1 A good is scarce (1) if the quantity available at a zero price is insufficient to provide the quantity demanded. 2 A low quantity supplied relative to NOTIONAL DEMAND, so that only a small proportion of those who want it can have it. For example, a postage stamp is said to be scarce (2) if only a few hundred copies exist, while thousands of collectors would like to have a copy.

Schalkenbach.   See ROBERT SCHALKENBACH FOUNDATION.

Scholes, Myron. (1941–)   Professor emeritus of Economics at Stanford University, he together with Robert Merton of Harvard University won the 1997 Nobel prize in economics for developing the methodology of valuing financial DERIVATIVES (2) such as OPTIONS (2). Fischer Black of MIT, who died in 1995, also worked with Scholes. Their work helped create the global market in derivatives that hedge (HEDGING) against RISK as well as provide speculation media, and contributed significantly to the understanding of markets.

Schumpeter, Joseph A. (1883–1950). Austrian-born and school economist at Harvard, famous for the concept of 'creative destruction' as well as his *History of Economic Analysis* (1954). He was a leading theorist of ENTREPRENEURS, who play key roles in his theories of trade cycles and economic development. Innovations by entrepreneurs upset the *status quo*, but then other producers copy the new products and methods. Schumpeter theorized that clusters of innovations create a boom and bust. He also argued that the success of market economies would lead to large bureaucratic corporations that would be taken over by government, leading to socialism; he underestimated the vitality of rivalry and technological change. He died leaving his manuscript on the history of economic thought, published posthumously by his wife.

science.   An organized body of KNOWLEDGE. The term usually refers to knowledge having an imprimatur by credentialed practitioners.

scientism. The misapplication of scientific methods to fields that are inappropriate or in a rigid way that excludes other useful methods. The term was used by Hayek for the inappropriate application of the methods of physical sciences to social science.

Scottish Enlightenment. The era in Scotland during the 1700s, when writers such as Adam Ferguson, DAVID HUME, Francis Hutcheson, and ADAM SMITH were influential. Their writing on NATURAL LAW, governance, and economics sought to use REASON to elucidate principles of social harmony, and Austrian (AUSTRIAN ECONOMICS) as well as classical-liberal thought continues to reflect ideas developed by this school of thought.

secession. Withdrawal of territory from a jurisdiction. Legalized secession would enable people to create new governments and even new countries, an exit option that would help reduce wasteful and oppressive government. The legal inability to secede creates a governmental ABSOLUTE MONOPOLY power over the territory under its jurisdiction and, globally, ENTRY MONOPOLY among countries.

seeing the cat. See CAT.

seignorage. The net revenue derived from creating new MONEY or MONEY SUBSTITUTES. As the DEMAND FOR MONEY increases, the issuer exchanges notes for real goods. The issuer can also obtain seignorage from inflating the money supply beyond demand.

seizure and forfeiture. The arbitrary confiscation of assets by government, often without any criminal conviction. It is alleged to be a civil action, the property committing the offense, even when the owner has no knowledge or control of it. The practice in the USA originated with English COMMON LAW. See also CIVIL ASSET FORFEITURE, *DEODAND*.

self-employment. The ownership of an enterprise, employing oneself as manager. The option of self-employment in a market ECONOMY prevents workers from being exploited by employers. A proprietor of an enterprise pays his wage, the opportunity cost of not working for others, out of his ACCOUNTING PROFIT, any extra profit being an ECONOMIC PROFIT.

self-esteem. The disposition to experience oneself as competent and worthy. Nathaniel Branden is a key author on this concept, which relates to individualism and the competency to make effective choices, and thus impacts the acceptance of liberty.

self-evident. 1 Evident without the need for further proof, evidence, or analysis. 2 Evident because reflection reveals that the denial of the proposition leads to a contradiction, hence a subset of (1).

self-interest. Narrowly, obtaining utility (UTILITY, MARGINAL) only from goals that exclude the WELL-BEING of others (except for one's immediate family) or any interest in others. Broadly, the utility one gains from the well-being of others is included. The INVISIBLE-HAND principle of self-interest is that the pursuit of narrow self-interest leads to social well-being, since producers satisfy the desires of consumers.

self-ownership. OWNERSHIP being a bundle of RIGHTS, self-ownership means having the rights to fully control one's own body and time. Hence it is the right to be FREE of any coercive HARM imposed by others, including any INVASION of one's body and any RESTRICTION of peaceful and honest ACTION (1). This implies that one has the right to one's own LABOR, its income as WAGES, and the PRODUCTS of labor.

Despite its invocation by libertarians (LIBERTARIANISM) and the seemingly useful application to POLICY, the concept of self-ownership is criticized by some philosophers as lacking coherence in the identification of subject and object. What does it mean to own oneself? The answer is that 'self-ownership' is just a metaphor, not to be taken that literally. Since rights are a correlative of moral wrongs, to have rights over my body means that it is morally wrong for others to invade my body. So self-ownership basically is a metaphor for the proposition that people have no rights to own others' bodies.

selfish. Concerned only with one's narrow SELF-INTEREST, doing no HARM to others but not aiding others even when they would fall into harm without assistance. Objectivist (OBJECTIVISM) followers of AYN RAND, regarding 'selfishness' as a virtue, may mean the absence of any feeling of obligation to others, and the absence of SACRIFICE.

Senior, William Nassau (1790–1864). British CLASSICAL economist at Oxford who held to a SUBJECTIVE theory of value rather than the labor theory. His theory of INTEREST as a return to capital funds was based on abstinence from consumption, almost but not quite a theory of TIME PREFERENCE. Senior regarded economic theory as universal to humanity, and he explicitly used AXIOMATIC-DEDUCTIVE methodology. His key work is *An Outline of the Science of Political Economy* (1836), the last chapter entitled 'Of Our Rational Expectations.'

service. A GOOD that is immediately consumed (CONSUME). Services are provided directly by human beings or by goods that are useful over a period of time. Services are regarded by some as intangible, but they are provided by tangible persons and goods. The distinction between a tangible good and a service is quite fuzzy and of little economic significance. The term 'goods' broadly includes services, though they are distinguished in the term 'goods and services.'

severable good. Goods which are not COLLECTIVE, whose quantity can be severed or divided among users; a synonym for PRIVATE GOODS.

severance tax. A tax on oil, minerals, or timber, proportional to output, taken when the resource is severed or separated from its natural state, similar in effect to a ROYALTY paid to government.

shadow economy. UNDERGROUND ECONOMY, or informal economy (INFORMAL SECTOR).

Sharpe, William F. (1934–). Professor at Stanford University and winner of the 1990 Nobel prize in Economics (shared with Miller and Markowitz) for his pioneering study of the CAPITAL ASSET PRICING MODEL, the relationship between RISK and return in INVESTMENT (2) theory. The Selection Sharpe Ratio compares a fund's return to that of a benchmark, dividing the average difference between them by the standard deviation of the differences, higher ratios providing better risk-adjusted returns.

shirking. Not working as hard and fully as the employer expects. Neoclassical (NEOCLASSICAL ECONOMICS) labor theory typically presumes that workers want to shirk, and so need to be monitored or paid extra 'efficiency' wages. However, in actuality, workers can take pride in their work and want to perform well if the work environment is conducive, that is, if their voice is heard, if they have some control over their operations, and if they sympathize (SYMPATHY) with the firm.

shock. An event affecting AGGREGATE DEMAND (for demand shocks) or AGGREGATE SUPPLY (for supply shocks) that quickly changes the level of output. A prime example is a sudden increase in the price of oil, which causes a supply shock, decreasing aggregate nominal output. In a flexible market ECONOMY, production can adjust to such shocks without causing a DEPRESSION or UNEMPLOYMENT, but if imported raw materials are more expensive, there is no way to avoid the decreased purchasing power of income.

shock therapy. The psychiatric term applied to the transition from a command (COMMAND ECONOMY) to a MARKET ECONOMY, where both LIBERALIZATION and PRIVATIZATION are sudden. The result is an immediate DEPRESSION, followed by an expansion that one hopes is more rapid than would be the case with gradual MARKETIZATION. Shocks could have been avoided with a physiocratic (PHYSIOCRACY) elimination of restrictions and taxes on productive effort, giving full reign to INCENTIVES, while pushing land to productive use by assessing a charge on the RENT (1), but such was not the advice proffered by most Western experts.

short run. As defined by Alfred Marshall, the time interval during which some assets are fixed.

short sale. The sale of an ASSET, followed by its purchase, the EXPECTATION being that one will PROFIT by the fall in PRICE.

shortage. The quantity demanded being greater than the quantity supplied at the prevailing price, leaving the inventory bare, most likely because of a PRICE CEILING, such as RENT CONTROL. A temporary shortage also occurs when a producer underestimates the DEMAND (1).

shut down cost. The cost incurred in the closing of an enterprise. If the shut down is permanent, then it is an ABANDONMENT COST.

silver. A bright whitish precious metal lighter than GOLD, which is easily shaped and conducts electricity well. Cheaper than gold for the past few centuries, it has been commonly used for lower-denomination COINS, as well as for jewelry and industrial uses.

silver certificate. Until the 1960s, the US dollar was a silver certificate convertible into SILVER. After silver coins went out of circulation, the $1 bill became fiat money like the rest of the currency.

silver dollar. A US coin with almost $1 of silver value when coins were made of SILVER. Dollar coins then become tokens made with metal of little intrinsic value.

sin tax. See SUMPTUARY TAX.

single tax. A TAX system with only one basic tax or family of taxes. The most famous one is the single tax on LAND RENT advocated by followers of HENRY GEORGE. This became the 'single-tax movement,' but later Georgists preferred to call it 'land-value taxation,' (LAND-VALUE TAX) and recently, in rejection of the 'tax' label, the term 'PUBLIC (or COMMUNITY) COLLECTION OF

RENT,' 'deed fee,' and 'rent assessment,' and 'community rent' are in use as alternatives. The geocratic single tax is actually a family of charges on the rent of sites, natural materials, and pollution dumps. Having one or a family of DIRECT TAXES has less FISCAL ILLUSION than having a multitude of taxes.

Sismondi, Jean (Jean Charles Léonard Simonde) (1773–1842). Swiss-born French economist from an Italian family, he was responsible for splitting LIBERALISM into two camps, the CLASSICAL LIBERALS and, following Sismondi, the WELFARE-STATE redistributionist economic-interventionist liberals. Having become a critic of markets and Say's law (SAY'S LAW OF MARKETS), he was a forerunner of MARX and KEYNES, originating the terms and concepts of the PROLETARIAT and class struggle. He was not a socialist, but paved the way for Marxism as well as the welfare state. Here too originated the statist-liberal failure to distinguish between the skewed markets causing the social problems and truly FREE MARKETS.

site. A plot of surface LAND with a particular LOCATION. Site value is a synonym for land value, and site revenue consists of rent generated by a site and paid to some COMMUNITY.

skeptic. One who neither naively believes nor cynically disbelieves on face value, but WARRANTS his belief with LOGIC and EVIDENCE, the proper scientific attitude. A skeptic is a doubter, but when presented with warrants, the cynic rather than the true skeptic continues to doubt.

skew. To twist, bias, distort, or slant. Starting with FREE-MARKET prices and profits, intervention skews them, rasing taxed prices, reducing subsidized prices, truncating profits and opportunities, shifting gains, eliminating incentives, confusing the knowledge conveyed by market signals. Outcomes are distorted and twisted from what they would be in an unhampered market.

skewed market. A market ECONOMY with INTERVENTION superimposed, skewing (SKEW) prices, reducing PROFITS, and truncating opportunity, resulting in more UNEMPLOYMENT and POVERTY and less growth. Critics of markets fail to see the skewing caused by intervention, blaming social problems on nonexisting 'free markets.' See also FREE MARKET, LARCENOUS.

slave. **1** CHATTEL SLAVERY, a person being explicitly under the total control of another. **2** Implicit slavery or peonage, an ADULT being in effect under control of other persons or institutions, especially the GOVERNMENT, that is, to the degree that one's WAGE is taxed, one is a slave to the government, being forced to work for the government rather than being able to work on behalf of one's self and family. **3** Slave (2) by feeling, though not in fact or law, as when one refers to oneself as a 'wage slave' or a 'debt slave' because one feels trapped in a job one does not like or by debt servicing.

slump.   A DEPRESSION.

small cap.   See CAP.

smart card.   A card containing a microchip which operates like a ledger. MONEY value can be transferred to and from the card. Some smart cards may be bearer claims against the issuer, similar to private bank notes. Smart cards are MONEY SUBSTITUTES.

Smith, Adam (1723–90).   Premier CLASSICAL free-trade Scottish economist, moral philosopher, and legal theorist. He opposed slavery and imperialism, and said war should be financed by taxes so people realize the burden. His famous book WEALTH OF NATIONS (1776, 1976), the first full treatise of political economy, popularized the metaphor of the INVISIBLE HAND and helped bring down the curtain on the mercantilist (MERCANTILISM) era. The book also presented the CANONS OF TAXATION, discussed the division of labor, theorized on rent, wages, profits, and prices, and spoke well of the PHYSIOCRATS. If these concepts were not original with Smith, he accomplished a great synthesis.

In addition to SELF-INTEREST as a motive in the *Wealth of Nations*, Smith presented the other great motivator, sympathy, in his book *The Theory of Moral Sentiments* (1790, 1982). There he wrote that there is an element of human nature by which a person is interested in the well-being of others, calling this sentiment 'sympathy.' His writing on law appears in Smith (1978, 1982).

Smith Center for Private Enterprise Studies.   Based in the California State University at Hayward, the privately funded organization sponsors lectures, research, and courses on the principles and practice of free enterprise.

social.   Referring to all the effects of an ACTION (1) on all the people in an ECONOMY, and to the common WELFARE (1). As Hayek noted, the term can be turned into a governmental meaning, as with 'socialization,' hence can be a weasel word taking out the original meaning.

social auditing.   An analysis of the impact of a company's operations and products on those other than shareholders, that is, communities, the environment and employees, a term coined during the 1970s as a social cost–benefit analysis. Ben & Jerry's Homemade, a prime example of a corporation that does this, hires the London-based New Economics Foundation to conduct the audit.

social choice.   The analysis of voting. Fiscal policy is often linked to social choice, as with the CLARKE TAX and the TIEBOUT MODEL of choosing among COMMUNITIES. The Arrow IMPOSSIBILITY THEOREM shows the difficulty of making collective decisions by simple voting methods. A different approach is that of CONSENSUS, in which large groups break up into smaller groups and discussion proceeds until some general agreement is reached. Voluntary associations, whether choosing among communities or seceding and forming new communities, are complementary to the internal choice methods.

social contract.   A unanimous (UNANIMITY) agreement by members of a SOCIETY (2) on the constitutional rules. This concept is used in political philosophy and theory.

social costs and benefits.   The PRIVATE COSTS, to the purchaser, plus the EXTERNAL EFFECTS, or likewise, the private benefits plus the externalities.

social evolution.   The change in CULTURE over time. HAYEK emphasized that the economic INSTITUTIONS we have now were not designed, but are the product of social evolution. The institutionalist school has emphasized economic evolution. Just as with biological evolution, organisms which are not fit do not survive, with social evolution, rules and practices which work better than others may tend to be adopted. The equivalent of biological genes are 'MEMES,' units of ideas, which get carried across generations. However, much historical change has also taken place through conquest and violence, so peaceful peoples without adequate defenses have often not been survivors.

social justice.   The implementation of NATURAL MORAL LAW by a governing agency. In essence, social justice is the absence of government-granted privilege. Individual justice is justice applied by one individual to another, giving the other his moral due. The key principle in social justice is the equal SELF-OWNERSHIP of each person. The concept of social justice is on one hand expanded by welfare statists to include WELFARE (2) and on the other hand denied by critics of natural moral law who claim there is no such thing as social justice. If there is no universal ethic, then there is no universal concept of justice, nor of liberty. See also ECONOMIC JUSTICE.

social problems.   Woes and maladies of SOCIETY (1), including poverty, unemployment, pollution, crime, and government intervention. The two ways of dealing with them is to treat the effects and to treat the causes. Most policy does the former, because it is visible, popular, and easy, though it is costly and does not solve the problem.

social science.   Science about human beings, including anthropology, psychology, psychiatry, history, sociology, economics, political science, and linguistics. The other two branches of science are the physical sciences and the biological sciences. Biology blends with social science in physical anthropology and the health sciences.

social security.   A combined national pension plan plus WELFARE (2) assistance to the old, sick, and poor. These are typically pay-as-you-go, taxing workers to fund the transfers. Large payroll taxes reduce savings available for investment, resulting in a smaller capital stock and lower national income. As the population ages, there is an ever larger ratio of recipients to providers. Various proposed reforms include a more realistically smaller inflation index, partial replacement with private investment plans, and the phase-out of the system.

social welfare function.   The WELL-BEING of society as a whole as a function of variables such as income, liberty, and culture. This raises the problem and possibility of aggregating individual WELFARE (1) into aggregate welfare, since individual utility cannot be measured. One way to resolve this is by the proposition that social welfare is maximized when individuals are free to each pursue his own well-being, in accord with SUBJECTIVE VALUES and NATURAL RIGHTS. Several organizations have devised indices of liberty and other variables, but none of these are definitive. Intuitively, most people can tell that some societies are better off than others; slave labor camps are worse places than free societies.

socialism.   A family of related concepts, the basic one being the ownership of the MEANS OF PRODUCTION by workers. In worker socialism, workers own their CAPITAL GOODS in worker cooperatives, unions (syndicalism), communes, tribes, ESOPs, and self-employment with no employees. In state socialism, the state controls the means of production, ideally as the agent of the workers. In practice, in the Soviet Union and other countries calling themselves socialist, the Communist Party was the RULING CLASS, and the workers were its employees, a situation some called 'state capitalism.' Aspects of state socialism include redistribution, administrative socialism (government ownership and control, or a command economy), and various types of substantial intervention, including social democracy (policy by vote) and industrial policy. See also ECONOMIC CALCULATION, MARKET SOCIALISM.

socialization. Conversion to common or governmental property.

society. **1** All the people in an ECONOMY or jurisdiction. **2** A nonprofit club or association.

socionomy. The theory and formulation of the basic or 'organic' laws of the organization and development society. Used by Spencer Heath.

Socrates (*c*. 470–399 BC). Greek philosopher who questioned the basic premises of his society, and was put to death for it. He showed that when people are questioned about concepts such as justice which they think they understand, they realize that they don't really know it. His philosophy and methods were recorded by Plato in dialogues, which makes it unclear what is Socrates's and what is Plato's. The Socratic method of teaching is to ask pointed questions and let the students find the answers or else admit they don't truly know.

Socratic questions. 'What do you mean?' and 'How do you know?' Answers to these two questions clarify and WARRANT *PROPOSITIONS.

solidarism. The belief that each person should defend and promote the dignity of others. The term was coined by the leading French anti-liberal economist Charles Gide in 1889.

space. **1** One of the three rudiments of the universe, encompassing distance in three dimensions. **2** The area beyond the surface and atmosphere of the earth and other cosmic bodies.

In economics, space (1) is manifested as the SITES in which economic ACTIVITY (1) takes place. Space is a type of LAND or NATURAL RESOURCE. Space is also involved in LOCATION THEORY. The economics of space thus involve both AREA (TERRITORY) and LOCATION.

Besides three-dimensional space, there are spaces in the electromagnetic spectrum, satellite orbits, and other natural phenomena by which matter exists in space (1).

Space (1) is one type of LAND which is not itself altered by use. Use does not use up, diminish, transport, or alter space. Usage only alters the material contents within a site. Hence, space remains land even in use, while material land such as minerals cease being land after alteration by HUMAN ACTION.

special assessments. Districts in which real estate is assessed for charges that finance public works within the district. Ideally, the increase in rent induced by the improvements is not less than the assessments.

special interests.   Groups with some common interest such as an INDUSTRY (2), who organize to fund political campaigns and to lobby for favors, and also to prevent intervention. Successful special interests have concentrated benefits, making it feasible to organize, while the costs are thinly spread among the taxpayers and consumers, who thus have less incentive to resist. Special interests also engage in propaganda to persuade voters that the special interest is also the general interest.

specie.   Precious metals used as MONEY in the form of COINS.

specie flow mechanism.   First formulated by DAVID HUME, it is the process by which trade balances with a GOLD STANDARD. Export surpluses are offset by gold imports, which raise prices and reduce net exports until trade in goods is balanced.

specific theory.   Theory that is specific to some event, place, culture, or particular phenomenon, rather than applying universally. An example is an explanation of the GREAT DEPRESSION.

speculation.   1 A guess as to the explanation of some phenomenon. 2 A prediction or EXPECTATION about some future outcome, especially a price change. 3 The purchase or sale of an asset on the EXPECTATION that the PRICE will change favorably, resulting in a gain. See also LAND SPECULATION.

spillover.   An EXTERNAL EFFECT.

spontaneous order.   The ORDER created by the MARKET PROCESS, which coordinates SUPPLY and DEMAND with the price system and profit and losses. When profits are higher than normal, supply increases and the profit and price goes down; when firms make losses, they reduce supply, and profits and prices increase. The process, however, is not automatic or a mechanism, since human ENTREPRENEURS drive the process by seeking out profitable opportunities, which are not always evident. HAYEK also called it the 'extended order.'

Spooner, Lysander (1808–87).   American postal entrepreneur, anarchist, and libertarian political theorist. He is called the 'father of the three-cent stamp' for setting up the American Letter Mail Company in competition with the US Post Office, which in response, lowered postage to 3 cents, and then forced him out of business. Spooner's *No Treason: The Constitution of No Authority* (1870) attacked imposed government, arguing for voluntary association. In *An Essay on the Trial by Jury* (1852), Spooner presented the history of the English jury system, showing how jurors had the right to judge both fact and law, and that independent jurors are a key protection against tyranny. He also wrote a treatise on *Natural Law* (1882), on *A new banking system* (1873), *A new system of paper currency* (1861), on *Poverty: its illegal causes and legal cure* (1846), *The unconstitutionality of slavery* (1847) and the *Unconstitutionality of prohibiting private mail* (1844). In *Vices are Not Crimes: A Vindication of Moral Liberty* (1875), Spooner argued that only harm to another is a true crime.

sprawl. See URBAN SPRAWL.

stable. Having a low variance, or an ECONOMY with mild or no BUSINESS CYCLES. MONEY which maintains its purchasing power. See also TURBULENCE, VOLATILITY.

stagflation. The presence of both price INFLATION and high UNEMPLOYMENT or economic stagnation, a phenomenon that challenged the notion of a stable PHILLIPS CURVE.

stamp duty. A TAX on goods, paid using a stamp attached to the good, common during the 1700s and 1800s, and into the 1900s with cigarettes and liquor. These revenue stamps are collectibles.

standard of living. The amount of CONSUMER GOODS a typical household can obtain during some time interval. Other factors that affect the quality of life can be added, such as crime, pollution, and persecution.

state. A government with supreme power over some territory and population. OPPENHEIMER (1914, 1975) held that the state necessarily involves a dominant class, originating in conquest, extracting tribute from a subordinate class, though the constitutional state offers protective services as well. Hence, Oppenheimer (1927) held the state to be 'the bastard offspring of might and right, of *ethos* and *kratos*.' Nock (1935, p. 60) regarded the state as the organization of the POLITICAL MEANS.

state capitalism. The ownership and operation of an ECONOMY by government, which becomes a monopoly FIRM. Some have called the Soviet economy 'state capitalism' rather than socialism, since to the worker, the state was the employer who exploited him, and the worker did not truly control the MEANS OF PRODUCTION.

state of being. An attribute of a PERSON not based on any ACTION (1). For example, the natural color of one's skin is part of one's state of being, as is one's race and the appearance of one's natural body. The laws of a free society neither DISCRIMINATE against (or for) nor criminalize a state of being.

static.   Analysis of a system, usually in EQUILIBRIUM, at a moment in time, in contrast to DYNAMIC analysis that examines a PROCESS over time. See also COMPARATIVE STATICS.

statistic.   A measure of data, such as a sum, a mean, or a variance.

status.   One's prestige, standing, and ranking in a social setting. Status is one motivator of ACTION (1).

status quo.   *Lat.* The currently existing situation.

step up of basis.   The exemption of unrealized gains, which steps up the taxable value to the current market value, for example on inherited property.

sticky.   Resistant to change, as a wage which is sticky downwards because workers will refuse to accept a lower wage. In Keynesian theory, wages, interest rates, and other prices are sticky, and with the market stuck, INTERVENTION is needed to push the market towards full employment. This raises the question of why a price would be sticky in the absence of intervention.

Stigler, George Joseph (1911–91).   Professor of Economics at the University of Chicago and winner of the 1982 Economics Nobel prize for his studies of markets and regulations. A leading microeconomist, he contributed to the topics of information and searching in labor markets.

stock.   1 A quantity of physical things at a moment in time. 2 A share of a corporation.

stock exchange.   An organization which facilitates exchanges among buyers and sellers of STOCKS (2) and other securities. Its key function is to provide a secondary market for shares as well as to facilitate raising funds in the primary market.

strategic behavior.   Non-cooperative action which attempts to exploit the ignorance or lack of power of another party. For example, one might attempt to deceive the other to gain an advantage. Game theory deals with such strategies. See also OPPORTUNISM.

strike.   A union's (UNIONS, LABOR) refusal to work until its demands are met. If the employer refuses to let the union members work, it is called a 'lockout.' From a social viewpoint, a strike is wasteful, since other parties can suffer losses that greatly exceed the gains that either side receive when the labor dispute is settled. Strikes occur in part because of legal privileges enjoyed by labor unions, but the greater reason is that without a union, workers in some industries have poor bargaining power due to job insecurity and unemployment. The poor relative position of labor is due to INTERVENTIONS which take much of the wage and make it costly for labor to pursue the alternative of SELF-EMPLOYMENT. The ultimate remedy for strikes is the elimination both of the taxation of wages and of the arbitrary regulation of enterprise. Then individual workers would have a more equal bargaining power with management, with greater opportunities for self-employment.

structure of taxes.   See TAX STRUCTURE.

structures of government.   Rules of government that determine the institutions. Representative government, division of power, method of voting, and ABILITY to exit a jurisdiction are examples of structures.

style.   The different categories or types of investments owned by a fund, the style return being that of indexes for these types. The selection return is the return from the particular stocks owned for those types.

subjective.   Stemming from the mind of the subject person.

subjective cost.   JAMES BUCHANAN distinguished between choice-influencing and choice-influenced cost. Choice-influencing cost is subjective. Market prices are objective, but one's opportunity costs depend on one's values.

subjective values.   The proposition that values are subjective is FOUNDATIONAL to economics. The economic value of a good depends on the interests of the person affected, relative to that of other goods. It is not just that persons subjectively have interests, but more radically that there are no values other than those of personal interests. Moral values are also subjective. The very subjectivity of values is itself an OBJECTIVE proposition from which an objective economic science and morality can be derived.

suborn.   Obtain through one's own or another's bribery, perjury, or other crime.

subsidiarity.   Decentralization that limits the scope of higher-level government, devolving policy to the lowest government levels in which it is efficient. This has been discussed as a policy goal for the EUROPEAN UNION.

subsidy.   A negative tax. A transfer of funds to an agent which is an ECONOMIC
RENT, not warranted (WARRANT) by economic performance, hence an INTERVENTION.

subsistence.   A household income that just barely enables it to obtain minimal food, shelter, and medicine. If income is below this level in the long run,
the population dies off.

substitute.   A good with a positive CROSS-ELASTICITY OF DEMAND for another
good. For example, if blue pencils are a substitute for red pencils, then if the
price of red ones rises, the demand for the blue ones will increase. The
presence of substitutes, close alternatives, prevents the exploitation of consumers and workers. See also PERFECT SUBSTITUTE.

sumptuary tax.   A tax imposed on ethical grounds on a good which the
government or the culture disfavors. *Syn.* SIN TAX.

supererogatory duties.   Acts that are a moral obligation, but which may
not be compelled.

supply.   1 The quantities of a good produced or in existence at a range of
prices during some time interval. 2 The quantities of a good offered to the
market at a range of prices at a moment in time.
   'Supply' refers to either or both (1) or (2) unless it is specified that it is a
supply of total quantity (1) or a supply of offers (2). 'Supply' in either case
refers to the whole range of quantities, while 'quantity supplied' refers to a
particular quantity at some price. A supply schedule is a list of prices and the
quantity supplied at each price. A supply curve is a graph with a line drawn
through the points of a supply schedule.
   For goods in current production, where all the product is offered to the
market and none is hoarded, supplies (1) and (2) coincide. This is the supply
curve typically implied in textbooks. Where there is some existing stock of
goods, some of which are offered to the market, such as the market for shares
of stock (excluding any new issues), supplies (1) and (2) differ.
   For shares of stock with no new issues, supply (1) is the number of shares in
existence; this supply curve is vertical. Supply (2) is the quantities of shares
offered for sale to the market at various prices. Supply (2) depends on supply
(1), since if supply (1) doubles (the stock splits in two), the market price would
be cut in half, and this would be reflected in supply (2).

The land market operates the same way. Supply (1) is fixed, the supply curve being vertical (the total quantity of land within some jurisdiction at various market rents). Supply (2) is upward-sloping, the quantity being lots offered to the market for sale. The confusion of those who deny that the supply of land fixed usually stems from the lack of recognition of the two different meanings of supply.

supply-side. Macroeconomic theory in which output is determined by the SUPPLY of factors and the PRODUCTIVITY of production, hence by the supply-side of the ECONOMY. AGGREGATE DEMAND therefore plays no role in determining output, or no long-term role; an increase in the money supply only drives up prices. Supply-side policy thus seeks to either increase the amount of factor inputs (such as labor and capital goods) or to increase productivity by reducing the wasteful costs imposed by government on production, namely taxes and regulations. The ultimate supply-side policy is GEO-ECONOMIC: the complete elimination of taxes and restrictions on wages, interest, capital goods, output, and transactions.

surplus. Having more GOODS than CLEAR (1) the market during a normal inventory cycle, as the quantity supplied is greater than the quantity demanded at that PRICE.

surplus value. The price of goods minus wages, including the wage component of capital goods. Marxists considered this properly belonging to LABOR, but with the ultimate factors being LAND and labor, and with labor paid its MARGINAL PRODUCT, the surplus, as glimpsed by QUESNAY, is actually ECONOMIC RENT, mostly land rent. Thus did Marx misidentify the surplus factor.

sustainable development. ECONOMIC DEVELOPMENT that sustains RENEWABLE RESOURCES. The current practice often is to subsidize the destruction of forests and wildlife with government-paid INFRASTRUCTURE.

sympathy. As analyzed by ADAM SMITH in the *Theory of Moral Sentiments* (1790, 1982), sympathy is 'our fellow-feeling with any passion whatever' (p. 10). As a complement to the INVISIBLE HAND, Smith presented what could be called a 'visible hand-out' theory of benevolent provision. Smithian sympathy is a feeling of affinity, accord, and empathy with a person, group, culture, organization, or other entity. 'Nature, therefore, exhorts mankind to acts of beneficence, by the pleasing consciousness of deserved reward' (p. 86). Sympathy differs from ALTRUISM in being part of the utility (UTILITY, MARGINAL) of the donor rather than some sense of duty or obligation.

synergy. A situation with increasing returns, economies of scale, positive externalities, a positive-sum game, or where individual goals promote the group's goals, as they do in markets.

synthesis. 1 A merging of two or more bodies of theory into one systematic theory, perhaps discarding some incompatible and unwarranted elements. 2 An artificial creation.

synthesized demand. DEMAND that is artificially created by advertising (ADVERTISE) that unduly influences consumers' preferences, an allegation of some institutionalist economics (INSTITUTIONAL ECONOMICS), particularly Galbraith (1958); see AFFLUENT SOCIETY. The concept is countered by the existence of subjective values and unlimited desires. The concept of creating wants is sound enough, but it goes deeper than the mere advertising of consumer goods; cultures inculcate values and wants in childhood which then carry over to adulthood, where they seem natural and universal, hence unquestioned and unexamined, and often inscribed into law, to the detriment of minorities with other values.

system. A set of interrelated elements. Economically, a system is a way of coordinating (COORDINATION) production and distribution.

T

tableau économique. *Fr.*The first macroeconomic model, developed by the PHYSIOCRATS.

takings. The CONFISCATION of PROPERTY by government or a reduction in the value or use of property because of government law and policy. The 5th Amendment to the US Constitution requires just compensation for private property taken for PUBLIC (2) use.

takings rights. So-called 'positive' rights to others' property, giving recipients the legal right to have government take others' property to redistribute (REDISTRIBUTION) it to the recipients.

tariff. A tax on imports. See PROTECTIONISM.

tâtonnement. *Fr.* The process of moving or 'groping' towards a Walrasian GENERAL EQUILIBRIUM as though an auctioneer were calling out prices to equilibrate (EQUILIBRATION) markets in all goods.

tax. A LIABILITY *IMPOSED by GOVERNMENT, other than penalties. A pure FREE MARKET has no ARBITRARY taxation, but may have levies in accord with the BENEFIT PRINCIPLE or RENT (1) charges for resources considered to be commonly owned.

See also ABSOLUTE TAX INCIDENCE, ACCESSIONS TAX, *AD VALOREM* TAX, AMUSEMENT TAX, ASSET TAX, AVOIDABLE TAX, BENEFIT PRINCIPLE, CAPITAL GAINS TAX, CARBON TAX, CLARKE TAX, CONSUMPTION TAX, CORPORATE INCOME TAX, DEATH TAX, DIRECT TAXES, ESTATE TAX, EXCESS BENEFIT, EXCESS BURDEN, EXCISE TAX, EXPENDITURE TAX, FISCAL DRAG, FLAT TAX, GIFT TAX, HEAD TAX, INCIDENCE OF TAXATION, INCOME TAX, INDIRECT TAXES, INFLATION TAX, INHERITANCE TAX, LAND-VALUE TAX, LUMP-SUM TAX, LUXURY TAX, NEUTRAL TAX, PAYROLL TAX, PIGOVIAN TAX, PROGRESSIVE TAX, PROPERTY TAX, PROPORTIONAL TAX, REGRESSIVE TAX, SALES TAX, SEVERANCE TAX, SINGLE TAX, STAMP DUTY, SUMPTUARY TAX, TARIFF, TRANSFER TAX, TURNOVER TAX, USE TAX, VALUE ADDED TAX, WEALTH TAX.

tax base. The item being taxed, such as income, sales, and property. When productive activity and mobile assets are taxed, there is usually some reduction in the tax base, while when fixed assets are taxed, the tax base is not reduced so long as the tax is not greater than the RENT (2) of the assets.

tax burden.   The negative effect of taxation on economic activity. The main effect of taxes on productive exertion is to shift SUPPLY curves upward to higher prices and lower quantities. See also EXCESS BURDEN. The more INELASTIC the supply of a taxed resource, the lower the social tax burden.

tax capacity.   The maximum amount of taxes a jurisdiction can pay, given the TAX STRUCTURE.

tax credit.   A reduction in the tax liability. Credits are typically provided for activities the government favors or does not wish to burden. Tax credits are also provided to avoid DOUBLE TAXATION. If the tax credit is greater than the tax liability, the extra amount can be paid to the filer as a subsidy. In contrast, see TAX DEDUCTION.

tax deduction.   A reduction in taxable income or other tax basis.

tax disincentive.   A reduction in the expected net gain from an activity because of a TAX or REGULATION, reducing current exertion as well as INVESTMENT.

tax efficiency.   The degree to which a portfolio has a low TAX liability relative to the return of a taxable account. A high FUND TURNOVER generates high taxes in short-term capital gains. Index funds tend to be tax efficient because there is relatively little buying and selling.

tax evasion.   Illegal escape of TAXATION.

tax expenditure.   A TAX DEDUCTION or TAX CREDIT for an activity which substitutes for what government would have paid for, and thus is regarded by government as equivalent to an EXPENDITURE. It is analogous to a thief who steals money and then donates it to the poor; if the victim instead agrees to donate the money himself, the thief considers this to really be his donation.

tax incidence.   See INCIDENCE OF TAXATION.

tax-push price inflation.   The situation in which workers demand and obtain higher WAGES because of higher taxes on wages. The higher wages then cause goods to have higher prices.

tax reform. An improvement in the tax system, such as to reduce the EXCESS BURDEN or to reduce some element of injustice. Fundamental tax reforms alters the TAX STRUCTURE rather than merely reducing tax rates or changing the deductions and credits.

tax shifting. Transferring the ultimate tax burden to other parties, as when an enterprise pays a sales tax to the government, but adds it to the price of the goods, shifting the tax in part to the consumer. The seller still bears some burden, because the increased after-tax price reduces the quantity demanded.

tax structure. The types of TAXES in a jurisdiction, the revenues of each type, and analysis of the impact of these taxes. Some tax structures induce greater EXPENDITURE than others, or have a greater EXCESS BURDEN for a given amount of revenues.

tax substitution. The policy of allowing people to substitute PRIVATE (1) services for government-provided services, and deduct the cost (or an average cost) from the user's tax liability. Some cities, for example, permit condominiums to hire a private garbage service and deduct the cost from property taxes. Tax credits for private tuition is another application.

tax wedge. The difference between gross-of-tax and net-of-tax prices. For example, the tax wedge on WAGES is the difference between the cost of labor to an employer, which includes taxes paid by the employer as well as indirectly imposed costs such as excessive litigation, and the net wage or take-home pay of the worker, after all taxes on the wage. In some cases, the wedge can greatly exceed the net wage. The effect of the tax wedge is to reduce the quantity demanded, which for the labor market, decreases employment. Taxes on fixed resources have no tax wedge.

taxation. The theory and practice of levying TAXES.

'taxation is theft.' This slogan was the title of the pamphlet by David Walter, published by the Society for Individual Liberty around 1969.

taxing everything that moves. The principle of taxation of tapping all EXPLICIT flows. It SKEWS production and exchange towards IMPLICIT returns.

taxonomy. The classification of the parts of some phenomenon or field of study. Examples in economics are the FACTORS OF PRODUCTION (land, labor, and capital goods) and the division of national expenditure into private consumption, private investment, and government ($Y = C + I + G$).

technological unemployment.   The increase in UNEMPLOYMENT due to a labor-saving technological improvement. In a pure market ECONOMY, this would be local and temporary, since there would be a demand for LABOR elsewhere. Policy that favors CAPITAL GOODS relative to labor induces such technology, which can increase unemployment if policy then subsidizes unemployment and erects BARRIERS to SELF-EMPLOYMENT.

technology.   The KNOWLEDGE embedded in HUMAN CAPITAL and CAPITAL GOODS. A change in the knowledge and its application which increases PRODUCTIVITY is a technological improvement, and the ongoing improvements constitute technological progress. Technology includes methods of organizing production.

teleological.   Directed to some ultimate end, goal, purpose, or outcome. In ethics, teleology evaluates acts in relation to such ends. In SUBJECTIVE ethics, however, each person has his own end.

Ten Commandments.   Ten moral laws inscribed in Exodus 20, presented by MOSES and at the core of Judaism and Christianity. The sixth forbids murder, the eighth forbids theft, and the ninth forbids fraud. The tenth warns against envy of the property of others. These form the basic tenets of a MARKET *ECONOMY, which is thus not only compatible with, but some would say, mandated by, Biblical authority.

tender.   To offer as payment or present for acceptance. To tender MONEY means to EXCHANGE it for goods. Money is backed when it is redeemed for some COMMODITY at a fixed rate. Money is thus not backed by the general productivity of an ECONOMY, but is tendered by the economy in being readily exchanged for goods. See LEGAL TENDER.

territorial gangsters.   A term used by some anarchists (ANARCHISM) for the domination of territory by COERCIVE *AGENTS (1).

territorial goods.   COLLECTIVE GOODS which impact a territory in which one must be located to use the goods. Territorial goods tend to generate LAND RENT, and can thus be self-financing if the rent is not less than the cost. Territorial goods preclude free riding (FREE RIDER), since users pay rent in order to be located there. (If a guest rides for free, his host pays for him.)

territory.   An area of LAND surface and the usable space above and below the surface.

theft. The TAKING of what properly belongs to another, thus a morally wrong or EVIL taking.

theonomy. 'God's law': a legal system based on theological, especially biblical, beliefs. Some theconomists favor shrinking the economic functions of the state to what they consider to be a limited God-ordained role. See also TEN COMMANDMENTS.

theorem. A PROPOSITION fully warranted (WARRANT) by LOGIC and EVIDENCE. Warrants imply justified belief but not CERTAINTY.

theory. An organized set of related THEOREMS. Sometimes, colloquially or loosely, 'theory' is used to mean CONJECTURE or HYPOTHESIS. In economics, theory is divided into positive (POSITIVE ECONOMICS) and normative (NORMATIVE ECONOMICS) branches. Positive theory in turn is divided into pure or universal theory and specific theory. The study of past theory is called the HISTORY OF ECONOMIC THOUGHT. Two major fields of economic theory are MICROECONOMICS and MACROECONOMICS, although there are phcnomena and concepts which intersect the two, such as the FACTORS OF PRODUCTION.

third parties. **1** Persons affected by market action, other than those who are party to an exchange. Third parties are thus those affected by EXTERNAL EFFECTS. **2** A generic term for minor political parties.

threat. A statement that someone will hurt the recipient of the statement, usually conditional on the victim not obeying a command of the perpetrator. A threat is itself a coercively harmful (HARM) act, like a bomb set now to explode in the future.

three-factor economics. Economic analysis based on the classical FACTORS – land, labor, and capital goods. GEO-ECONOMICS emphasizes three-factor analysis. Neoclassical (NEOCLASSICAL ECONOMICS) and some Austrians' analysis (AUSTRIAN ECONOMICS) use two factors, labor and 'capital' to which land is merged.

Thünen, Johann Heinrich von (1783–1850).   German pioneer of LOCATION THEORY who also developed a theory of RENT (1), the distribution of income, and diminishing returns.

Tideman, Nicolaus (1943–).   GEO-ECONOMIC *PUBLIC-CHOICE economist at Virginia Polytechnic Institute. He served as Senior Staff Economist, President's Council of Economic Advisers, 1970–71. He has written on land-value taxation, economic justice, the measurement of concentration, and the de-

mand-revealing (DEMAND REVELATION) process. He has also been a consultant on economic reforms in the former Soviet republics and organized an open letter to Mikhail Gorbachev signed by 30 economists urging that LAND RENT be used as a source of government revenue rather than 'make unnecessarily great use of taxes that impede' the ECONOMY (Appendix in Noyes, 1991).

Tiebout model.   A model of the provision of LOCAL PUBLIC GOODS among multiple communities which residents may choose from, based on a landmark paper by Charles Tiebout (1956).

tight joint.   MONEY whose expansion beyond the DEMAND FOR MONEY immediately increases the PRICE LEVEL, having no effect on output, as in some classical models. See also, BROKEN JOINT, LOOSE JOINT.

time.   1 A moment. 2 A duration. 3 A historical process or event.
   Time (2) is one of the three rudiments of the universe, along with space and matter/energy. Time (2) is thus not a FACTOR OF PRODUCTION but an element of all factors and processes. An analysis that examines a phenomenon over a duration is called DYNAMIC, versus a STATIC analysis of a moment.

time preference.   The PREFERENCE for goods at the present time relative to those at future times. This preference is based on the limited human lifespan, the UNCERTAINTY of the future, economizing (ECONOMIZE), and unlimited desires. The premium for present-day goods over future foods constitutes a rate of discount of future goods, or the rate of INTEREST paid on loans to those who wish to use present-day goods and have no SAVINGS to fund them. The Austrian theory of interest (AUSTRIAN ECONOMICS) is based on time preference.

title.   A RIGHT to the ownership of an item, possibly including a document demonstrating the right.

title fee.   A fee paid to maintain TITLES conditional on such payments.

token.   MONEY or a MONEY SUBSTITUTE without intrinsic value.

tool.   A non-human instrument used in production. CAPITAL GOODS can briefly be described as tools.

total return.   The total percentage change in the value of an INVESTMENT (2), including CAPITAL GAINS and reinvested income.

totalitarianism. The system in which the central GOVERNMENT attempts to control the entire ECONOMY and all significant aspects of human life.

tradable permits. See MARKETABLE DISCHARGE PERMITS.

trade. EXCHANGE.

trade creation. The increase in net international trade caused by the formation of a FREE-TRADE area. There is a net increase in EFFICIENCY (2).

trade cycle. An alternative name for BUSINESS CYCLE.

trade diversion. A decrease in international trade (INTERNATIONAL ECONOMICS) caused by the formation of a FREE-TRADE area due to a shift in trade from countries outside the bloc, which may be more efficient, to those inside the bloc due to the elimination of TARIFFS within the bloc. Diverting trade from lower-cost to higher-cost producers reduces world EFFICIENCY (2).

trade union. See UNIONS, LABOR.

tragedy of the unmanaged commons. Garret Hardin's (1968) widely used phrase the 'tragedy of the commons,' refers to the overuse and destruction of common-access resources. When the resources are managed and access is controlled, such as by charging RENT (1), then the tragedy does not arise.

training for performance. Investing in HUMAN CAPITAL geared to specific business needs.

transaction. An economic ACT (2). The cost of the act includes both the resources directly exchanged for an item and the TRANSACTION cost, the OPPORTUNITY COST of attaining the transaction. For example, the transaction cost of food is the time and resources expended in obtaining the food, aside from the price of the food. These resources have alternative uses which constitute the opportunity cost. Since transaction costs are real-world costs, any real-world MARKET FAILURE to perform transactions would need to take these costs into account.

transaction cost. See TRANSACTION.

transfer payment. A transfer of resources, usually FUNDS to recipients of assistance or SUBSIDIES, not in exchange for any service. Voluntary transfers are gifts; the term is usually used for REDISTRIBUTION transfers mandated by

GOVERNMENT. In the case of SOCIAL SECURITY, there is some link between the tax payment and the eventual receipt of the transfer, but the link is weak and often non-existent.

transfer-seeking.   Financing political campaigns and making other payments to office holders and political parties in the attempt to obtain transfers of resources, protection from competition, laws suppressing cultural practices they disfavor, and seeking other PRIVILEGES. It is often called 'rent-seeking' because the transfer is an ECONOMIC RENT; it is also LAND-RENT-seeking when real-estate developers and owners seek public works that increase their rents, paid for by taxes on labor and enterprise. When farm interests obtain transfers and price supports, the public pays for it both as consumers and as taxpayers. Besides the loss due to taxes and higher prices, the seeking of transfers is itself costly, and a social WASTE. See also PUBLIC CHOICE.

transfer tax.   A special SALES TAX on the transfer of certain assets, such as REAL ESTATE.

transitivity.   Consistency of rank ordering, so that if A is preferred to B and B to C, A is preferred to C. If in experiments transitivity seems to be violated, then one could inquire as to the nature of the questions and procedure before concluding that the behavior is irrational.

triangle.   See HAYEKIAN TRIANGLE.

trickle down.   The proposition that WEALTH and growth mainly benefit the rich, from which trickle a few jobs. The expression is a favorite epithet of critics of MARKETS, which may well be so in SKEWED MARKETS with BARRIERS to employment. In a market ECONOMY, the high productivity and absence of barriers to employment would quite likely create a gusher of OPPORTUNITY rather than a trickle.

TRIM.   Trade-related investment measure. A law requiring a multinational corporation to export a minimum proportion of their production and/or refraining from importing certain goods. Such BARRIERS to trade are to be phased out under the Uruguay round of GATT/WORLD TRADE ORGANIZATION.

true.   A PROPOSITION in accord with perceived reality. Some deny that we can know what is true, while others believe that we can have an adequate intersubjective understanding of observed reality, that is adequate enough to be useful.

trust. **1** An amalgamated company. **2** A legal entity having title to property, managed by trustees for the designated beneficiaries.

truth. A PROPOSITION which is TRUE.

Tullock, Gordon (1922–). A PUBLIC-CHOICE economist, Tullock has written on a wide variety of topics in PUBLIC ECONOMICS, including bureaucracy, war, voting, law, and property rights. He co-authored with JAMES BUCHANAN the famous book *The Calculus of Consent* (Buchanan and Tullock, 1962). Formerly at Virginia Polytechnic Institute and State University and then at George Mason University, Tullock now teaches at the University of Arizona in Tucson.

turbulence. Complex, swift, ever-changing movements, so that they are difficult to track, predict, and follow. Tornadoes and stock-market crashes are examples. Seemingly disordered, such events have causes and structure and follow scientific laws. The field that studies turbulence is misleadingly called 'chaos theory.' See CHAOS. Markets may sometimes be turbulent, but seldom chaotic.

turbulence theory. Better known as 'chaos theory,' it analyzes turbulent behavior such as the weather or stock markets, which are not really chaotic. One concept is the butterfly effect, which states that small changes in inputs can create major changes in the outputs. An implication for policy is that regulators will be unable to predict or control such outcomes.

Turgot, Anne-Robert Jacques (1727–81). French economist associated with the PHYSIOCRATS. As controller general of finance (1774–76), he abolished (ABOLISH) the *CORVÉE*, eliminated SALES TAXES on grain, attempted to remove BARRIERS to trade, and enacted other reforms; he was removed due to opposition to his policies, including his advocacy of the *IMPÔT UNIQUE* on LAND RENT. In his *Réflexions sur la Formation et la Distribution des Richesses* (1766), Turgot presented a theory of free trade and *laissez-faire*, as well as concepts such as DIMINISHING RETURNS.

turnover tax. A SALES TAX on the transfer of an asset. It is more inefficient than a VALUE ADDED TAX, since the price paid for the item is not deducted from the tax base, and is thus a greater BARRIER to the transfer of assets.

U

unanimity. Voluntary participation by all members of a group, and governance by the consent of each member. It can most feasibly be implemented
at the constitutional level of forming an organization or joining it. At this
high level, the members agree to operational decision making by majority
voting or some other rule. The unanimity principle is associated with Knut
Wicksell.

unanimous improvement. A change in circumstances which makes at least
one person better off, without any objections from others, that is without
making them worse off by their judgment.

   In a free market, unanimity is only a limit for acts which are morally
wrong by the universal ethic. Acts which merely offend others or inciden-
tally injure them (for example financially, through competition), making
them less well off but not invading their domains, are not unanimously agreed
to, but are not legally restricted.

uncertainty. Lack of certainty, especially about the future. The future is not
only unknown, but the probability of an uncertain event is unknown, so it is not
feasible to insure against. Uncertainty is a fundamental axiomatic proposition
in economics, one emphasized especially by the Austrian school (Austrian
economics). As Frank Knight theorized, entrepreneurial profits arise out of
the uncertain future, as those who best discern the demand for a product, as
well as costs and other variables, are rewarded with an economic profit.

underclass. The class of people living in poverty who persist in it generation after generation, since most cannot overcome the barriers to improve
their condition.

underground economy. See informal sector.

undesigned order. Another name for the spontaneous order.

unearned income. See earned income.

uneasiness. The term used by Ludwig von Mises, who stated (1949, 1966,
p. 92) that the relief from a felt uneasiness is the goal of an action. Uneasi-

ness is the feeling or sentiment of having less utility (such as having discomfort or feeling a longing) than one would if goals were achieved, such as obtaining some item.

unemployment.   The workers who are willing and able to work at prevailing wages, but cannot find EMPLOYMENT. Actual unemployment rates are affected by unemployment insurance as well as not counting those who are too discouraged to seek work, but would be willing to work. In FREE-MARKET thought, unemployment is caused by BARRIERS such as the TAX WEDGE on wages and regulations making it difficult to fire workers or imposing RESTRICTIONS on employment. See also NATURAL RATE OF UNEMPLOYMENT.

unintended consequences.   Results of a policy that were not intended and often not foreseen by the decision makers. INTERVENTION typically has unintended consequences, as people react to circumvent and avoid RESTRICTIONS and IMPOSED costs.

union shop.   A legal requirement that a worker in a firm must join a union after beginning employment. US states with right-to-work laws prohibit the enforcement of union shops.

unions, labor.   Organizations of workers which bargain with the owners and managers of firms. In many countries, labor unions are exempt from antitrust laws and have various legal privileges. The STRIKE is the prime weapon of a union. If the LABOR market is divided into a union and non-union sector, the outcome is typically a higher-than-market WAGE LEVEL in the union sector and a lower-than-market wage level in the non-union sector, as the higher union wage reduces employment in that sector, shifting the workers to the non-union sector. High-paid unions in manufacturing, however, run the risk of pricing themselves out of a global market. See also LABOR.

unit of account.   The unit of a CURRENCY, such as dollar or franc. With a GOLD STANDARD, the unit is a weight of gold. With fiat money, the unit has a historical basis.

universal.   Applying to an entire field, hence UNIVERSE (2). A universal PRINCIPLE or THEOREM in economics applies to all people, places, cultures, and times. A UNIVERSAL ETHIC applies to all human beings. See also general (GENERAL EQUILIBRIUM), PURE. Contrasts: cultural (CULTURE), specific (SPECIFIC THEORY).

universal economics.   Economic THEORY that synthesizes warranted (WARRANT) theory from all known schools of thought into an integrated whole.

universal ethic. The formulation of NATURAL MORAL LAW into a set of ethical rules for good, evil, and neutral acts, derived from two aspects of human nature: the moral equality of persons, and the independence (or separateness of mind) of persons. The principle ethical rule for evil, as recognized by JOHN LOCKE, JOHN STUART MILL, and others, is that it is morally wrong to invasively HARM others. Morally good acts are those which are welcomed benefits to others. All other acts, including those which only affect oneself, are morally neutral.

The universal ethic determines which acts are VOLUNTARY, namely those which are not evil. LIBERTY then consists of law in accord with the universal ethic, prohibiting coercive harm and not prohibiting any other acts. NATURAL RIGHTS are then defined as the correlative of moral wrong as designated by the universal ethic: a right to do X means that the negation of the act is morally wrong. Thus, the right to own property means that it is morally wrong to take or destroy the property of others (Foldvary, 1980).

universe. 1 Everything that exists. The rudiments of the physical universe are time, space, and substance (mass and energy). 2 The set of all elements within a particular field, such as economics. Hence, a universally valid proposition of economics is universal within economics, but not necessarily in other fields, just as a universal terrestrial biological principle may apply only to life on earth.

urban economics. A branch of applied economics dealing with cities. Urban economics applies economic theory to topics concerning cities and towns, such as LOCATION THEORY, LAND use, housing, the growth of cities, and urban problems such as slums and crime. It overlaps with regional economics.

FREE-MARKET urban policy would ABOLISH the local TAXATION of labor, enterprise, sales, and buildings; eliminate ARBITRARY permits, zoning, building codes, restrictions on jitneys, and other REGULATIONS. GEO-ECONOMIC policy would finance the government with the assessment and collection of the site RENTS (1), which would limit both URBAN SPRAWL and blight. COVENANTS would replace zoning, while many of the neighborhood collective goods would be provided by contractual and consensual PRIVATE COMMUNITIES.

urban sprawl. Urban development that spreads out unevenly, using up excessive space, relative to the benchmark of a pure FREE MARKET with the COMMUNITY COLLECTION OF RENT. When people voluntarily choose to live in low-density communities, this is a market-warranted use of space, but when development skips over undeveloped LAND or does not fully develop land due to zoning restrictions and land speculation due to rental gains from anticipated public works not funded by the landowner beneficiaries, then it creates INFRASTRUCTURE and land costs not warranted by the pure MARKET PROCESS.

use tax.   A tax on goods brought into a state which would be subject to SALES TAX if sold within the state. This tax attempts to limit the avoidance of sales tax by purchasing from out of state.

user fee.   A PRICE which one voluntarily (VOUNTARY) pays for a service provided by GOVERNMENT, the payment being directly related to the service and its cost. An example is a charge for obtaining a passport. If the charge is compulsory, then it is not a genuine user fee, but an earmarked (EARMARKING) or EXCISE TAX (Wagner, 1991). A user fee may, however, be a requirement in order to use some service or property.

usufruct.   The RIGHT to use the PROPERTY of another so long as its VALUE is not diminished.

utilitarianism.   The ethical (ETHIC) philosophy of judging acts according to the CONSEQUENCES, that is their effect on the utility (UTILITY, MARGINAL) of persons. Rule-utilitarianism consists of ethical RULES which are then judged for consequences, rather than judging types of act.

NATURAL MORAL LAW (or NATURAL RIGHTS, or the UNIVERSAL ETHIC) has a different basis, but can also be complementary (COMPLEMENT) to utilitarianism. The universal ethic's rule that evil is what coercively HARMS others provides the utilitarian harm rule. Hence, natural moral law is needed by rule-utilitarianism to provide the rules, and also to preclude the utilitarian problem of having some rule that pleases a majority but severely harms a minority.

utility, marginal.   1 In neoclassical (NEOCLASSICAL ECONOMICS) theory, the satisfaction obtained by an extra unit of a GOOD; or more precisely, the PREFERENCE for a good relative to other goods. More broadly, the utility of a person or group is its WELL-BEING or welfare. Neoclassical utility is often mathematized into a function of goods variables. 2 In CARL MENGER'S (1871, 1976) definition, marginal utility is the importance of a good in achieving an end. 3 In modern Austrian theory (AUSTRIAN ECONOMICS), the marginal utility of a good is its ordinal (ORDINAL UTILITY) preference relative to other goods as they help achieve a ranking of ends.

Both neoclassical and modern Austrian utility theory are ordinal, a matter of relative preference. However, some economists believe that utility is fundamentally CARDINAL, not in being measurable, but in its being a quantity. Intuitively, for example, one can feel that A is a bit preferred to B, while B is much preferred to C. Utility is also cardinal in having a sign: one cannot measure utility as a number, but one can determine whether the utility is positive, negative (an unwanted good), or neutral.

There is also theory, not well developed so far, on the DYNAMICS of utility as people learn and grow. See also DIMINISHING MARGINAL UTILITY.

Utopia.   A visionary ideal of a society with the best possible policies and other desired elements.

V

valence. The capacity of an element to combine with another. By extension, the capacity of a FACTOR OF PRODUCTION to combine with, hence COMPLEMENT, other factors, high valence being high complementarity. For example, cattle have a high valence for land and a low valence for labor. (Gaffney, 1996).

value. Economic values are the relative importance that a person assigns to his various ends. Goods acquire value in achieving those ends. The value of goods is thus determined subjectively (see SUBJECTIVE VALUES). The use value of a good is its subjective value to a person.

The intrinsic value of an item is not any objective value but the market value of the substance a good is made of rather than the good itself, as the intrinsic value of a gold COIN is the market value of the gold.

A market value is the EQUILIBRATION of bids and offers based on the values persons place on goods. Goods exchange at prices where a bid and offer are matched at a price. Higher offers and lower bids do not trade. The EXCHANGE value of a good is its market value.

There have also been labor and labor-saved theories of value, which at best are explanations for the market price of goods in current production. See LABOR THEORY OF VALUE.

As theorized by CARL MENGER, the value of factors of production are imputed from the value of the goods they produce.

A MORAL (1) value is also subjective, according to the subjective theory of values. Objectivists (OBJECTIVISM) and others posit objective values from teleologies (TELEOLOGICAL) such as human flourishing or life. Subjective moral values do not preclude an objective ethic, just as subjective economic values do not preclude an objective theory of economics. From independent subjective values and their equal position, premises which JOHN LOCKE presented, one can derive a rational, culturally objective, UNIVERSAL ETHIC (Foldvary, 1980).

value-added tax. A TAX on the value added to a product by a firm, the value consisting of the factor payments (wages, rent, and return on capital goods, including interest) and economic profit. The tax is broader and more efficient than turnover and other sales taxes, and does not burden individual worker-taxpayers with COMPLIANCE COSTS. The cost of inputs is subtracted from the cost of outputs in determining the tax basis. The VAT is widely used in Europe. One advantage relative to income taxes is that exports can be exempt from the tax. Usually, as implemented, there are exceptions and complications, government is exempt, and there are compliance costs for the firms. Some of the tax is passed on to consumers, and some borne by labor and landowners. There is an excess burden to VAT, unlike taxes or charges on LAND RENT.

value-free science.   See NON-VALUED SCIENCE.

VAT.   VALUE ADDED TAX.

velocity.   The number of times the MONEY SUPPLY turns over per year, that is the speed of the circulation. The measure of the velocity depends on the measure of the money supply, because the narrower the measure of money, the greater its velocity. The effect of money on the PRICE LEVEL depends on the velocity multiplied by the money stock. See also the EQUATION OF EXCHANGE.

Virginia school of political economy.   A school that has been based at the Center for Study of Public Choice at three universities in Virginia, now at GEORGE MASON UNIVERSITY. The Center was established by JAMES BUCHANAN and G. Warren Nutter in 1957 at the University of Virginia. The members sought to revive the CLASSICAL emphasis on POLITICAL ECONOMY. A key work of the school was *The Calculus of Consent* (1962) by James Buchanan and GORDON TULLOCK. RONALD COASE was associated with the school and there wrote his paper on social cost. Mancur Olson gave the program the above title in 1985. Charles Rowley (1996) has contrasted the public-choice approach of the Virginia school with that of the CHICAGO SCHOOL. The Virginia school places greater emphasis on institutions and focuses more specifically on GOVERNMENT FAILURE (or political market failure). But the school also investigates political reforms, institutions that are less conducive to failure. See also Mueller (1985).

volatility.   The amount of fluctuation in the price of an asset, usually measured per year. Often, what is called the 'risk' of an investment is the volatility, as opposed to the possibility of the complete collapse of the value of the asset.

volenti non fit injuria.   *Lat.* To the willing, no injury is committed.

volitional.   Having and exercising FREE WILL, a defining characteristic of PERSONS.

voluntary. Performed completely from one's own volition. In the context of a MARKET, voluntary means that acts are uncoerced not just among the actors in a TRANSACTION but also for THIRD PARTIES. The meaning of 'voluntary' is determined by an ethic; see UNIVERSAL ETHIC.

voting. See AGENDA, APPROVAL VOTING, BORDA COUNT, BOTTOM-UP VOTING, COMMUNITARIAN DEMOCRACY, IMPOSSIBILITY THEOREM, MASS DEMOCRACY, PARADOX OF VOTING.

voucher. Tickets that are valid for the purchase of a particular good or service or shares of stock. Vouchers have been suggested for EDUCATION, where parents use them to choose a school, making an even financial choice among government and private schools.

W

wage level. The prevailing WAGE paid to unskilled workers in an ECONOMY, the more productive workers being paid a premium over the basic wage level. In CLASSICAL ECONOMICS, the wage level is determined by the productivity of labor at the extensive MARGIN OF PRODUCTION. Neoclassical (NEOCLASSICAL ECONOMICS) wage theory has an economy-wide supply and demand curve for labor determining the wage, but the demand comes from the AGGREGATE PRODUCTION FUNCTION which shows productivity at the margin where the last worker is employed, and the supply is a short-run function, whereas the classical supply of labor is horizontal at subsistence until all households are employed, after which it slopes up or becomes vertical. The two theories are thus complementary (COMPLEMENT). See also LAW OF WAGES, WAKEFIELD.

wages. The earnings of LABOR. Wages take many forms, including hourly payments, monthly salaries, commissions, profits from self-employment, and in-kind wages such as home-grown produce.

Wakefield, Edward Gibbon (1796–1862). He organized and promoted the colonization of Australia and New Zealand. In his book *England and America* (1833), Wakefield examined the Swan River Colony in Western Australia, inquiring as to why WAGES there were high. The reason was that immigrants had the option of obtaining their own land for farming. The government there later fixed the price of land at a pound per acre in order to reduce wages. This thus provides empirical evidence for the classical relationship between wages and RENT.

Walras, Léon (1834–1910). One of the three major pioneers of MARGINAL UTILITY theory, Walras also developed a mathematical model of GENERAL EQUILIBRIUM. Walras (1896) also proposed that LAND RENT provide the means for funding government. In a more modern form, Walras thus continued two French physiocratic themes, the *tableau économique* (model of the entire ECONOMY) and the *IMPÔT UNIQUE*.

'War is the health of the state.' See RANDOLPH BOURNE.

warehouse banking. Also called '100 per cent reserve banking,' it is the BANKING practice of maintaining deposits equal to RESERVE assets, so deposit accounts are safeguarded from possible loss due to default. Some advocates of 100-percent reserve banking argue that FRACTIONAL-RESERVE BANKING is fraudulent, but it seems that so long as the practice is disclosed, fractional-reserve banks could freely and honestly compete with warehouse banks in a FREE-MARKET banking system, paying higher interest to depositors than warehouse banks.

warrant.   To justify, prove, or provide sufficient grounds for belief. A THEO-REM is warranted by LOGIC and EVIDENCE.

waste.   The reduction in utility (UTILITY, MARGINAL) from a loss of resources which could have served more desired uses. Some waste results from accidents and the inability to predict demand, while other waste results from the EXCESS BURDEN of TAXATION and REGULATION, which directly wastes resources from COMPLIANCE COSTS, and also inserts a TAX WEDGE between the marginal social cost and the marginal social benefit (SOCIAL COSTS AND BENEFITS), a distortion that wastes resources. 'Waste' is also a term for POLLUTION.

wealth.   Anything with positive market VALUE. Human beings are excluded, since in the absence of CHATTEL SLAVERY, human beings are not purchased in a market, but hired. However, some theorists include HUMAN CAPITAL. Some geo-economists (GEO-ECONOMICS) also exclude NATURAL RESOURCES, including as wealth only produced goods.

Wealth of Nations.   The first full treatise on economics, written by Adam Smith (1776, 1976), and a major influence on economic theory, policy, and CLASSICAL LIBERAL thought.

wealth tax.   A tax on the value of one's WEALTH or ASSETS. See ASSET TAX.

weasel word.   Hayek's term for words that are used in a way that sucks the original meaning from them. 'SOCIAL,' for example, can refer to the people or to governmental agencies, and the term is used in ways that seem to merge the two, as though they were not distinct.

weighted average maturity.   The average time until the securities in a portfolio mature, weighted by the dollar amounts.

welfare.   **1** Social WELL-BEING. **2** Governmental assistance and TRANSFER PAYMENTS. Transfers to corporate interests are called 'corporate welfare.'

welfare economics. The economics of WELFARE (1), which evaluates the effects of various policies. In FREE-MARKET welfare thought, welfare is considered to be greatest when individuals are free to peruse their own conception of well-being and when there is a minimum of EXCESS BURDEN imposed on the ECONOMY.

welfare state. GOVERNMENT assistance to the poor as well as to others in the provision of schooling, housing, food, medicine, pensions, senior centers, and other services. For SOCIAL SECURITY and, in some countries, nationalized medicine, participation in programs is mandatory. In effect it is a REDISTRIBUTION program from taxpayers to various classes of recipients, with a major overhead burden. The FREE-MARKET approach to welfare, in contrast, is to leave income with those who earned it, while having no BARRIERS to entrepreneurial (ENTREPRENEUR) opportunity, which would then leave households with the means to obtain their own services more suitably to their individual wants.

well-being. The amount and degree to which individuals in an ECONOMY are able to pursue and attain their ends.

Wicksell, Knut (1851–1926). Swedish economist who was perhaps the first geo-Austrian (GEO-AUSTRIAN SYNTHESIS) and universalist economist (UNIVERSAL ECONOMICS), synthesizing SYNTHESIS (1) CLASSICAL, Austrian (AUSTRIAN ECONOMICS), PUBLIC-CHOICE and neoclassical (NEOCLASSICAL ECONOMICS) concepts into an integrated theory of interest, land and rent, capital goods, labor and wages, monetary theory, and public finance. He originated the distinction between the natural and the market rate of INTEREST. In PUBLIC FINANCE, Wicksell's (1958) benchmark was UNANIMITY, and with regard to TAXATION, Wicksell recognized LAND RENTS as an efficient and equitable source of revenue.

widget. Either cylindrical containers for carrying messages or, in the UK, bulbs containing carbon dioxide in canned beer, which when pierced, releases the gas. The word is used in hypothetical examples of a manufactured good.

Wieser, Friedrich von (1851–1926). Austrian-nation, Austrian-school economist (AUSTRIAN ECONOMICS) who originated the concept of opportunity cost and furthered the theory of imputation (IMPUTATION OF VALUE). He also analyzed urban RENT (1).

winner's curse. When people have different beliefs about the value of some item, the highest bidder is the person who makes the greatest upward error in valuation.

workable competition.   The name given to real-world COMPETITION, which cannot feasibly satisfy the criteria for PERFECT COMPETITION. However, criteria proposed for competition policy have been criticized for not having a sound theoretical basis. See ANTI-TRUST.

World Trade Organization.   Successor name to GATT.

X, Y, Z

X goods. Physical goods, in contrast to Y GOODS and Z GOODS.

Y. Symbol used for NATIONAL INCOME.

Y goods. THE CHARACTERISTICS of physical goods (X GOODS). See Z GOODS.

yield. The return on an asset, usually computed on an annual basis as a percentage of the asset value. Generally, the yield is some INTEREST RATE times the price of the asset. The real yield is the nominal yield after subtracting INFLATION.

yield curve. A graph depicting the maturity of a fixed-income security versus its yield. The curve normally slopes up as a higher yield is paid for a longer maturity with higher RISK.

Z goods. An abstract good such as music, proposed by GARY BECKER (1965). STIGLER and Becker (1977) define Z goods as the ultimate items entering a utility (UTILITY, MARGINAL) function. For example, the physical X good of an orchestra produces the ultimate Z good of music. The Lancastrian CHARACTERISTICS of X goods can then be labeled Y goods, and these properties make up the Z goods.

zero coupon bonds. Bonds that, instead of paying cash INTEREST, are sold at a discount and then redeemed for face value. Though the RETURN is not paid until maturity, the implicit interest is taxed annually by the US government.

zoo effect. An upward bias in measuring CONGESTION versus population (Oates, 1988). Large cities have zoos, so such services increase with population.

Zube, John. Australian libertarian (LIBERTARIANISM) panarchist (PANARCHY) ENTREPRENEUR of microfiche publishing, holding peace plans, 'social inventions,' and FREE-MARKET, *CLASSICAL-LIBERAL texts.

BIBLIOGRAPHY

Amariglio, Jack, Antonio Callari, Stephen Resnick, David Ruccio, and Richard Wolff (1996), 'Nondeterminist Marxism: the birth of a postmodern tradition in economics,' in Fred E. Foldvary (ed.), *Beyond Neoclassical Economics*, Cheltenham, UK: Edward Elgar, pp. 134–47.

Anderson, Terry L., and Donald R. Leal (1991), *Free Market Environmentalism*, San Francisco: Pacific Research Institute for Public Policy.

Arrow, Kenneth (1951, 1966), *Social Choice and Individual Values*, New York: Wiley.

August, Eugene R. (ed.) (1971), *The Negro Question [by] John Stuart Mill*, New York, Appleton-Century-Crofts.

Auld, D.A.L., and Lorraine Eden (1990), 'Public Characteristics of Nonpublic Goods,' *Public Finance*, **45** (3), 378–91.

Baetjer, Howard (1993), *Software as Capital*, Doctoral dissertation, George Mason University.

Becker, Gary (1965), 'A Theory of the Allocation of Time,' *The Economic Journal* (September), 493–517.

Becker, Gary (1971), *The Economics of Discrimination*, 2nd edn., Chicago: University of Chicago Press.

Becker, Gary, and Guity Nashat Becker (1996), *The Economics of Life: From Baseball to Affirmative Action to Immigration, How Real-world Issues Affect our Everyday Life*, New York: McGraw-Hill.

Bell, Tom W. (1991), 'Polycentric Law,' *Humane Studies Review*, **7** (1) (Winter 1991/2) (http://mason.gmu.edu/~ihs/w91issues.html).

Benson, Bruce (1990), *The Enterprise of Law*, San Francisco: Pacific Research Institute.

Berman, Harold J. (1983), *Law and Revolution: The Formation of the Western Legal Tradition*, Cambridge, MA: Harvard University Press.

Blaug, Mark (1985), *Great Economists since Keynes*, Cambridge: Cambridge University Press.

Blaug, Mark (1986), *Great Economists before Keynes*, Cambridge: Cambridge University Press.

Block, Walter, and Michael Walker (1989), *Lexicon of Economic Thought*, Vancouver: Fraser Institute.

Boettke, Peter (1993), *Why Perestroika Failed: The Politics and Economics of Socialist Transformation*, New York: Routledge.

Boettke, Peter (1996), 'What is wrong with neoclassical economics (and what is still wrong with Austrian economics)?' in Fred E. Foldvary (ed.), *Beyond Neoclassical Economics*, Cheltenham, UK: Edward Elgar, pp. 22–40.

Böhm-Bawerk, Eugen von (1898), *Karl Marx and the Close of his System: A Criticism*, Alice M. Macdonald (trans.), London: T. F. Unwin.

Böhm-Bawerk, Eugen von (1921, 1959), *Capital and Interest* (three volumes), George Huncke, and Hans Sennholz (trans.), South Holland, IL: Libertarian Press.

Brown, Harry Gunnison (1942), *Basic Principles of Economics*, Columbia, MO: Lucas Brothers.

Brown, Harry Gunnison (1924, 1979), *The Economics of Taxation*, reprinted, Chicago: University of Chicago.

Buber, Martin (1983), *A Land of Two Peoples*, Paul R. Mendes-Flohr (ed.), Oxford: Oxford University Press.

Buchanan, James (1965), 'An Economic Theory of Clubs,' *Economica*, **32** (February), 1–14.

Buchanan, James (1990), 'The Domain of Constitutional Economics,' *Constitutional Political Economy*, **1** (1) (Winter), 1–18.

Buchanan, James M., Charles K. Rowley, and Robert D. Tollison (eds) (1986), *Deficits*, New York: Basil Blackwell.

Buchanan, James M., and Tullock, Gordon (1962, 1965), *The Calculus of Consent*, Ann Arbor: University of Michigan Press.

Burris, Alan (1983), *A Liberty Primer*, Rochester, NY: Society for Individual Liberty.

Campa, José, and Linda Goldberg (1997), 'The Evolving External Orientation of Manufacturing: A Profile of Four Countries', *Economic Policy Review*, **3** (2).

Carlson, Benny (1994), *The State as Monster: Gustav Cassel and Eli Heckscher on the Role and Growth of the State*, Lanham, MD; New York; London: University Press of America.

Chandler, Tertius (1983), *Chandler's Half-Encyclopedia*, 2nd edn, San Francisco: Gutenberg Press.

Chandler, Tertius (1986), *Moses and the Golden Age*, Bryn Mawr, PA: Dorrance and Company.

Clarke, Edward (1971), 'Multi-part Pricing of Public Goods,' *Public Choice*, **11** (Fall), 17–33.

Coase, Ronald H. (1937), 'The Nature of the Firm', *Economic*, **4**: 386–405.

Coase, Ronald H. (1960), 'The Problem of Social Cost', *Journal of Law and Economics* **3** (October): 1–44.

Coase, Ronald H. (1974), 'The Lighthouse in Economics', *Journal of Law and Economics*, **17** (October): 357–76.

Cobb, Charles W., and Paul Douglas (1928), 'A Theory of Production,' *American Economic Review*, **18** (March), 165.

Crews, Clyde Wayne, Jr. (1996), *Ten Thousand Commandments*, Washington, DC: Competitive Enterprise Institute.

Davenport, Herbert J. (1908), *Value and Distribution*, Chicago: University of Chicago Press.

Davenport, Herbert J. (1914), *Economics of Enterprise*, New York: Macmillan.

De Soto, Hernando (1989), *The Other Path*, New York: Harper & Row.

Demsetz, Harold (1964), 'The Exchange and Enforcement of Property Rights,' *Journal of Law and Economics*, **7** (October), 11–26.

Demsetz, Harold (1967), 'Towards a Theory of Property Rights', *American Economic Review*, **57** (May), 347–73.

Demsetz, Harold (1970), 'The Private Production of Public Goods', *Journal of Law and Economics*, **13** (October), 293–306.

Dos Passos, John (1932), *1919*, New York: Harcourt, Brace & Co.

Feder, Kris (1996), 'Geo-economics,' in Fred E. Foldvary (ed.), *Beyond Neoclassical Economics*, Cheltenham, UK: Edward Elgar Publishing, pp. 41–60.

Feenstra, Robert C., and Andrew K. Rose (1997), 'Putting Things in Order: Patterns of Trade Dynamics and Growth,' NBER Working Paper 5975.

Finneran, John P. (1996), 'A Tale of Two Dictionaries,' in Wilson Mixon, Jr. (ed.), *Private Means, Public Ends: Voluntarism vs. Coercion*, Irvington-on-Hudson: Foundation for Economic Education, pp. 21–4.

Foldvary, Fred (1980), *The Soul of Liberty*, San Francisco: Gutenberg Press.

Foldvary, Fred (1994a), 'Poverty and the theory of wages: a "geoclassical" analysis', in Nicolaus Tideman (ed.), *Land and Taxation*, London: Shepheard-Walwyn, pp. 141–56.

Foldvary, Fred (1994b), *Public Goods and Private Communities*, Aldershot, UK: Edward Elgar Publishing.

Foldvary, Fred (1995), 'The Measurement of Inequality, Concentration, and Diversification', Working paper E95-09, Virginia Polytechnic Institute and State University, Blacksburg, Virginia.

Foldvary, Fred (ed.) (1996), *Beyond Neoclassical Economics*, Cheltenham, UK: Edward Elgar Publishing.

Foldvary, Fred (1997a), 'Government and Governance', *The Freeman* **47** (1) (January), 33–7.

Foldvary, Fred (1997b), 'The Business Cycle: A Georgist-Austrian Synthesis', *American Journal of Economics and Sociology* **56** (4) (October), 521–41.

Foldvary, Fred (1997c), 'Franz Oppenheimer, the state, and land', in Kenneth C. Wenzer (ed.), *An Anthology of Single Land Tax Thought*, Rochester, NY: University of Rochester Press, pp. 403–38.

Foldvary, Fred, and George Selgin (1995), 'The Dependency of Wage Contracts on Monetary Policy', *Journal of Institutional and Theoretical Economics*, **151** (4) (December), 658–72.

Gaffney, Mason (1994), 'Neo-classical Economics as a Stratagem against Henry George,' in Mason Gaffney and Fred Harrison (eds), *The Corruption of Economics*, London: Shepheard-Walwyn, pp. 29–163.

Gaffney, Mason (1996), 'Taxes, Capital, and Jobs,' Manuscript.

Galbraith, John Kenneth (1958), *The Affluent Society*, Boston: Houghton Mifflin.

Garrison, Roger W. (1978), *Austrian Macroeconomics*, Menlo Park: Institute for Humane Studies.

Garrison, Roger W. (1984), 'Time and Money: The Universals of Macroeconomic Theorizing,' *Journal of Macroeconomics*, **6** (2) (spring), 197–213.

Garrison, Roger W. (1997), 'Time and Money,' Core chapter in *Time and Money: the Macroeconomics of Capital Structure*, Work in progress.

George, Henry (1871), *Our Land and Land Policy, National and State*, San Francisco: White & Hauer.

George, Henry (1879, 1975), *Progress and Poverty*, New York: Robert Schalkenbach Foundation.

George, Henry (1883), *Social Problems*, New York: Robert Schalkenbach Foundation.

Grapard, Ulla (1996), 'Feminist Economics: Let me Count the Ways,' in Fred E. Foldvary (ed.), *Beyond Neoclassical Economics*, Cheltenham, UK: Edward Elgar Publishing, pp. 100–14.

Greaves, Percy L., Jr. (1974), *Mises Made Easier*, New York: Free Market Books.

Gunning, J. (1997a), 'Herbert J. Davenport's Transformation of the Austrian Theory of Value and Cost,' *Perspectives on the History of Economic Thought*, **14**, London: Routledge.

Gunning, J. (1997b), 'H. J. Davenport's Loan Fund Theory of Capital,' Manuscript.

Gwartney, James, Robert Lawson, and Walter Block (1996), *Economic Freedom of the World 1775–1995*, Vancouver: Fraser Institute.

Hall, Marshall, and Nicolaus Tideman (1967), 'Measures of Concentration,' *Journal of the American Statistical Association*, **62** (March), 162–8.

Hardin, Garrett (1968), 'Tragedy of the Commons', *Science*, **162**, 1243–8.

Harrison, Fred (1983), *The Power in the Land*, New York: Universe Books.

Hayek, Friedrich A. (1960), *The Constitution of Liberty*, South Bend: Gateway Editions.

Hayek, Friedrich A. (1973), *Law, Legislation, and Liberty*, vol. I, Chicago: University of Chicago Press.

Hayek, Friedrich A. (1990), *Denationalisation of Money: The Argument Refined*, 3rd edn, London: Institute of Economic Affairs.

Hazlitt, Henry (1959), *The Failure of the 'New Economics': An Analysis of the Keynesian Fallacies*, Princeton: Van Nostrand.

Hirschman, Albert O. (1970), *Exit, Voice, and Loyalty*, Cambridge: Harvard University Press.

Hodgkiss, F. T. (1942), 'Raffles of Singapore,' *The Freeman*, **5** (5) (March), 106–7.

Hoyt, Homer (1933), *One Hundred Years of Land Value in Chicago*, reprinted NY: Arno Press and The New York Times, 1970.

Kirzner, Israel M. (1987), 'Austrian School of Economics,' in John Eatwell, Murray Milgate, and Peter Newman (eds), *The New Palgrave: A Dictionary of Economics*, London: Macmillan Press, pp. 145–51.

Laffer, Arthur B. (1979), 'Statement Prepared for the Joint Economic Committee, May 20,' reprinted in Arthur B. Laffer and Jan P. Seymour (eds), *The Economics of the Tax Revolt*, New York: Harcourt Brace Jovanovich, pp. 75–9.

Littlechild, Stephen (1978), *The Fallacy of the Mixed Economy*, London: Institute of Economic Affairs.

Locke, John (1690, 1947), *Two Treatises of Government*, Thomas I. Cook (ed.), New York: Hafner Press. Includes 'First Treatise of Government', pp. 3–118, and 'Second Treatise of Civil Government', pp. 119–247.

McClelland, David (1976), *The Achieving Society*, New York: Irvington Publishers.

Menger, Carl (1871, 1976), *Principles of Economics*, James Dingwall and Bert Hoselitz (trans.), New York: New York University Press.

Mises, Ludwig von (1924, 1980), *The Theory of Money and Credit*, 2nd edition. H.E. Batson, (trans.). Indianapolis: Liberty Classics.

Mises, Ludwig von (1949, 1966), *Human Action*, New Haven: Yale University Press and Henry Regnery Company.

Mixon, Wilson, Jr. (1996), *Private Means, Public Ends: Voluntarism vs. Coercion*, Irvington-on-Hudson: Foundation for Economic Education.

Mueller, D. (1985), *The 'Virginia School' and Public Choice*, Fairfax: Center for Study of Public Choice.

Neill, A.S. (1960), *Summerhill: A Radical Approach to Child Rearing*, New York: Hart Publishing.

Nock, Albert J. (1935), *Our Enemy the State*, reprinted, Caldwell, ID: Caxton Printers.

Noyes, Richard (ed.) (1991), *Now the Synthesis: Capitalism, Socialism, and the New Social Contract*, New York: Holmes & Meier.

Oates, Wallace E. (1988), 'On the Measurement of Congestion in the Provision of Local Public Goods,' *Journal of Urban Economics*, **24** (July), 85–94.

Oppenheimer, Franz (1914, 1975), *The State*, New York: Free Life Editions.

Oppenheimer, Franz (1917, 1997), 'Collective and Private Ownership of Land,' in *Land Tenure in Palestine*, The Hague: Jewish National Fund, pp. 5–18. Reprinted in Foldvary, Fred (1997), 'Franz Oppenheimer, the state, and land', in Kenneth C. Wenzer (ed.), *An Anthology of Single Land Tax Thought*, Rochester, NY: University of Rochester Press, pp. 414–34.

Oppenheimer, Franz (1927), 'The Idolatry of the State,' *Review of Nations*, **2** (February), 13–26.

O'Quinn, Robert P. (1991), 'The Americans with Disabilities Act: Time for Amendments,' CATO policy analysis no. 158.

Panayotou, Theodore (1993), *Green Markets*, San Francisco: Institute for Contemporary Studies.

Reed, Terrance G. (1992), 'American Forfeiture Law: Property Owners Meet the Prosecutor,' CATO policy analysis no. 179.

Rothbard, Murray N. (1963, 1975), *America's Great Depression*, Kansas City: Sheed and Ward.

Rowley, Charles, and Michelle Vachris (1996), 'The Virginia school of political economy,' in Fred E. Foldvary (ed.), *Beyond Neoclassical Economics*, Cheltenham, UK: Edward Elgar, pp. 61–82.

Ryan, Christopher K. (1987), *Harry Gunnison Brown: Economist*, Boulder: Westview Press.

Samuelson, Paul A. (1954), 'The Pure Theory of Public Expenditure,' *Review of Economics and Statistics*, **36** (4) (November), 387–9.

Schumpeter, Joseph A. (1954, 1986), *History of Economic Analysis*, Elizabeth B. Schumpeter (ed.), New York: Oxford University Press.

Schumpeter, Joseph A. (1976), *Capitalism, Socialism and Democracy*, 5th edn, New York: Harper.

Selgin, George A. (1988), *The Theory of Free Banking*, Totowa, NJ: Rowman & Littlefield, and Washington, DC: CATO Institute.

Smith, Adam (1790, 1982), *The Theory of Moral Sentiments*, Indianapolis: Liberty Classics.

Smith, Adam (1978, 1982), *Lectures on Jurisprudence*, Indianapolis: Liberty Classics.

Smith, Adam (1776, 1976), *The Wealth of Nations*, Vols 1 and 2, Edwin Canaan (ed.). Chicago: University of Chicago Press.

Smith, Gerald Alonzo (1996), 'Humanist economics: from homo economicus to homo sapiens,' in Fred E. Foldvary (ed.), *Beyond Neoclassical Economics*, Cheltenham, UK: Edward Elgar, pp. 83–99.

Sowell, Thomas (1974), *Classical Economics Reconsidered*, Princeton: Princeton University Press.

Stigler, George, and Becker, Gary (1977), 'De Gustibus Non Est Disputandum,' *American Economic Review*, **67** (March), 76–90.

Tiebout, Charles M. (1956), 'A Pure Theory of Local Expenditure,' *Journal of Political Economy*, **64**, 416–24.

Tideman, T. Nicolaus, and Tullock, Gordon (1976), 'A New and Superior Process for Making Social Choices,' *Journal of Political Economy*, **84** (6) (December), 1145–59.

Vaughn, Karen I. (1980), *John Locke, Economist and Social Scientist*, Chicago: University of Chicago Press.

Wagner, Richard (ed.) (1991), *Charging for Government*, London: Routledge.

Walras, Léon (1896), *Studies in Social Economics*, Mason Gaffney, Lausanne: F. Rouge and Co. (unpublished trans., 1967).

Wanniski, Jude (1978), *The Way the World Works: How Economies Fail and Succeed*, New York: Basic Books.

Whalen, Charles (1996), 'The institutional approach to political economy,' in Fred E. Foldvary (ed.), *Beyond Neoclassical Economics*, Cheltenham, UK: Edward Elgar, pp. 83–99.

White, Lawrence (1984), *Free Banking in Britain: Theory, Experience and Debate, 1800–1845*, New York: Cambridge University Press.

Wicksell, Knut (1958), 'A New Principle of Just Taxation,' in R.A. Musgrave and Alan T. Peacock (eds), *Classics in the Theory of Public Finance*, London: Macmillan & Co., pp. 72–116.

Yolton, John W. (1993), *A Locke Dictionary*, Cambridge, USA, and Oxford, UK: Blackwell.